D0577681

THE RIGHTEOUSNESS OF THE KINGDOM

WALTER
RAUSCHENBUSCH

THE RIGHTEOUSNESS OF THE KINGDOM

Edited and Introduced by
MAX L. STACKHOUSE

Abingdon Press
Nashville New York

THE RIGHTEOUSNESS OF THE KINGDOM

Library of Congress Catalog Card Number: 68-17441

SET UP, PRINTED, AND BOUND BY THE PARTHENON PRESS, AT NASHVILLE, TENNESSEE, UNITED STATES OF AMERICA

FOREWORD

The stature of Walter Rauschenbusch as a Christian thinker and social prophet has been increasing. To be sure, he has been criticized from various points of view, and much that he wrote was of significance primarily for his own time. But the seriousness and the quality of his effort to relate Christian faith to social thought and action have won for him new attention in our day. As important later figures in American theology and ethics have emerged, it has seemed natural to compare them to him. He has been treated in a number of useful doctoral studies. It was in the course of such a study, one which focused on the ethical method of Walter Rauschenbusch and Reinhold Niebuhr, that Max L. Stackhouse discovered the Rauschenbusch manuscript now published for the first time.

In view of the continuing significance of Rauschenbusch's social ethical theory and practice, there has been increasing interest not only in his well-known major books but also in his lesser-known articles, addresses, and occasional pieces. Study of them illumines his famous books and deepens our understanding of this leading social prophet of the early twentieth century. It is of particular value to have in print at this time of the fiftieth anniversary of his passing an early Rauschenbusch manuscript on the central theme of his life as minister, scholar, and prophet—the Kingdom of God.

Thanks to the acumen of Dr. Stackhouse, who teaches Christian ethics at the Andover Newton Theological School, we now have this formative work of the young Rauschenbusch, carefully edited and illuminatingly introduced.

To a great extent, the continuing fascination of Rauschenbusch lies in the fact that his challenge has not yet been fully met. He called for the blending of evangelical concern with social passion in thought and action and worked sensitively at that task. Only pieces of the work he laid out have been done; the many unpredictable and momentous things that have happened in the half-century since he died make the job more difficult and yet more important. So the work he saw as so crucial is still largely before us; his challenge is still not answered. This early work of Rauschenbusch can help us more profoundly to understand that prophet of a social Christianity and to think through for ourselves for our time the relationship between religious faith and social issues.

Robert T. Handy
Professor of Church History
Union Theological Seminary
New York City

ACKNOWLEDGMENTS

One becomes aware, when editing and introducing a manuscript, how indebted to others he is and how communal his personal efforts are. I want to thank Carl Raushenbush, son of Walter Rauschenbusch, and Edward M. Starr of the American Baptist Historical Society for permission to use and publish this material; Robert T. Handy, Amos N. Wilder, Winthrop Hudson, and James Luther Adams for encouragement in this project; Elise Arnold and Barbara Morse for typing the manuscript in the various stages of editing; and Frederic M. Hudson and Frank Lloyd Dent for assistance in bringing my 1965 bibliography of Rauschenbusch up to date. Mr. Dent also provided invaluable technical assistance.

CONTENTS

PART I—EDITOR'S INTRODUCTION

The Continuing Importance of Walter Rauschenbusch 13

a. The Man and the Manuscript 14
b. The Context of Recovery 20
c. The Structure of Christian Social-Ethical Thought 27
d. The New Testament as a Resource for Social Ethics 45

PART II—THE RIGHTEOUSNESS OF THE KINGDOM

Author's Introduction 63

1. Christianity Is Revolutionary 70
2. The Kingdom of God 79

a. The Messianic Theocracy 79
b. Ideal Vindicated 98

c. What Is and Was and Is to Come 105
d. Sanctification of This Life 110

3. The Revolutionary Power 117

a. Christ 118
b. The Spirit of God 132
c. The Church 149
d. The Church and the World 162

4. The New Law 179

a. Social Rank 195
b. Wealth and Poverty 206
c. Sex and Family 236
d. The State 244

5. The New Morality 251

a. Duty to Self 251
b. The Practice of Religion 264
c. Present Prospects 279

PART III—BIBLIOGRAPHY

1. The Works of Walter Rauschenbusch 289

a. Books 289
b. Published Articles, Reviews, Pamphlets 291
c. Unpublished Material 304

2. Selected Secondary Literature 308

INDEXES

Index of Scripture References 313

Index of Persons and Subjects 315

PART I

EDITOR'S INTRODUCTION

THE CONTINUING IMPORTANCE OF WALTER RAUSCHENBUSCH

Fifty years ago America's greatest prophet of social Christianity died. Three quarters of a century ago he wrote his first book as a struggling young pastor of an immigrant church in the slums of New York City. That book was never published. Other writings later gave him instantaneous fame; but this seminal work, *The Righteousness of the Kingdom,* where he first worked out the foundations of his life's concern for the Social Gospel, was never submitted to a publisher. Many bits and pieces, notions and motifs from that early work can be traced in widely scattered religious periodical literature of the day; but only with the recovery of this document can we come to a fuller assessment of this man's thought and his continuing significance. It is appropriate to commemorate the fiftieth anniversary of Walter Rauschenbusch's death by publishing, for the first time, his first major effort.

Not only is it appropriate, it is important. America's fragile contribution to prophetic and intellectually compelling Christianity is not secure enough to ensure its survival in the context of contemporary life and international relations. America has produced relatively few great religious thinkers, in spite of the indelible marks on her character and culture left by religious concerns and movements. Yet those few have left a distinctive legacy. Walter Rauschenbusch belongs on the list of those who shaped an inheritance that can be traced from Jonathan Edwards, Ralph Waldo Emerson, Horace Bushnell, and, in their own ways, Herman Melville, Abraham Lincoln, and William James. Out of its concern for righteous holiness, American Christianity has concentrated more on the conditions, personal and social, that are necessary for a significant relationship to the holy and the concrete consequences of that relationship than on the precise character of the holy itself. While that tradition has frequently given rise to moral pretension and self-righteousness, it has also often resulted in a prophetic, humanly concerned, ethically rooted faith. It is important to recover, at least in part, that prophetic tradition as exemplified in Walter Rauschenbusch, for we are in a day when "cheap prophecy" is as much a danger to the American churches as "cheap grace" was to the Germany of Dietrich Bonhoeffer a generation ago.

a. The Man and the Manuscript

Who was this prophet of social Christianity? Why has there been no mention of this manuscript until now? And why is it of more than antiquarian interest?

Son of an immigrant German Baptist minister of Lutheran extraction, Walter Rauschenbusch was a pastor turned professor of church history. From his earliest memory at the age of four, when he argued with his father as to the amount of mourning cloth that should be hung on the door after hearing of Lincoln's assassination,[1] until one of his last known letters, wherein he discusses the significance of President Wilson's attitude toward the Russian Revolu-

[1] "Reminiscences of my Life," manuscript booklet sent to his wife during their courtship, 1892 (D. R. Sharpe Collection). Cf. also D. R. Sharpe, *Walter Rauschenbusch* (New York: The Macmillan Company, 1942), p. 1.

tion,[2] he was a spokesman "For the Right." [3] At no time did he lose his contact with the issues that moved men's souls and shaped their lives. Educated in Germany and in this country, he returned after his New York pastorate of eleven years to his own seminary in Rochester. There he was to teach until his death.

Walter Rauschenbusch wrote a number of books. *Christianity and the Social Crisis* (1907) and *Christianizing the Social Order* (1912) are the most characteristic. A little book, *Prayers of the Social Awakening* (1909), sometimes titled *For God and the People,* and a study guide written for the YMCA, *The Social Principles of Jesus* (1914), were the most widely read books during his lifetime. His *A Theology for the Social Gospel* (1917) is the most enduring and the best-known work today.

Reinhold Niebuhr, in spite of his sometimes devastating critique of the old liberals, called him "not only the real founder of social Christianity in this country but also its most brilliant and generally satisfying exponent to this present day." [4] A. W. Beaven, former president of the Federal Council of Churches, later wrote: "It is clear, it seems to me, that the greatest single personal influence on the life and thought of the American Church in the last fifty years was exerted by Walter Rauschenbusch." [5] And even more recently, a contemporary student can write,

At the very peak of ecumenical studies and dialogue concerning the church two forces have emerged which reopen the questions Rauschenbusch raised. The first . . . must be raised over a simple identification of our religious institutions with lofty conceptions like Body and Bride of Christ. The second . . . from the Civil Rights movement, revealing the ambivalence of

[2] Letter to Vida Scudder, professor at Wellesley College, February 18, 1918 (personal library of M. L. Stackhouse).

[3] This is the title of a radical, independent paper for the working people founded by Rauschenbusch with his friends Elizabeth Post, J. E. Raymond, and Leighton Williams in New York, 1889. Cf. *The New York Times* article on "For the Right," November 16, 1890 (D. R. Sharpe Collection).

[4] Reinhold Niebuhr, *An Interpretation of Christian Ethics* (New York: Harper & Brothers, 1935), p. 1.

[5] Letter from A. W. Beaven to Mrs. Rauschenbusch in 1937. Quoted by G. Bromley Oxnam, *Personalities in Social Reform* (Nashville: Abingdon-Cokesbury Press, 1950), p. 74.

a church which produces a cleavage [in response to] . . . prophetic voices in the church.[6]

The ideas which were to have such power that they persist when few in the churches know the name of their author were generated in the early years of Walter Rauschenbusch's life. Walter Rauschenbusch himself gave the best statement of this early period when he spoke of it in an informal talk to a Sunday school class in 1913:

I was born and brought up in a religious way, and when I was about sixteen or seventeen my religious experience began to come to me. At this time, it had no social expression in it. . . . Then I began to work in New York and there, among the working people, my social education began. I began to understand the connection between religious and social questions. I had no social outlook before. I hadn't known how society could be saved. When I began to apply my previous religious ideas to the conditions I found, I discovered they didn't fit. At this time my friends were urging me to give up this social work and devote myself to "Christian work." Some of them felt grieved for me, but I knew the work was Christ's work and I went ahead, although I had to set myself against all that I had previously been taught. I had to go back to the Bible to find out whether I or my friends were right. I had to revise my whole study of the Bible. . . .

People didn't want to hear my message; they had no mind for it; they would take all I said about religion in the way they had been used to it, but they didn't want any of this "social stuff." All my scientific studying of the Bible was undertaken to find a basis for the Christian teaching of a social gospel. I kept on that way for eleven years in New York. I lived among the common people all the time. . . .

All this time I began to have a desire to write a book. I had six books in mind—I still have—but I didn't know which one to write. Most of the books I had in mind were scholarly books on church history which would have increased my standing as a scholar and a professor. They were not dangerous books; they would have been hailed without adverse criticism.

I decided, however, to write a book on social questions for the Lord Christ and the people. This was a dangerous book and I entered upon my

[6] Donovan E. Smucker, "Rauschenbusch's View of the Church as a Dynamic Voluntary Association," *Voluntary Associations*, ed. D. B. Robertson (Richmond: John Knox Press, 1966), p. 169.

task with fear and trembling. It was part of my Christian ministry, a religious book to me.

Three times I started and each time I was compelled to stop in the middle on account of work. When I went back to my book, I found each time I had out-grown the book.[7]

By far the most significant of these early manuscripts is *The Righteousness of the Kingdom,* recently discovered in the archives of the American Baptist Historical Society. The precise history of this manuscript is not known. It must have been something like this: Rauschenbusch completed a good bit of his projected book, sending it off to his close friends Leighton Williams and Nathaniel Schmidt for comment. There are some indications that it was to be a joint project with Schmidt.[8] Williams returned it quickly after reading it and making some comments in the margins. Schmidt probably held it for quite a long time. There are, in total, some ninety pages of comment on Rauschenbusch's text by Schmidt—comments that Rauschenbusch used in revisions. Rauschenbusch, during the period that his manuscript was away, not only fell in love with the charming Pauline Rother, later to be his wife, but also became involved in the formation of the Brotherhood of the Kingdom, a group of pastors who dedicated themselves to study, discipline, the propagation of the notion of the Kingdom of God, and the implementation of the social dimensions of Christianity in general.[9] Rauschenbusch also had become active in the writing of church school literature and in the Baptist Congress, an annual meeting for discussion of church polity, social problems, theology, and ethics. For a while he was secretary of this organization, a task that, in addition to his pastoral work and frequent writings for journals, denominational publications, and lectur-

[7] Reported in the *Rochester Democrat and Chronicle,* January 25, 1913.

[8] Schmidt, New Testament scholar at Colgate University, ran into difficulties with the conservatives over the use of higher criticism and over his skeptical understanding of the Virgin Birth. A battle ensued, and it is likely that this matter so preempted his time that Rauschenbusch proceeded to write the whole first draft alone. Schmidt moved to Cornell.

[9] A study of the Brotherhood of the Kingdom has recently been completed. See Frederic M. Hudson, "The Reign of the New Humanity" (Ph.D. dissertation, Columbia University, 1968).

ing, kept him from returning quickly to the document. He spent part of the year 1891 studying sociology and New Testament in Germany. Very possibly, some of this manuscript was written in Europe.

The influence of Albrecht Ritschl, who dominated the European theological scene, may be a significant factor here, for many passages have the Ritschlian ring. But Ritschl also suggested on several occasions that "righteousness" is not a central Christian notion, is not integral to a Christian understanding of God or religion, and should not be linked with concepts of "wrath" and "holiness." Ritschl did think that "righteousness" had at best an eschatological reference and thus shows an undeveloped suggestion that could lead to this work; but it seems more likely that the influence of Ritschlian theology dulled Rauschenbusch's enthusiasm for such a strong statement. Thus the influence of Ritschl that shows in Rauschenbusch's later writings may have partially truncated rather than assisted Rauschenbusch's early "realism." Such softening was a common pattern in German theological circles of the day.[10]

Rauschenbusch himself softened his style in his later works. As the movement of the Social Gospel gained not only tolerance but wide acceptance and a constituency, it broadened its appeal. It is interesting, for example, to compare the approach of this early book with a little sermon that is in several ways characteristic of some of his later writing.[11] In *The Righteousness of the Kingdom* he begins with the proclamation, on biblical grounds, that Christianity is revolutionary, that it demands a radical restructuring of thought and life and society. He then specifies the implications for daily life and ordinary values. In contrast, a sermon delivered before a women's gathering in 1912 begins with a rehearsal of the ordinary loyalties of American Christianity and the nature of a woman's concern for her children; his examples are grounded in everyday experiences. He then

[10] Cf. the excellent work by W. O. Shanahan, *German Protestants Face the Social Question* (South Bend, Indiana: Notre Dame University Press, 1954).

[11] "The Church and Social Questions," *Conservation of National Ideals,* ed. Margaret E. Sangster (New York: Fleming H. Revell Company, 1911), pp. 99-122.

proceeds, however, to press the boundaries of these already present concerns, pointing out that Christianity broadens our concern with *our* children to reach to *all* children. Then he concludes by suggesting that if women really want to preserve Christianity in America and to love children in a Christian way, they will mobilize against the prevailing child labor practices and see to it that society is transformed. At first Rauschenbusch was bringing social Christianity to the people. Later he brought people to social Christianity.

Except for his own hint that he outgrew some earlier efforts, it is not known why the plan to publish this material was never carried through. It surpasses much that was published in this period. Yet there are clearly loose moments in the document when the fact that he was a young preacher overcomes tight argument. There are many times when he thinks by association and example rather than by sustained logic or careful biblical scholarship. Yet such moments add to the charismatic power of the document, offer insight into the developing thought of this man, and make it open to the audience for whom he wrote—plain church people.

To point out the simplicity and sometimes oversimplicity of *The Righteousness of the Kingdom* does not compromise its integrity or its significance, as we shall shortly see in a more systematic way. The drive, the passion, and the rhetoric of later years were already taking shape. And many motifs that serve as hidden presuppositions for later work are here explicit. But recognition of the seeking, and hence provisional, character of the total work may help us to understand Rauschenbusch's own hesitancy to publish prematurely.

How this material found its way into the American Baptist Historical Archives in Rochester is not clear either. Dr. D. R. Sharpe, Rauschenbusch's biographer, makes no mention of it in his book. The curator of the archives, Mr. Edward Starr, our best authority, believes nevertheless that it was part of the unorganized material sent to the archives by Sharpe. One librarian at the Colgate-Rochester Divinity School, who had known Rauschenbusch, suggested that these manuscripts were lost for a while in a basement of a Rochester house, recovered by someone who recognized the name Rauschenbusch, and were sent to the school where the American Baptist Historical Society Archives are located. When they arrived, the librarian said, they were filed by a secretary under several titles and remained unrecognized as part of a single manuscript for some time. In any case, the manuscript was found scattered amidst several boxes of Rauschenbusch papers and not recognized as a total document until a chapter outline and correspondence with Schmidt in Rauschenbusch's handwriting allowed this writer to piece it together.[12]

b. The Context of Recovery

The Righteousness of the Kingdom appears today in a time of rapid transition for the churches. They are socially concerned and ecumenically slanted, but somewhat unsure of their footing and direction. What they see ahead often looks totally different from the past. No firm social philosophy seems to guide their mission or their own community life.

In the summary of his monumental work *The Social Teaching of the Christian Churches,* Ernst Troeltsch states that only two major Christian social philosophies have ever been developed—the Catholic and the Calvinist. This contemporary of Rauschenbusch speculates as to the possible survival of both, for the social-ethical influence of Christianity seemed precarious fifty years ago. Since that time the Nazis, the Stalinists, the wars of liberation and the reaction to them, rapid social change, and the troubled consciences of many Christians

[12] The document as it was found was not in final form. Several short sections listed in an outline are found in the manuscript only as a list of topics, and others stand in only partially revised form. Still others are revisions of chapters in Rauschenbusch's private variety of shorthand and speed writing, seemingly revised in response to Schmidt's criticisms. In reconstructing the manuscript, I have attempted to use the latest and most complete statements. I have revised or reorganized only in those instances where it seemed necessary by virtue of grammar, where a phrase might lead to misunderstanding today, where the organization required transitions, where Rauschenbusch's notes indicate that he intended it, where the joining of a partially revised chapter to the rest of an unrevised version demanded word or sentence changes. In two places three points were made in the text, and only two were used in a summary paragraph. I supplied the missing point in his language. I struck out one full paragraph that was badly written and unrelated to the flow of argument.

force us to ask again whether the social-ethical power of Christianity is still viable.

In their old forms Catholicism and Calvinism as social philosophies are dead. (Some have mistaken the deceased for God.) The vision of an organic, hierarchical order sanctified by objectified means of grace, and that of an established theocracy of elect saints who are justified by grace through faith, must both be judged as no longer live options for social reconstruction. This is not to suggest that these visions do not still hold power. The residue of periods in which such patterns dominated, however tenuously, lingers in surrogate form in our interpretations of the past, in various contemporary concepts of good community, in the theological formulations that are the tools of Christian ethics, and quite explicitly in many nostalgic critics of modern culture who see it as unauthentic, fragmented, depersonalized, and unfaithful. But this *is* to suggest that these two forms of "Christendom" have ended—or rather, have played their part and now must yield the stage after their immeasurable contribution to the drama of Christianity in modern culture.

Further, recent attempts to revive the theological and ecclesiological frameworks that gave rise to these social philosophies have been of little help in the ethical reconstruction of contemporary moral and social life, although they have served as a corrective to those who think everything must begin *de novo* in each generation. For all the recent "Neo-Reformation" concern about a positive theology, there is no positive social ethic. Although Karl Barth could courageously and vigorously utilize a Neo-Calvinism to oppose Hitler when naziism threatened to usurp the salvific claims of the gospel and the liberals saw their naïve sentimentalism repeatedly shattered, one searches in vain among his voluminous writings and those of his disciples to find suggestive new directions for culture and politics. One finds no new *Institutes*. And although the entire world rejoices at the spirit and intentions of Vatican II, it is now becoming clear that it represents more tinkering to bring the church up to date than substantive social and ethical reconstruction. Of course, all data are not in. Judicious tinkering in the 1960's may well set a pattern for continual revision and institutionalized processes of sustained reform that will, in the long run, outstrip the most sanguine expectations.

But the question of Troeltsch still remains: Can Christianity develop another articulate "social philosophy," or is the social-ethical power of Christianity at an end? Troeltsch is frequently criticized by sociologists of religion for making little room in his thought for the denomination, that peculiar mode of church organization that now seems to be in a process of rapid transition. Theologians sometimes see the end of the denomination in the new ecumenical spirit, in the new conversations and patterns of merger among the present denominations in this country, and in the already established "United Churches" of, for example, Canada and South India. Nonetheless, the case can be made that larger, indeed massive, denominations are being formed, and that emerging ecclesiological patterns are not so strikingly different from most denominational patterns as they may seem. New networks of trust, authority, and communication have to be forged; but structural similarity with the denominations is clear. The patterns that are emerging are not Catholic or Calvinist in the classical molds. Further, the "United Churches" are forming a single rather than a divided front with which to confront, to compete, to oppose where necessary, and to cooperate where possible with both heterodox social religions of nationalism, domestic and foreign, Islam and Marxism, and with Catholicism and Judaism to which it feels closer affinity. Indeed, these religious organizations and ideologies are structurally similar to earlier denominational patterns within American piety now transferred to an international setting. American Catholicism that was so influential in Vatican II is already more a "denomination" than a "church," and it seems likely that it will be so also in the younger nations. The new denominational pattern, a "conciliar denominationalism" if you will, has interior analogues to, as well as objective historical connections with, the "free church" denominational tradition and looms as the dominant mode of church organization throughout the world. The question is this: Is it capable of providing a third alternative to the social and ethical orientation of Catholicism and Calvinism in their older forms?

Rauschenbusch did not see the day of "conciliar denominationalism"; but deeply connected in his thought are two conflicting motifs that are part of conciliar denominationalism also: sectarianism and Christendom. On the one hand, Rauschenbusch comes from an evangelical background from which he gained a sense of intense and explicit faith that could only be held by fully committed members. On the other hand, Rauschenbusch lived in the age of lingering hope for a catholic "Christian culture" and in an age that, especially through the developing social sciences,[13] saw the legitimacy of secular realms. He, like the developing "conciliar denominations," saw the necessity of the select body of believers anticipating the Kingdom in word and deed in good sectarian fashion, and of taking the world seriously on its own terms, as did all visions of Christendom. These motifs conspire in his thought to produce a vision of a revolutionized responsible society for which a socially understood gospel is the catalyst.

The predominant orientation of the "conciliar denominations" is a modified Social Gospel, in spite of the contempt often expressed for the term. It does not take very extensive analysis of the publications, debates, addresses, reports, new forms of mission, new creeds, or orders of service of the new denominations to realize that a somewhat chastized new Social Gospel is shaping the major bodies. Such analysis also reveals more continuity than discontinuity between the Social Gospel of the pre–World War I variety and the "Christian realism" of the 1930's and 1940's than is usually acknowledged, in spite of striking shifts in rhetoric and selected policies.

The critics of the conciliar denominations on the right and left are keenly aware of that similarity, both in this country and abroad. The "right" feels that the church should be spiritual alone and that it has no business involving itself in political theology and social change. Indeed, the "right" frequently accuses the denominations of

[13] The importance of the social sciences to the Social Gospel is not often accented. Yet the relationship is a crucial one. Among contemporary writers, Robert T. Handy has given this aspect of the movement special accent by including Richard T. Ely, one of the leading social theorists and economists of the day, in his collection, *The Social Gospel in America*, in *A Library of Protestant Thought*, ed. John Dillenberger, *et al.* (New York: Oxford University Press, 1966).

stirring up trouble on account of a second "fall" of the church under the influence of the Social Gospel.[14] The "left" chastizes the denominations for becoming involved in social amelioration on the pattern of the Social Gospel just at the moment a genuine violent revolution seemed possible, or for coming into areas of social change after "true radicals" have made the initial steps, and then taking all the glory and modifying the radicality of the program.[15] In the midst of these criticisms, however, we have seen for more than three decades a parade of new theologians and ethicists who have a lover's quarrel with the denominations. In this country, for example, they accuse them of not taking the dilemma of moral man and immoral society seriously, of not understanding social salvation, of celebrating a middle-class piety, of enjoying a suburban captivity, of having noise in their solemn assemblies, of sitting in comfortable pews, of falsely resisting the secular city. These critics of varying stature are the heirs of the Social Gospel, as their Neo-Calvinist friends and political enemies recognize, both in their appeal to a massive audience through tractarian theology and in their constructive attempt to link theology with the political and social sciences and with social action.

Can conciliar denominationalism, now of worldwide significance, develop a social philosophy that can provide a constructive third alternative to moribund forms of "church type" Christendom on the basis of this heritage? And can the new Social Gospel, already deeply

[14] Such an accusation can be found in a widely circulated paperback written during the Goldwater campaign and still available through the John Birch Society. "The weapons . . . by which the collectivists have moved a generation of Americans to sell their freedom and integrity for security would never have worked had American roots in basic Judaic-Christian traditions not first been severed. . . . Dr. Walter Rauschenbusch and Dr. Harry F. Ward were probably the most responsible for the 'revolution in religion.' . . . Rauschenbusch was a shrewd practitioner of the Fabian methodology who realized that if he identified socialism as such in his preaching and teaching, many people in the church would be repelled. . . . Rauschenbusch and his 'social gospel' provided the philosophy for the collectivist movement which has drained much of American Protestantism of its effect on man and his life" (John A. Stormer, *None Dare Call It Treason* [Florissant, Missouri: Liberty Bell Press, 1964], pp. 124-25. Stormer sees the Rauschenbusch-inspired "fall" of the church most clearly manifested in the National Council of Churches (*Ibid.*, pp. 125-26), in *The Christian Century* (*Ibid.*, pp. 128-29), and in some thirty of the ninety-five scholars who produced the Revised Standard Version of the Holy Bible (*Ibid.*, p. 128).

[15] From personal conversations in Selma, Alabama, and in Boston, Massachusetts.

influential in the infrastructure of the conciliar denominationalism, provide resources for such an alternative? In some respects the reconstruction is well on its way. The responses of the church to the problems of civil rights, in spite of much self-flagellation about "too-little-too-late," have had considerable effect. Again and again it is the workers from these new bodies that stay, organize, teach, preach, and serve after the reporters are gone and the federal budgets are cut. Other particular issues have been addressed frequently, but not always so well. A persistent malaise suggests confusion about the theological or social-ethical tools to meet the challenge.

No one is interested in a bodily resurrection of the old Social Gospel, although its heirs keep its memory alive in action, publication, and preference. It was and is primarily concerned with *ad hoc* judgments on *ad hoc* problems, even if there are distinctive elements of style that have continuity. It was and is a movement peopled not by Augustines, Aquinases, or Calvins, who at each juncture of their life and thought seemed to give a fresh and intellectually compelling definition to the whole of Christian life and thought. Instead, it was and is, like most of church history, populated by those who made significant shifts and accents within a more restricted frame. It was and is susceptible at many points to the charges of idealism, immanentism, perfectionism, and culture-Christianity, not to mention a longer list of more formal heresies.

A rehabilitation of the old Social Gospel is neither possible nor desirable. Yet we must ask what themes developed by the Social Gospel and especially by Rauschenbusch are in fact of continuing relevance in view of the continuity of that period with the present and in view of the demands facing the denominations that feel it part of their Christian vocation to establish justice and righteousness in the community.

In seminaries and graduate schools, the reexamination of the theology of the last two centuries is becoming increasingly intensive. Though some theologians and moralists still feel compelled to apologize to their peers for their interest in Schleiermacher, Ritschl, Troeltsch, or in philosophy and the sciences, a revolution as important as that of the Barthian era is quietly taking place. A new apologetic theology and a new culturally and socially concerned ethic springs from the ashes of liberalism ploughed, harrowed, and fertilized by Neo-Calvinism, other Neo-Reformation theologies, a new harvest of Catholic thinkers, and some modest efforts at conversation with Jews. The recovery of a primary document by one of the greatest proponents of the Social Gospel allows the reexamination to extend in a new direction and provides an auspicious occasion to renew the search for elements of continuing validity that may help conciliar denominations discover a third Christian social philosophy amid a changing ecclesiological and theological scene.

The Righteousness of the Kingdom opens several areas of ethical reflection for us. Not only does it allow us to see the basic insights of a prophetic figure in the process of formation, but it raises both concrete and general issues that are of enduring pertinence. It points out the perils of affluence and the sin of allowing pauperism to exist in a way that has immediate relevance for a nation that only speaks occasionally of a war on poverty. The manuscript treats Christian perspectives on civil disobedience and resistance, it warns of the dangers of an "industrial-military complex," it treats questions of consumer rights and sexual morality, and it points out the impact and moral significance of urbanization and industrialization in rapidly developing areas. On these topics Rauschenbusch's manuscript belies those contemporary "cheap prophets" who say that the church has never been concerned with such problems before they came along.

At quite a different level of ethical discourse, this document allows a reinterpretation of his total work and a refocusing of the questions that should be of concern to proponents of social Christianity. With *The Righteousness of the Kingdom* in hand, two related areas in the thought of Rauschenbusch that concern every serious moralist come to the fore: What is the structure of Christian social-ethical thought, and in what way is the New Testament a resource for social ethics? [16]

[16] Some readers may wish to proceed directly to Part II at this point, for the remainder of Part I presupposes some familiarity with Rauschenbusch's writings.

c. The Structure of Christian Social-Ethical Thought

The major theological and ethical achievements of the twentieth century are not based on shifts of content, but on shifts of form. Barth's commentary on the *Epistle to the Romans,* that shook the theological world, begins by accenting a "dialectic" of the "infinite qualitative distinction between God and Man." In many ways, the whole of Karl Barth's effort may be seen as an imaginative recovery and recasting of major biblical, creedal, and Reformation themes in terms of this formal principle of the dialectic. Paul Tillich also sets the character of his thought in the Introduction to his *Systematic Theology* by establishing the foundations of the method of correlation. Emil Brunner begins his *Divine Imperative* with an extensive discussion of method and procedure, and the principle-contextual debate in Christian ethics that raged for more than a decade centered on the form of ethical procedure. The methodological process sets the tone and draws the limits of the content. So also the formal structure of the Social Gospel is that which defines its character.

Those who write on Walter Rauschenbusch and the Social Gospel are not usually concerned about the structure of his thought. Indeed, Rauschenbusch himself, not unlike the other major figures of the Social Gospel movement, appears little concerned about method. The contemporary celebrants and heirs of the Social Gospel are frequently more dedicated to diffusing the immediate message of social action among the people than to stressing a conceptual framework that can sustain and transform man, society, and the church. Neo-Reformation critics of the Social Gospel who should know and consider the logic of theological thinking all too frequently damn the movement on a thematic basis, because it does not affirm the Word of God as its dominant idea. But such judgment is premature, for in no case known to this author has it been rendered after analysis of the intrinsic logic of thought involved. Although there are undoubtedly areas of serious inadequacy, the transplanting of Barthian critiques of Ritschl to the thought of Rauschenbusch, or the uncritical adopting of Reinhold Niebuhr's initial castigation of the Social Gospel—the usual forms of Neo-Reformation criticism—may have to be judged inadequate themselves if a substantial analysis of the structure of Rauschenbusch's social-ethical thought is taken into account. Such an analysis is doubly necessary, since so many references polemically caricature Rauschenbusch as a straw man.

The fundamental category of Rauschenbusch's thought is history. It is history wherein God reveals his will for man, and where man experiences the holy. It is therefore history which teaches man, it is history in which man lives, it is history that is to be redeemed. It is history rather than ideation or nature that is the arena of experience, ethics, and decision. History is the drama of man's struggles with the forces and spirits of good and evil.

But Rauschenbusch does not merely affirm the centrality of history; he gives it theological and empirical grounding. Theologically, Rauschenbusch accepts the historical revelation of the Christ. "When God revealed himself," Rauschenbusch wrote,

> it was not by communicating abstract propositions or systems of doctrine. The fundamental fact in the Christian revelation was that the Word became flesh. Therewith, Truth became History. Christianity was first a single life, then a collective life, then a stream of historical influences, and always a healing and saving power. Let us not reverse God's process. . . . The future of Christian theology lies in the comprehension of Christianity in history.[17]

The theological affirmation has an empirical reference. There are marks of the Christian faith and life in history. Rauschenbusch is not only dependent in this matter upon the nineteenth-century studies of the historical Jesus, but he saw the early church's ability to establish new forms of social life on a basis of universal values and voluntary commitment as crucial *marks* of authentic revelation.[18] Regarding

[17] "The Influence of Historical Studies on Theology," *American Journal of Theology,* XI (January, 1907), 127. Contrast Rauschenbusch's own statements with the treatment of him in W. A. Visser 't Hooft, *The Background of the Social Gospel in America* (Haarlem: H. D. Tjeenk Willink & Zoon, 1928).

[18] "Jesus as an Organizer of Men," *Biblical World New Series,* XI (1898), 102-11. See also his "The Deacons of the New Testament," *The Homiletic Review,* XXXVIII (December, 1899), 539-43.

later periods, the church provided the "leaders, the protectors of the poor, and the organizers of the forces of law and order" in the provincial cities of the medieval world that became a haven amid the flood of barbarian life of the fifth century.[19] He emphasizes the church's role in preserving intellectual culture and extending the range of education as well as the establishment of law where it was absent or faltered. He points out the historical connection of Protestantism with the willingness to use nature to subdue and humanize nature. And in reply to an objection that Christianity has done little, in spite of these accomplishments, to shape history and to make history alive to the Truth incarnate in it, he asks:

> Has it not lifted woman to equality and companionship with man, secured the sanctity and stability of marriage, changed parental despotism to parental service, and eliminated unnatural vice, the abandonment of children, blood revenge, and the robbery of the shipwrecked from the customs of Christian nations? Has it not abolished slavery, mitigated war, covered all lands with a network of charities to uplift the poor and the fallen, fostered the institutions of education, aided the progress of civil liberty and social justice, and diffused a softening tenderness throughout human life? [20]

Rauschenbusch's concept of history, thus, is one which has theological and empirical undergirding, and his identification of crucial events and movements serves as an ethical apologetic for Christianity understood as a historical movement.

The identification of the crucial events and movements of history, however, requires a conceptual framework. Not all events are of equal significance, not all events and movements reveal their meaning di-

[19] *Christianity and the Social Crisis* (New York: The Macmillan Company, 1907), p 144.

[20] *Ibid.*, p. 147. Some time ago, I located several of Rauschenbusch's former students who still had his lecture notes in their files. With the help of Edward Starr, some were persuaded to turn them over to the American Baptist Historical Archives. New research on these materials show that Rauschenbusch carried his socio-theological apologetic for the church's activity onto the American scene in considerable detail. He especially attempts to document the church's "noble scars" in regard to slavery and race relations, economic injustice, church-state relations, and the struggle of ecumenical unity. Cf. the striking treatment of this material in H. W. Bowden's "Walter Rauschenbusch and American Church History," *Foundations*, IX (1966), 234-50.

rectly, and some events and movements were evil. The most significant ones are those which promise a fuller reconstitution in the future and hence are only present in nascent form. Some richly structured set of concepts is necessary to comprehend and to articulate theologically laden history and the empirically grounded theological concern which was Rauschenbusch's passion.

Many of the conceptual theological frameworks dominant in his day were empty for him. The evangelicals, who deeply influenced him, were too personalistic to be concerned about the ebb and flow of social history. The Calvinists whom he admired in an earlier form, were far too concerned with doctrine that had lost contact with the historical movements which first brought them to life. The liberals with whom he had a natural affinity were frequently more concerned with the relation of theology and scientific theories than the relationship of religion and a society in rapid social change. Further, none of the available theologies had a radical sense of future transformation and fulfillment. Only the socialist movement spoke in eschatological-social terms.[21] Theologians all too often confined themselves to rehearsing and rationalizing tradition. The result of his quest was the highly complex concept, the Kingdom of God.

The Kingdom of God functions as the interpretative concept by which Rauschenbusch exegetes history. It is a concept that excludes any flat, positivistic reading of history but demands concrete historical reference at each point of theological and moral concern.[22]

Before setting forth the constituent elements of the concept of the Kingdom of God and its relationship to history, two observations are

[21] Rauschenbusch wrote frequently and with considerable discernment on socialism. He finds some of its practical measures more helpful than its philosophical baggage. See especially his booklet *Kann ein Christ auch ein Sozialist sein?* (Philadelphia: H. R. Grassmann, 1894); his article "Christian Socialism," *A Dictionary of Religion and Ethics*, ed. Shailer Mathews (New York: The Macmillan Company, 1921), pp. 90-91; and his manuscript of a 1901 talk "Dogmatic and Practical Socialism" (D. R. Sharpe Collection), partially reproduced in D. R. Sharpe, *Walter Rauschenbusch*, pp. 203-16.

[22] See esp. "The Kingdom of God," *Cleveland's Young Men*, XXVII (January 19, 1913), and "Die Geschichte der Idee des Reiches Gottes" (address published as a pamphlet, September, 1902). Cf. also M. L. Stackhouse, "Eschatology and Ethical Method" (Ph.D. dissertation, Harvard University, 1965).

required about how the concept functions. First, history and the Kingdom of God have, for Rauschenbusch, both descriptive and prescriptive functions. Although the Anglo-American philosophical traditions since Hume, with the exception of pragmatism, have maintained the importance of the distinction between the "is" and the "ought," and although German liberal theology which influenced the American Social Gospel frequently speaks of the difference between the "*est*" and the "*significat*," Rauschenbusch was unwilling entirely to divorce from each other the prescriptive and descriptive functions either with respect to history or the Kingdom. There are, in history, especially in its social and institutional dimensions, demands and obligations, structures and dynamics, which one can *describe* that have a prescriptive character. The very fact of their presence imposes obligations upon man, and the failure to fulfill the obligations brings ruin to the man and the society or institution. But some obligations structured into the society also destroy. Some demands built into history threaten its dynamic. The Kingdom of God functions as a discriminating principle as to what is authentically historical and what is destructive of the historical. Thus, for Rauschenbusch, the Kingdom itself is not only normative but refers to some actual dimensions of history that are describable. If there is nothing in history to which one can point and say that the Kingdom is at work, the Kingdom idea has no more validity than any religious concept conceived by any of the world's religions, a possibility he is loathe to countenance.

Second, the Kingdom of God, while clearly having immanental aspects, actually functions in two ways as a mode of protecting transcendence. On the one hand, it preserves the "otherness" of God. It is the *Kingdom* of God, representing the righteousness and truth, the power and will of God that are at work in the world. God himself remains the living God whose center and being are distinct from the historical stream of influences that flow from Jesus Christ. On the other hand, the Kingdom points toward an eschatological fulfillment and transformation that provides a transcendent openness to the future. Man acts purposefully and acts with most sense of significance when his purpose involves a transcendent goal.

The ways in which the concepts of history and the Kingdom of God function in Rauschenbusch contain elements of continuing validity. If the church intends to have anything to say in regard to the massive social and historical problems today, it is obligated to recast its understanding of the relationship between the "is" and the "ought," in order to assure that its conception is open, indeed, integrally related to the technical data of human historical experience. In his social and institutional understanding of history, in his concern for the historical concreteness of theological reference, and in his pointing toward the eschatological openness of history, Rauschenbusch anticipated themes which today are common among theologians who speak of "God acting in history," or "the politics of God." [23]

The complex concept of the Kingdom of God can best be understood if we see that it has three principal dimensions which manifest themselves historically in three specific ways. The three fundamental dimensions are ideational, natural, and institutional.

Ideationally, at the highest level of theological conception the Kingdom of God means messianic theocracy. As a matter of fact, the "entire religious ideal of Israel was the theocracy . . . the complete penetation of the national life by religious morality. It meant politics in the name of God." [24] Theocracy is a concept that Jesus adopted and adapted and gave historical power. Although this messianic theocracy was also "a popular idea that shaded off into innumerable tints and not a rigid formula or scheme that had to be accepted or rejected entire," [25] there are several distinguishing marks which continually appear in this ideal conception so persistently bound to historical reality. The idea of the messianic theocracy is universalistic, spiritual, voluntary (noncoercive by force or miraculous display), and it establishes the value and responsibility of the human personal-

[23] These motifs pervaded the 1966 Geneva Conference on Church and Society sponsored by the World Council of Churches. Cf. *World Conference on Church and Society: The Official Report* (Geneva: World Council of Churches, 1967).

[24] *Christianity and the Social Crisis,* p. 8.

[25] *The Righteousness of the Kingdom,* below, p. 82.

ity. In these four characteristics which Rauschenbusch develops in *The Righteousness of the Kingdom* are elements that are necessary to the definition of theocracy and that point toward historical moments where racial, class, and ethnic barriers are overcome, where a holy *esprit de corps* is developed in a covenantal community, and where individuality is evoked by institutional pattern and legal protection.[26]

Traces of the Kingdom of God, however, do not only find sanction in those ideas that have ever commended themselves to man; it is also possible to see traces of it in *nature*. Here again the notion of universality finds a central place. "There is a large sense in which all the universe is a revelation of God . . . [and] the mere fact that all over the world men have had a religion of some kind . . . is a serious and pathetic fact." [27] Rauschenbusch is under no illusion about the ability to prove Christianity on naturalistic grounds; "the argument from design has collapsed before the doctrine of natural selection." [28] One

[26] *Ibid.*, p. 67. Rauschenbusch and the Social Gospel movement in general have been criticized of late for failure to deal strongly with racial issues. (Cf., for example, Thomas F. Gossett, *Race: The History of an Idea in America* [New York: Schocken Books, 1965], pp. 175-97, and Purvis M. Carter, "The Astigmatism of the Social Gospel" [Master's thesis, Howard University, 1962]) Rauschenbusch is not fully satisfying today in this matter any more than he is fully satisfying in his economic theories (cf. Harry Emerson Fosdick, "Introduction," *A Rauschenbusch Reader,* ed. B. Y. Landis [New York; Harper & Row, 1957]). Yet three aspects of his thought must be taken into account to get an accurate appraisal of his views: first, his understanding of the anti-ethnic character of the Christian movement that drives toward universalism. Race in this context refers to the human race. Superiority or inferiority within the race depends upon the superiority of democratic institutions over other varieties (see *Christianity and the Social Crisis,* p. 222; *Christianizing the Social Order* [New York: The Macmillan Company, 1912], p. 154; and esp., *Die politische Verfassung unseres Landes* [Cleveland: Bickel, 1902], pp. 7-9, wherein he contrasts the North with the South in terms of the tradition of town meetings as against the aristocratic traditions of the county). Second, against some of his Social Gospel colleagues at a time of anti-immigration agitation, Rauschenbusch argued that this country should leave its immigration doors open as wide as possible. The mixing of peoples and bloods in an atmosphere of freedom is a healthy thing (see "Limits of Immigration," *Seventh Annual Session of the Baptist Congress* [New York, 1888], pp. 86-87). And finally, he anticipated some of the recent reflections in the situation of the Negro when he specifically related the question of economic suppression to the question of personal identity (see "The Problem of the Black Man," *American Missionary,* LXVIII [March, 1914], 23).

[27] "Revelation: an Exposition," *Biblical World New Series,* X (1897), 95.

[28] "Religion, the Life of God in the Soul of Man," *The Baptist Magazine* (May, 1909), p. 2.

can only presume to read theological notions or moral laws from the realm of nature in a very minimal sense.

But there are ways in which nature impinges upon history and the Kingdom of God. Therefore, nature must be taken into account in any descriptive or normative ethical account. The sexual instinct, for example, is a natural social drive that "is always weaving new combinations of lives, reaching out to the right and the left and knitting threads that had no connections before, bringing whole groups of families into friendly cooperation . . . , [causing us to laugh] at the efforts of the proud to isolate themselves from the rest of their kind." [29] Sex cuts across class and cultural loyalties. The case is similar to "natural" associational loyalties of neighborhoods, lodges, work or professional groups, colleges, the city, state, or country. While these can become the occasion for the most unmitigated group selfishness, they can also become the way to channel our "natural" preferences and concerns "into the love of many and weave more closely the web of social life." [30] Thus, as nature and natural drives sometimes provide sensitivity to universality, they also drive toward new concrete centers of human concern, producing a potential basis for the social solidarity and interdependence of larger groupings of humanity.

Under the influence of Henry George, the author of *Progress and Poverty,* another "natural" phenomenon, land, became central in Rauschenbusch's understanding of how nature must be included as one of the dimensions of the Kingdom of God. Land is the root metaphor for Rauschenbusch's understanding of the economic system. Land is the primary means of production. Land is a natural resource and the fundamental form of property. When land passes from the control of the community to the control of a few, both the resources and the community are plundered, whether or not the few consider themselves Christians. He decries the destructive effects of the logging and mining industries in the rural areas and condemns slum housing and accompanying destruction of family life caused by land speculation and absentee landlords in the cities. Rauschenbusch sees in such

[29] *Dare We Be Christians?* (Boston: The Pilgrim Press, 1914), p. 2.
[30] *Ibid.*, p. 32.

conditions a "natural" economic potential at work that demands community control over land and, by implication, all economic resources by which the few exploit the many. "The only alternatives are government interference by taxes and royalties or government ownership. Both are in operation in other countries and are feasible." [31]

We can see, then, that besides the *idea* of the messianic theocracy, there is a "necessary" development toward an *organon*, a fraternal socialistic order implied by fundamental structures of "nature" such as sex and land. It is necessary not in the sense that it is inevitable, but in the sense that it is required for *good* social order. Both the ideational and the natural structures are included in the primarily eschatological term Kingdom of God. Both the ideational and the natural structures involve descriptive and prescriptive responses. It is at the points where the idea of the righteous messianic theocracy links directly with the genuinely natural uses of natural resources and drives man toward the historical actuality of fraternity and socialism that the Kingdom can be said to be manifest. It is at these points that history is most creative.

But the Kingdom of God is neither inevitable nor exhausted in history. It always stands as a transcendent future possibility, an eschatological possibility, even if it is partially manifest in the present. It is always "already" and "not yet." "The Kingdom of God is always but coming; . . . you can never lay your hand on it to say 'It is here.' " [32] It is not until the eschatological transformation of heaven and earth that the vision and nature of the Kingdom of God will be fully realized. "Even a Christian social order cannot mean perfection. As long as men are flesh and blood the world can be neither sinless nor painless. . . . The justest and most sympathetic human society conceivable would unknowingly inflict injury and wrong and only slowly realize it when it heard the insistent cry of pain." [33] "The continents are strewn with the ruins of dead nations and civilizations.

[31] "Lecture Notes on the Social Question," Manuscript in the D. R. Sharpe Collection, Part. I, p. 19. Cf. also *Christianity and the Social Crisis*, pp. 221-27, and *Christianizing the Social Order*, pp. 235-36 and pp. 377 ff.

[32] *The Social Principles of Jesus* (New York: The Association Press, 1914), p. 177.

[33] *Christianizing the Social Order*, p. 126.

History laughs at the optimistic illusion that nothing can stand in the way of human progress. . . . What guarantee have we, then, that our modern civilization with its pomp will not be one with Nineveh and Tyre?" [34]

The term which Rauschenbusch repeats in the context of such statements, "christianized social order," is crucial to an understanding of the relation of the Kingdom and history in the *institutional dimensions* of Rauschenbusch's thought. At the outset, it is necessary to point out that there is an important distinction between a christianized social order and the Kingdom of God, although they are related. We have already seen that Rauschenbusch believes that a Christian social order is not a fixed entity. Both slow and rapid social change in history makes any constant state soon outmoded. Perfection cannot sustain itself in history. The Kingdom of God is transcendent in spite of its partial presence. Yet within the confines of the historical change a relatively better order can improve the human situation if based on Christian principles of social life driving toward the institutional realization of the values of the messianic theocracy and the fraternity and socialism of "natural" relationships.

An unchristian social order can be known by the fact that it makes good men do bad things. It tempts, defeats, drains, and degrades, and leaves men stunted, cowed, and shamed in their manhood. A Christian social order makes bad men do good things. It sets high aims, steadies the vagrant impulses of the weak, trains the powers of the young, and is felt by all as an uplifting force which leaves them with the consciousness of a broader and nobler humanity as their years go on.[35]

A Christian social order can be provisionally established in history while the Kingdom of God, although active in history, cannot; but the two are clearly related. History is the realm of human existence, and it is there that men become aware of the possibilities and character of the Kingdom of God. The Kingdom of God becomes the ideal, the hope, and the power by which the social order can be christianized

[34] *Christianity and the Social Crisis*, pp. 279-89.
[35] *Christianizing the Social Order*, p. 127.

in history. The more we christianize the social order, the more clearly can we see further significance and implications of the Kingdom of God. But this christianizing does not mean putting Christ in the Constitution, having Christian political parties, or having an established church. Rather, it means actualizing in the secular world by secular means patterns of justice and universality.

The three major dimensions of the Kingdom of God manifest themselves and thereby affect history and the christianization of the society in three ways. First, history has been altered by the "Kingdom event" of Jesus Christ. "Jesus Christ was the initiator of the Kingdom." [36] Although the Kingdom of God is never fully realizable in history, since Jesus Christ "it is within us, and among us." [37] There were others, of course, who pointed toward the Kingdom of God, broadened its definition by pointing beyond nationalistic politics, and heightened sensitivity to it. But Jesus was different from them. He did not speak revelations and he did not receive revelations; "he was the revelation." [38] And from the Messiah directly came the historical reality of a new epoch that transforms society toward the rule of God.

Second, the Kingdom of God is mediated by individuals.[39] Jesus began his ministry with the words, "Repent, the Kingdom of God is at hand." And a man can only repent in his own heart. "The ABC of social renewal and moral advance is for us to face our sins sincerely. . . . [Then] we realize that what we call peccadillos in ourselves are the black sins that have slain the innocents and have hagridden humanity through all its history. That is the beginning of the social vision." [40] Rauschenbusch points out that Jesus worked on individuals and through individuals; nevertheless,

[36] *The Social Principles of Jesus,* p. 176.

[37] *Ibid.,* p. 176.

[38] *Ibid.,* p. 81. Note the difference between rules and principles. The term "principle," for Rauschenbusch, is not an ideational "law" that one applies to all situations of a certain sort; rather, it is essentially an interpretive guideline for discerning the core meaning of historical demands and events. Cf. *The Righteousness of the Kingdom,* below, pp. 167, 181.

[39] Rauschenbusch's understanding of personality and the person, especially as related to his organic theories and metaphors, is presently being worked out in a promising Ph.D. dissertation under preparation at Harvard University by Frank Lloyd Dent.

[40] *The Social Principles of Jesus,* p. 81.

his real end was not individualistic, but social, and in his method he employed strong social forces. He knew that a new view of life would have to be implanted before the new life could be lived and that the new society would have to nucleate around personal centers of renewal. But his end was not the new soul, but the new society; not man, but Man.[41]

For those who are grasped by the social vision of the Kingdom of God as Christ offered it, there are special tasks.

The life and fate of these individuals anticipate the issues of history. . . . Working out the moral and intellectual problems in their minds before the masses have realized them, they become the natural leaders in the fight, clarifying the minds of others, and thus become not only forerunners, but invaluable personal factors in the moral progress of the race.[42]

However, insofar as these pioneering individuals remain within themselves, they are not fulfilling their task.

Those who received it [the vision, hope, and power of the Kingdom] declared it to others with that instinct of the fellowship and communication which God has attached to the knowledge of the truth as a spiritual instinct of propagation. . . . So especially the *Bible,* in which we have the record of the revelations of God to holy men; their visions of the character of God; their inspired interpretations of history; and their outlooks into God's purposes for the future.[43]

On the one hand, their insight becomes, indeed, must become, a part of the total "capital of religious thought which is handed down from generation to generation," [44] a part of the collective memory of man. And on the other hand, personal regeneration must recognize its limitations, for it cannot define the full conception of what is right. "That is defined for [the person] in the main by the religious community whose ideas he accepts." [45] This definition by the community,

[41] *Christianity and the Social Crisis,* pp. 60-61.
[42] *The Social Principles of Jesus,* p. 176.
[43] "Revelation: an Exposition," pp. 95-96.
[44] *Ibid.,* p. 97.
[45] *Christianity and the Social Crisis,* p. 354.

however, does not mean the acceptance of implicit faith, but rather a self-conscious explicit faith on the part of each member of the community. In short, the eschatological Kingdom is mediated to the present by the individual insofar as that individual is socialized. "Jesus never fell into the fundamental heresy of later theology; he never viewed the human individual apart from human society." [46]

Third, the Kingdom of God is mediated by the church. "She does not exist for her own sake; she is simply a working organization to create the Christian life in individuals and the Kingdom of God in human society." [47] Indeed, the meaning of baptism into the church, derived from the practice of John and other prophetic figures of the day, is indicative of the church's mediating functions. "The men who were baptized by John were . . . [baptized] to the coming of the Kingdom of God and of his Messiah. . . . Baptism was the mark of a . . . movement toward a new era." [48]

But for Rauschenbusch, the church is not only an institutional means of perpetuating the stream of concrete historical influence that derives from Jesus and drives toward the future. It functions also as a model for optimal social organization—or at least, it has and should. Rauschenbusch, of course, is heavily dependent upon the "free church" model as manifest in the Baptist Church of which he was a part, but his use of this model is not simple. He uses a modified "free church" ecclesiology to construct an organizational model of what might be called a "universalized, aggressive sect," [49] structurally similar to some aspects of the conciliar denominations now on the

[46] *Ibid.*, p. 65.

[47] *Ibid.*, p. 185.

[48] *The Social Principles of Jesus,* p. 52.

[49] The character of Rauschenbusch's primarily sectarian understanding of the church and its relationship to ecumenical Christianity is discussed in R. Müller, *Walter Rauschenbusch: ein Beitrag zur Begegnung des deutschen und des amerikanischen Protestantismus* (Leiden/Köln: E. J. Brill, 1957), especially pp. 65 ff. It should also be pointed out that Rauschenbusch was influenced by his father, who left Lutheranism for the "free church" tradition, who was one of the first in America to become deeply concerned about the sources and development of the "Radical Reformation," and who was one of the first to attempt bringing denominations into working relationships. Rauschenbusch completed and published his father's unfinished autobiography, *Leben und Wirken von August Rauschenbusch* (Kassel: J. G. Oncken, 1901).

horizon. Speaking on the topic in 1912, Rauschenbusch recounted the background of the "universalized sect" that he defended. Such an organization is the institutional form that links in history the ideas of the messianic theocracy and the "natural" inclinations toward social solidarity. It becomes an instrument that implements aspects of the Kingdom in history by christianizing society. Rauschenbusch refers to the anticipations of this mode of organization in the early church, in the monastic and some heretical movements, in the industrial cities growing in twelfth-century Europe, in the Anabaptists, and in the English reformation. In each of these, "men were reaching out toward a simple gospel, toward a fraternal organization of all life, and wherever they had a little freedom of action, instinctively . . . [they] converged towards the same results to which we have come today." [50] "The church is a picked company of soldiers whose efficiency depends more on their quality than on their number. The Broad Church thinkers are entirely right in insisting that the church is to benefit not only a small circle of the elect, but all men and the entire life of humanity. But they are wrong in thinking that this can best be accomplished by admitting everybody into the church . . . at birth." [51]

The model of the free church having a vocation that reaches into the whole of society as an institutional reality is, according to Rauschenbusch, dependent upon actual organizational work of Jesus and the early disciples. "Organization," according to Rauschenbusch, "is the process of creating a social organism. It consists of giving formal recognition to social relations already existing and giving increased strength and durability by the recognition, or of creating new relations." [52] Jesus did both. Although Jesus was concerned, for example, about the "fundamental obligations written deep in the constitution of human society, such as filial reverence and family solidarity," he extended this instinct into a wider context.[53] The disciples and

[50] "Baptists and Social Progress," *Centenary of Organized Baptist Work, 1912* (Pittsburgh, 1913), p. 76.

[51] *The Righteousness of the Kingdom*, below, p. 159.

[52] *Biblical World*, XI, 104.

[53] *The Social Principles of Jesus*, p. 141.

the early communities were quite in line with the intentions of Jesus when, after the death of Jesus, "they continued a family life among themselves and shared what they had . . . , expressed their organic unity by calling [leaders] 'the Twelve' long after there were no longer twelve in number," and developed forms of differentiated leadership and organization directly opposed to dominant patterns by acknowledging qualities and abilities no longer based on class, clan, or social influence.[54] Rauschenbusch carried out his analysis also with regard to the economic structure of the early church, the structure of church political authority, and the redefinition of the role of women in the life of the community.[55]

Thus the structure of human existence, which is historical in its very nature, has been already constitutionally affected by forces deriving from the life and death of Jesus Christ. The final meaning of human life—the Kingdom of God as synthesis of messianic theocracy and fraternal socialism—seen by Rauschenbusch as meditated to history and as a force therein by Jesus Christ, by individuals who catch and communicate the social vision of the Kingdom of God, and by the church, which, in spite of its perversions, can never fully deny its implicit witness to the Kingdom in its history of having christianized some areas of the social order. The Kingdom of God stands beyond history; yet it is a force in history, actually changing the structure of human thought and relations.

From the viewpoint of the interaction of history and the Kingdom of God, Rauschenbusch reads the events and phenomena of the present and attempts to construct, on occasion, a theology and a social analysis to sustain and support biblical and historical sensitivities. In fact, the majority of Rauschenbusch's writings can be characterized as bringing this logic to bear on the particular questions and institutions of his day. He discusses the structure and dynamics of the family, of urbanization, of government, of labor and professional organizations, of business and of education, of doctrines of

[54] *Biblical World,* XI, 105-6.

[55] Cf. "Social Ideas in the New Testament," *The Treasury,* XVII (1899), 155-59. Rauschenbusch began a book on "The Woman Problem" that was never finished.

sin and theories of redemption, of notions of inspiration and prophecy as they represent, fail to represent, or resist elements of the Kingdom of God in history. But his discernment of his own age is less pertinent here than the fundamental structure of his thought.

Rauschenbusch moves from the context wherein man finds himself a historical creature to the ideational, natural, and institutional structures that are the crucial categories and powers that inform historical existence. And he argues that these dimensions of the Kingdom are most dramatically manifest in Jesus Christ, in persons, and in the prototypical social organ, the church. As the New Testament is a synthesis of conceptual, natural, and organizational structure of the first century, so Rauschenbusch, with the Bible as his model, welds together a theological-social vision of the Kingdom of God—an interpretive frame for reading the dimensions and directions of history and a goal that ever transcends man's accomplishments. The structure of Rauschenbusch's thought, therefore, can be clearly contrasted with two groups: those who begin in doctrine and then deductively or intuitively work out the implications for human historical existence (orthodoxy and neo-orthodoxy); those who begin in an interpretation of the nature of Nature and use religious symbols that have emotive power in human history to express the structure of creation (modernism and natural or ontological theology). We may even say that Rauschenbusch's historical sensitivity is more appropriate to contemporary interpretations of man and society and to the demands of a new conciliar denominationalism then either of those two.

Rauschenbusch may well be criticized for reading the various aspects of the Kingdom in so moralistic a fashion and for failing to explicate fully the tragedy he sees in the historical drama that concerns him. Nonetheless, he resists and qualifies the pervasive optimism of his age. In any case it is hardly fair to criticize him for being born in America or for having lived a generation too soon. To be sure, he frequently operated from superficial sociological knowledge and was too much influenced by Americanist motifs of the age of Theodore Roosevelt. But if the above analysis of his fundamental structure of thought is correct, then these are not the central problems. We shall have to reckon Rauschenbusch as providing a structural framework that deserves reexamination. His own failure to fulfill the implications of his method is of little importance in this effort. The attempt to construct a historical theology of history that is socially sensitive has been the continuing problem of twentieth-century Christian ethics and is an undoubted requirement for an adequate social philosophy in the emerging worldwide denominationalism.

But our apology for a fresh look at Rauschenbusch needs further qualification theologically. He reaches toward the "highest" theological conception and derives the concept of the "messianic theocracy." But he nowhere gives an adequate doctrine of the God implied by theocracy. He strives to incorporate an appreciation of nature, and although he rightly resists naturalism and scientism, he does so without asking fundamental questions about the relationship of science and metaphysics to the theological interpretation of history that is his primary concern. He synthesizes an understanding of governing theological motifs with sensitivities to nature and institutional life to produce a highly suggestive, eschatological vision of the Kingdom of God, which he sees as part of a "natural law of history." This Kingdom has been given concrete historical impetus by Jesus Christ and the church and stands as the ultimate vision of the future. But he does not develop an adequate understanding of Creation, the Incarnation, or Eschatology where one might expect these relationships to be worked out in their full systematic significance. Nevertheless, it can be asked whether Rauschenbusch's failures are "blunders" because he was wrong about the whole enterprise, or whether they are "limitations" because he was parochial where suggestive.

Three criticisms frequently leveled at Rauschenbusch clearly need correction. The first was made by Reinhold Niebuhr and has been uncritically echoed ever since, although Niebuhr himself has modified it. That is that Rauschenbusch idealistically overestimated the teaching power of the gospel and did not emphasize the need for organizational instrumentalities. This document which allows an altered reading of the later Rauschenbusch reveals, I think, that the criticism applies more to other figures than to Rauschenbusch.

The second criticism is that he does not treat the central question of Christianity: salvation. His whole mode of thinking in many ways presupposes "salvation history," although he can never really equate the historical process with the fullness of salvation. Rauschenbusch holds that salvation is ultimately in God's hands, not ours. And that fact frees us from the ultimate question to ask the penultimate one of obedience to his will and ways in history. A more just and righteous society is within the purview of human action and is the this-worldly sign of our obedience to the divine desire for the Kingdom of God. On several occasions, we must recognize, Rauschenbusch seems to confuse the penultimate and the ultimate questions. There are moments when the experience of full personhood and the establishment of a just society seem to be the "earning" of social salvation. With one exception, however, he never sustains the argument and always introduces strong qualifications (as quoted above, pp. 35-36, for instance). He is quite convinced that no definition of salvation is sufficient that does not take account of the social matrix of human existence and a social interpretation of the self, and that the most appropriate interpretation of history would reveal imperatives for Christian social concern.

The third criticism that one reads so often about Rauschenbusch is that his concern for universal man is sentimental. There are undoubtedly sentimental and idealistic elements in his work. But although we have seen illusions about the prospects of easy universalism rudely dispelled, we have also witnessed new forms of international relations as well as a creative if often violent and painful mutual restraint rise out of the ashes of shattered nationalism. Indeed, it may prove to be nationalism, not universalism, that is shattered on the rocks of twentieth-century conflict.

There were, however, two areas of Rauschenbusch's thought that were to be examined for their continuing significance. The first, the structure of Christian social-ethical thought, will have to be judged upon a reappraisal of the structure of Rauschenbusch's ethical thought as informed by this new document. The second is perhaps more controversial: the use of the New Testament as a resource for social ethics.

d. The New Testament as a Resource for Social Ethics

Throughout Rauschenbusch's life, there is a clear biblical dependence. The recovery of the manuscript included in this volume suggests that he was even considerably more of a biblical theologian than he is given credit for having been. The fundamental relationship between history and the Kingdom was first worked out on biblical grounds. It is, therefore, incumbent upon us to inquire into the continuing utility of his view of the biblical sources.

To see what is of continued pertinence in his use of Scripture, it will be most useful to contrast Rauschenbusch's effort with that of the most influential New Testament scholar today, Rudolf Bultmann.[56] One might, of course, also compare C. H. Dodd, F. Grant, O. Cullmann, A. Wilder, and other outstanding New Testament scholars, but they (with the exception of Wilder) seldom speak, either positively or negatively, to the issues raised by the Rauschenbusch manuscript. Bultmann clearly does so at almost every point. Not only will this comparison and contrast throw some of the central questions into sharper focus, but there are good historical reasons for making the comparison. Both Rauschenbusch and Bultmann are heirs of the nineteenth-century theological orientation from Schleiermacher, Dilthey, Ritschl, and Harnack. Under the influence of this tradition, which Rauschenbusch has adapted to an aggressive free church orientation and Bultmann to existentialism, both scholars are antidogmatic, antimystical, anticeremonial, antilegalistic, and antiscientistic in their understanding of the meaning of the gospel. Both presuppose and

[56] Besides the work of Bultmann himself, several secondary sources have been very helpful in sorting out the central concerns of Bultmann as they are pertinent to this effort: the two volumes of essays edited by Carl E. Braaten and Roy A. Harrisville, *Kerygma and History* (Nashville: Abingdon Press, 1962), and *The Historical Jesus and the Kerygmatic Christ* (Nashville: Abingdon Press, 1964); Thomas C. Oden, *Radical Obedience: The Ethics of Rudolf Bultmann* (Philadelphia: The Westminster Press, 1954); and H. Ganse Little, "History, Decision and Responsibility" (Ph.D. dissertation, Harvard University, 1965).

heavily emphasize the historicity of man's existence and see the will as the center of man's nature, thus accenting decision in history. Both want to demythologize, desacramentalize, and retranslate the core of the gospel into meaningful contemporary terms. Both want to desecularize and put into fresh perspective the world of nature. Both are interested in an interpretation of existence characterized by openness toward the future. Both believe that the Kingdom of God is futuristic but determinative in the present. Both want believers to take up Jesus' cross as their own in radical obedience. Both see a sharp distinction between Greek and Hebrew modes of thought. And although both presuppose the reality and the necessity of the historical Jesus as the foundation of Christian thought, neither is ultimately willing to rest his case on the ability of historians to reconstruct the self-consciousness of Jesus. All these similarities make the differences between them somewhat intramural. But precisely the similarities throw the crucial differences into more dramatic relief so that some of the continuing questions of the relationship of New Testament studies to Christian social ethics raised by the recovery of this document can be the more clearly seen. For in the midst of the chastised liberalism of the world denominations, a division is growing between the existential and the social interpretations of the gospel.

Several things need to be said, however, before we proceed to compare these interpretations in their relation between the Old and New Testaments, the meaning of eschatology, and the underlying assumptions of their views. Pitting Rauschenbusch against Bultmann is a bit like sending David against Goliath, in view of the impact these two have had on contemporary theological scholarship. But if we ask which way of approaching the New Testament has had the greatest influence in the life of the modern denominations and councils of churches, or even in the curriculum structures of theological education developed in the twentieth century, the roles are reversed. These two figures are, in several ways, representative of two styles of neo-liberal thought that confront the denominations in the last half of the twentieth century. The choice between them—even in the form of qualified acceptance of one or the other that the choice is sure to entail—will have long-range consequences for the life of the church. The existential, neo-Lutheran position of Bultmann stands in direct conflict on many points with the sociological, semi-Calvinist position of Rauschenbusch.

Both Rauschenbusch and Bultmann see the New Testament in the context of the Old Testament. Christianity is a Jewish sect. For Rauschenbusch, however, the relationship is primarily one of continuity. For Bultmann, it is one of contrast. Rauschenbusch begins his first chapter with the accent on the relationship of Jesus to the prophets:

> Jesus was the successor of the Old Testament prophets. The common people of his day discerned this kinship and whispered that he must be Elijah or Jeremiah or some other of the prophets. Although he denied his identification with them, he himself repeatedly drew the parallel between the work and lot of the prophets and his own.[57]

The implication of this relationship, seen also in John the Baptist, is that Christianity is revolutionary. Jesus, to be sure, did not have an explicit political program for nations. Rather, Jesus and his disciples were, like the prophets, tribunes of the people, appealing to a Messianic hope that relativized existing social and political institutions or loyalties by envisioning the possibilities of new, more just relationships, and turning the popular values of people on their heads so that the so-called divine would appear demonic, while the negligible would emerge supremely significant. Rauschenbusch insists that it was not mere misunderstanding when John was beheaded and Jesus was crucified as a religious and political insurgent any more than when Paul was accused before Felix of being a mover of insurrections. John prophetically anticipated, Jesus embodied, and Paul proclaimed an event that initiated a new social movement. The authorities perceived correctly what the effects of such movements were, whether or not these were conscious intentions of political change.

Rauschenbusch reinforces his view by appealing to New Testament

[57] *The Righteousness of the Kingdom*, below, p. 70.

materials that seem to him to provide insight into the dominant historical influences through which the New Testament must be interpreted. The books of Revelation and James are the product of Jewish Christianity with powerful ethical concerns, and present most accurately the ethos that was shared by Jesus. These books represent the radical social wing of the primitive church.[58]

> The Jewish Christian communities were numerically and spiritually an important part of earliest Christianity. In many respects they most faithfully preserved the direct impress of Jesus. . . . The hope of the immediate return of Christ dominated the life of primitive Christianity. . . . Their preaching was with a view to that event. . . . The Christian hope of the Parousia was the Jewish hope of the Messianic kingdom, except that the person of the Messiah had gained wonderfully in concreteness and attractiveness and the hope had become far more vivid and intense. . . . Moreover, this branch preserved the social-historical consciousness of Christianity by focusing attention on "signs of the times" and having a "theory of ages," in a way that Paul and John did not, even though they had "a scheme of the future . . . that is unreal, unhistorical and mechanical." [59]

Bultmann too regards the early Christian movement as related to the prophets, especially as seen in Jesus' relationship to John. Not only does their preaching (especially that of Jesus) represent "in fact a tremendous protest against contemporary Jewish legalism, thus renewing under changed conditions the protest of the ancient prophets against the official Hebrew religion," [60] but "*both movements, that of John and that of Jesus, were Messianic.* Their connection with each other and also with other Messianic movements is recognizable in the fact that disciples of the Baptist came over to Jesus, and that there was even a Zealot among Jesus' followers." [61]

In contrast to Rauschenbusch, however, Bultmann holds that Jesus' concern had really nothing to do with social problems. "Un-

[58] Condensed from *Christianity and the Social Crisis,* pp. 101-12.
[59] Cf. *Ibid.,* pp. 95 ff.
[60] *Primitive Christianity,* tr. R. H. Fuller (New York: Meridian Books, 1956), p. 73.
[61] *Jesus and the Word,* tr. L. P. Smith and E. H. Lantero (New York: Charles Scribner's Sons, 1934), p. 25.

like the ancient prophets . . . he was not concerned with social righteousness. Such a concern would have been irrelevant now that Israel had lost her independence." [62] The efforts of John and Jesus were essentially unpolitical, even antipolitical, although there were some political Messianic groups active at that time. Any "outsiders certainly could not recognize the essentially unpolitical character of the leadership of both John and Jesus, especially as both aroused considerable popular excitement. Both movements were therefore suppressed quickly by the execution of their leaders." [63] Thus Bultmann attributes the beheading and crucifixion to misunderstanding, while Rauschenbusch sees them as due to the attempt of the establishment to preserve the status quo in the face of revolutionary effects of religious and social-ethical charisma.

Rauschenbusch appeals to Revelation and James, while Bultmann points to influential movements through which to interpret Jesus and John.

> Clearly ancient eastern, non-Jewish conceptions influenced this Baptist movement; old mythology of Persia or Babylon perhaps also influenced the Baptist's preaching of the coming Judge. . . . Possibly the Mandaean Gnostic sect which emerged later is a development of this old Baptist sect. . . . It is worth noting that the Mandaeans called themselves "Nazarenes"; and that Jesus is often so called in the early Christian tradition.[64]

Thus Bultmann, both at this point and more extensively in his discussion about the appropriateness of Paul's use of Gnostic categories,[65] sees the center of Jesus' teaching and preaching to be in no way political or eschatological in the sense of social transformation. Rather, Christianity like Gnosticism is a redeemer religion in which the eschatological refers to a renewal of the inner man while the present signifies the decay of the outward man. "Hence it follows that for Christianity as well as for Gnosticism, the present salvation is not

[62] *Primitive Christianity,* p. 73.
[63] *Jesus and the Word,* p. 25.
[64] *Ibid.,* p. 24.
[65] *Primitive Christianity,* esp. pp. 196 ff.

visible like an event in history." [66] Although Jesus probably expected some future events that would involve the action of God, the significance of this expectation does not lie in any view as to what might or should happen in the course of time. Indeed, it only means that the future is open, radically so, and that therefore man is called to existential decision in the present, a decision that accepts the openness of the Kingdom, its judgment, and its blessing. Apocalyptic concerns are a deviant attempt to be specific about a future that should remain open and to objectify what is ultimately only subjective. Such an interpretation strikingly contrasts with Rauschenbusch's appreciation of apocalyptic literature as an attempt to preserve the historical and social dimension of Christianity from Gnostic influences.

Both writers deal with these concerns in the first chapters of their initial books on early Christianity and proceed to a discussion of the Kingdom of God in the next sections. For both, the concept of the Kingdom is crucial. We have already seen something of Rauschenbusch's interpretation of the Kingdom in another connection, but we need now to contrast it with Bultmann's. Rauschenbusch and Bultmann are in accord that the Kingdom is already present in Jesus Christ and that the Kingdom is nevertheless transcendent. Yet any agreement must be carefully qualified. For Rauschenbusch, the possibilities of the Kingdom are historically borne by new righteous social institutions growing directly and indirectly from the influence of Jesus. For Bultmann,

> The Kingdom of God is deliverance for men. It is that *eschatological* deliverance which ends everything earthly. . . . [It] is diametrically opposed to all relative values. . . . It is not a good toward which the will and action of men is directed, not an ideal which is in any sense realized through human conduct. . . . [It cannot be understood] in the light of the modern conceptions of "nature" and "evolution" . . . . [It is nonsocial, for] the Kingdom . . . tears men up by the roots from their business life and from their social relationships and commands the dead to bury their dead. "The saints," [as] the company of disciples of Jesus soon called themselves . . . are sepa-

[66] *Ibid.*, p. 39.

rated from the present world and have their life in the beyond. . . . It is *supernatural, superhistorical.*[67]

Bultmann, however, does ask whether there are any empirical references in the discussion of the Kingdom. That is, are there any conditions or consequences implied by such language? He acknowledges that the early church and perhaps Jesus expected the resurrection of the dead and eating and drinking in the Kingdom, but Bultmann insists nevertheless that "men are forbidden to make any picture of the future life . . . [and are denied] the calculation of the time and the watching for signs." [68] Programmatic action on the grounds of an eschatological ethic is forbidden. Thus the only historical reference that is implied in language about the Kingdom of God is the moment of existential decision of the person. In each moment man is confronted with a radical "either/or" which determines his authenticity or inauthenticity.

Just as Rauschenbusch attributes nationalistic apocalyptic overtones of some of the Kingdom rhetoric to the limitations of the disciples (citing Matt. 19:28 and Luke 22:29, 30),[69] so Bultmann says that "these are indeed not genuine words of Jesus; they reflect the hope of the earliest community." [70] But while for Rauschenbusch these passages indicate that Jesus was groping toward a more universal conception of the Kingdom of God, Bultmann states flatly that "the fact that in the thought of Jesus the national connotation of the Kingdom of God remains in the background does not mean that he taught its universality." [71] Jesus does not think in universalistic terms, for that would only mean that Man instead of the Jew is attempting to exercise a claim against God. "Man as such is not predestined for the Kingdom. The Kingdom is an eschatological miracle, and those destined for it are not thus destined because of their humanity but because they are called of God." [72]

[67] *Jesus and the Word,* pp. 35-38.
[68] *Ibid.,* p. 39.
[69] *Christianity and the Social Crisis,* pp. 62-63.
[70] *Jesus and the Word,* p. 43.
[71] *Ibid.,* p. 43.
[72] *Ibid.,* p. 46.

Rauschenbusch sees universalistic ideas as clear implications of the message of Jesus and sees also universal aspects of nature as pertinent to the decision for and structure of the Kingdom. Bultmann rejects both of these.[73] A similarity appears when both insist that it is finally not the individual but the church that is called.[74] But that similarity crumbles upon closer scrutiny. Rauschenbusch sees the church as a gathering and dispersing instrument by which those catching the vision of the Kingdom serve all men. Bultmann sees it as a gathered company of the faithful. Rauschenbusch attributes its creation to the concrete concern of Jesus to form a new institutional center of loyalty and righteousness in contrast to the dominant patterns of social organization. In a situation of family and tribal loyalties, the church calls all men brothers and all women sisters. In a situation of rigid controls on property, the church establishes a common purse and even later a semisocialist means of economic distribution. In an open society where wealth and title are the marks of honor and worthiness, Jesus establishes a voluntary hidden society

[73] In contrast, Amos N. Wilder evaluates Rauschenbusch's work in the following manner on these points: "For one thing, I notice six areas in which I would find Rauschenbusch on the right side historically in assessing the eschatology of Jesus: (1) the theocratic conception of the Kingdom as against an individualistic one; (2) a revolutionary view as against a policy of waiting; (3) a social . . . view of the Kingdom as against one conceived of in terms of inner spirituality; (4) a view of Jesus' eschatology as identifying itself with what we might call "secularity" as against a view of the Kingdom associated with shrine piety; (5) a view of the Kingdom as involving conflict as against views of Jesus' program as one of smooth education in society; (6) a view of the coming of the Kingdom involving . . . setbacks and detours as against an evolutionary view of the Kingdom. (However, on this last point one does find phrases . . . where Rauschenbusch . . . [seems] to hold a very optimistic view of a progressive Kingdom). . . . Again, Rauschenbusch holds that Jesus' outlook was marked by universalism, meaning that Jesus expected the gospel and instructed his disciples to extend the gospel beyond the land of the Jewish people. [Rauschenbusch] . . . here cites Matthew 28, the great commission, and one wonders about this use of post-resurrection [material] . . . as a saying of Christ." (Personal correspondence to the editor, July, 1966.)

[74] Cf. Rauschenbusch's formulations above, pp. 37-38 to Bultmann's statement: "It is not the individual who attains, in the Kingdom of God, to the realization of his latent capacities, to the cultivation of his personality, or to perfect happiness. That *God* should cause His sovereignty to appear, that *His* will should be done, that the promise to the community should be fulfilled, this is what the realization of the Kingdom of God means. Thus the individual indeed finds deliverance, but only because he belongs to the eschatological community, not because of his personality." *Jesus and the Word,* p. 47.

where the faith and trust and suffering of the poor are honored in anticipation of the Kingdom.

Bultmann, by contrast, says: "It is probable that such sayings as betray no church interests at all really go back to Jesus." [75] Further, insofar as the early church established new patterns of society, it failed to follow in the footsteps of Jesus, for it instituted a new variety of legalism whereas Jesus opposed every form of it. The early church, according to Bultmann, just "did not understand the double edge of certain of the sayings of Jesus about the Law." [76]

In this connection, we might point out comparative responses to a turning point in New Testament scholarship. Bultmann is critical of the "interim-ethic" view of the New Testament. Late in Rauschenbusch's career and early in Bultmann's, Albert Schweitzer argued that early Christian expectation of the end of the world meant that "Jesus had no interest in the different aspects of moral life, in marriage and work, in the value of property and civil order." [77] Instead, he developed only a radical interim ethic for the time between his coming and the end of the world. Since the end did not come as expected, it is of dubious continual import. Bultmann takes issue with this view, but not with its social and ethical implications. Rather, he is concerned with particular aspects of the eschatological theory as it affects existential decision making. The eschatological language does imply the radical importance of immediate decision, but it has nothing to do with moral action to shape the future. Bultmann thus insists "it is certainly true that as a result of the expectation of the imminent end of this world, Jesus was not interested in many of the concrete possibilities in which man's obedience can be proved on earth." [78]

From a standpoint informed by nascent sociology of theological knowledge, Rauschenbusch responds quite differently to the whole issue after reading Schweitzer's book:

[75] *Ibid.*, p. 124.
[76] *Ibid.*, p. 126.
[77] Quoted by Bultmann, *Ibid.*, p. 127.
[78] *Ibid.*, p. 127.

My own conviction is that the professional theologians of Europe, who all belong by kinship and sympathy to the bourgeois classes and are constitutionally incapacitated for understanding any revolutionary ideas, past or present, have overemphasized the ascetic and eschatological elements in the teachings of Jesus (in the sense of the end of the world). They have classed as ascetic or apocalyptic the radical sayings about property and non-resistance which seem to them impractical or visionary. If the present chastisement of God purges our intellects of capitalistic and upper-class iniquities, we shall no longer damn these sayings by calling them eschatological, but shall exhibit them as anticipations of the fraternal ethics of democracy and prophecies of social common sense.[79]

The responses of these two figures to Schweitzer is significant because each would perhaps criticize the other in the same way that he criticizes Schweitzer. Bultmann would surely say that Rauschenbusch understands little about existential decision making and the way in which the future impinges upon man's historicity in it. Rauschenbusch would undoubtedly classify Bultmann as one who is ideologically blinded to the direct implications of historical-social movements under the impress of the Kingdom. The differences between them seem, thus, to involve some fundamental philosophical differences that need exploring.

One could continue to recount the divergences between Rauschenbusch and Bultmann within a common frame by pointing to differences in their understanding of particular passages, and in their selection of particular portions of the New Testament for accent or by spelling out their opposing interpretations of the command of love. But on the basis of the disagreements so far discussed, the task is to inquire why they are so different given their similar theological tradition and the same material to interpret.

In part, their differences are similar to the problem that the sociologists face in the "fully-only" question. When the correlation between factors is, say, 42 percent, is this to be reported as "fully" or "only"? For Rauschenbusch and Bultmann, this takes form in the

[79] *A Theology for the Social Gospel* (Nashville: Abingdon Press, 1960 [first published New York: The Macmillan Company, 1917]), p. 158.

comparisons between Christianity and Judaism, Jesus and John, Jesus and Paul, Jesus and Gnostic movements, Jesus and Jewish eschatological Christianity, primitive Christianity and subsequent transformationist movements that have claimed sanction in the New Testament. Are the relationships between these sets of factors to be seen as "fully" similar in so many respects, or as "only" reflecting minimal correlation? At many points, the choice between "fully" and "only" depends upon the direction and consequences of the whole argument, for that will determine whether a particular analogy is relatively significant or not.

In part Rauschenbusch and Bultmann are each merely children of their respective periods. Their choices can be understood in the context of their times. But we need to seek a deeper level to comprehend more fundamental disagreements between them.

The central difference is one which runs through the history of Christian thought. One stream can be found in the Pauline, Augustinian, Lutheran, and Pietist interpretations of the law as essentially contradictory to the gospel. Indeed, the distinctions of sin and grace, exteriority and interiority, are often quite easily correlated to the distinction between law and gospel. Recent bearers of this tradition fear "objectification" in doctrine, institution, or program. In contrast, the synoptic, non-Pauline, semi-Augustinian, and Calvinist "free church" interpretation sees the gospel as that which transforms and redefines but does not invalidate; universalizes and idealizes, but does not sentimentalize; fully utilizes and influences, but is not dominated by law. In the latter view, the relationship between interiority and exteriority is seen as a reciprocal one, and the distinction is certainly not correlated with the distinction between being in grace or being under sin. "Objectification" is recognized to have danger, but it is seen to be necessary: "By their fruits ye shall know them." In regard to both the life of the person and the life of the church, there is a direct correlation between its objective functions, its acts and involvements, latent and manifest, and its subjective existence. Personhood and koinonia are deeply influenced by the social context and cannot be divorced from it. What people and groups *are* is apparent from what they in fact *do* as they act on and are acted upon by their environment. Radically stated, the former view insists that "stone walls do not a prison make, nor iron bars a cage"; there is still the reality of spiritual freedom and grace. The latter view insists that stone walls and iron bars are not irrelevant to spiritual freedom; they can and often do destroy it. The latter calls men, under mandate of the gospel, to redesign the institutionalized walls and habits that separate men and establish new structures that positively influence social and personal liberty. But according to Bultmann, "any attempt on man's part to establish the security of his existence on the basis of determinate facts in the world, over which he can exercise control, leads to being bound to the past and shut in sin." [80]

There are several implications of this fundamental difference. First, how much are we to allow technical historical data to influence our understanding of the New Testament? Both men, according to the standards of their days, consider themselves thoroughly historical. But, even granting the differences in current material available to them and the differences in professional competence, there is an underlying divergence. Rauschenbusch sees the meaning of the New Testament primarily in terms of what the historical event of Jesus Christ and the historical life of the church actually did, sociologically, to the structure of human relationships. The genuine revelation is not "in" the New Testament but "in" history and historical consequences. He intentionally went to Germany to study sociology and the New Testament simultaneously, and he consciously developed a view in which the New Testament is a prism through which we see what God was doing in the midst of human life.

In contrast, Bultmann uses his sophisticated historical tools, especially form criticism, in order to isolate the essential "message" of the New Testament. The historical context shapes the message but is not in itself informative. We study the historical context to extricate the intended message. Revelation occurs in history, but it is in

[80] H. Ganse Little, "History, Decision and Responsibility," p. 223.

fact something other than history. It is an eternal message or word that characterizes and provokes man's need for immediate decision and radical obedience. The message and the decision are the crucial "events" that have no "objective" reference. Although Rauschenbusch does not use this language, revelatory "events" are, for him, historical occasions, when social processes, personal commitments, and organizations shift the structure of human relations under the influence of the power and reign of God. On this point one is tempted to suggest that for Rauschenbusch the medium is the message, and the medium is history. In any case, we must say that Rauschenbusch is more thoroughly historical than Bultmann in that he does not think that the central meaning of the New Testament is a supernatural, superhistorical formal "word" or message. The meaning instead is to be found in what it does as a historical dynamic. Of course, in several passages Rauschenbusch sees ethical imperatives as rather formal superhistorical principles coming from the New Testament, and as ideals to be transplanted across the centuries. But in contrast to other figures of the Social Gospel, he takes considerable pains to show that there are structural historical continuities and analogies between the New Testament world and the present that allow such transplanting.

Bultmann says that "the incarnation is . . . an eschatological event and not a datable event of the past; it is an event which is continually being re-enacted in the event of proclamation." [81] Elsewhere he writes that "what God has done in Jesus Christ is not an historical fact which is capable of historical proof. The objectifying historian as such cannot see that an historical person (Jesus of Nazareth) is the eternal Logos." [82] To this, Rauschenbusch would reply: Of course not, but we can see that history has been constitutionally affected by Jesus and the movement in his name. We can see how the Fourth Gospel adopted and adapted the term "logos" both to express the transforming but noncoercive power of this historical pattern of events and to call the attention of others to its significance. Then, in confrontation

[81] *Kerygma and Myth* (New York: Harper & Row, 1933), ed. by H. W. Bartsch, p. 60.
[82] *Jesus Christ and Mythology* (New York: Charles Scribner's Sons, 1958), p. 80.

with the movement, its discipline, its direction, its vision, one decides either to join or not. The conditions and consequences of decision are as much a part of the Christian understanding of revelation as the "message" and the decision. They are constitutive.

The second presupposition beneath the different approaches of Rauschenbusch and Bultmann is their understanding of how man's historicity influences his decision making. For Bultmann, man's historicity means that all reliances and securities pass away and are transient, allowing for pure faith.[83] Rauschenbusch sees a positive relationship between history and faith. Bultmann, more in the Lutheran mold, sees history as that which undercuts and condemns securities. It drives man to purity of faith in the gospel. The future impinges on the present in every moment, destroying the residues of the past. Therefore, man stands in his historicity under an "eternal now" wherein free decision must be existentially made. For Rauschenbusch, the historicity of decision making means that men and societies become aware of alternatives and obligations by claims that are made upon their time, money, effort, loyalty, skill, and sometimes life. Demands for radical obedience to God are part of these claims. Decisions as to how one person or nation is to allocate the various resources at its command are concrete historical decisions that demand both adjudication between competing claims and calculation of consequences. The weighing of claims and the allocation of one's resources in obedience to God's will demand a historically sensitive interpretive framework and some principles of discrimination. Actual authentic existence demands a "new hermeneutic" that cuts to the quick of historical and institutional as well as personal life. To sustain or create demands that compromise the totalitarian effects of a single historical person or institution, one must establish historically enduring institutions geared to secure freedom. Thus historicity is related to free decision making, but in a way that leads us directly

[83] Rauschenbusch says of the view that wants to separate pure Christianity from the world that it "asks for a pure gospel and means a disembodied spirit that haunts churches." *The Righteousness of the Kingdom*, below, p. 87. Cf. also, "Ethical versus Forensic Conceptions of Salvation," *Eleventh Annual Session of the Baptist Congress* (New York, 1894), pp. 76-77.

into social ethics, institutional life, and concepts of "good order" rather than away from all reliance upon institutions and historical programs.

The issues raised by *The Righteousness of the Kingdom* take on larger dimensions when placed in the context of the most dominant movement in contemporary New Testament scholarship. The conflicts between the approach of Rauschenbusch and that of Bultmann are centered not only in disputes about the meaning of particular passages but also in the understanding of eschatology, the principles of interpretation, and in basic assumptions that have long-range consequences.

The Righteousness of the Kingdom forces us to ask whether there may not be an alternative to the contemporary consensus in New Testament scholarship. Is it not possible that a socially and ethically sensitive "new hermeneutic" of the New Testament can be developed without violating the texts and their role in history, and without speaking only in an *ad hoc* fashion to contemporary problems—as is the wont of much social ethics? [84] The developing world denominations will soon be demanding and producing such interpretations, if there is any substance to the foregoing analysis, and it is not unlikely that some of the motifs of Walter Rauschenbusch's *The Righteousness of the Kingdom* will find resonance again. It is the hope of this author that the quality of the man and the material itself, the context of its recovery, the new light that it sheds on the structure of ethical thought, and the prophetic insight that he brings to his unfinished quest for a historical and ethical interpretation of Christianity will add to that likelihood.

[84] James Gustafson, for example, laments the over-accent on the immediate in much contemporary ethics that prevents serious research of a fundamental sort. ("Christian Ethics," *Religion*, ed. Paul Ramsey [Englewood Cliffs, N. J.: Prentice Hall, 1965], p. 287.) He points out the necessity of research in the area of biblical ethics and suggests that, in contrast to present practices engendered in part by the state of biblical scholarship, "broader theological use of the Bible is particularly necessary where the Christian community desires to interpret theologically and ethically the importance of Christian faith for the extensive and complex issues of human morality in politics, economics, and other areas, and where the community accepts some responsibility for the temporal good of the whole society" (*ibid.*, p. 310).

PART II

THE RIGHTEOUSNESS OF THE KINGDOM

AUTHOR'S INTRODUCTION

It would be a mistake to represent Jesus merely as an ethical teacher. His purpose above all things was to make God known and loved among men. To leave the Father out of Christ's teaching is to blot the sun out of the day. But on the other hand he was not merely a guide in mystical religion. He came to found a new society on earth, and he laid down the principles of conduct which were to govern men in this new society. Nor did he regard this as a matter of secondary importance. The bulk of his teachings as recorded in the first three Gospels is on questions of conduct. Questions of ceremonial were slighted by him; he took them up only when they were thrust upon him by others, and then it was only to unwrap and rescue some question of justice or mercy which was tangled up in the ceremony and in danger of suffocation. In doctrinal discussions also he frequently showed the ethical aspect was the one that mainly interested him; that in fact he refused to consider theological questions when divorced from their ethical outcome. "Will the number of the saved be smaller?" "See that you are saved yourself." (Luke 13, 23-24.)

We cannot conceal from ourselves the fact that the Christian church has not, on the whole, apportioned its interest in the same way. It has split on questions of ceremonial, like the use of leavened or unleavened bread in communion, but not on the question of violent resistance to wrong. It has been shaken for centuries on doctrinal questions, like the relation of the persons of the Trinity, but not so much on the relation of rich and poor. There is a clean-limbed vigor in the discussion of doctrine, which seems to change to the halting step of the half-blind in the treatment of human relations as affected by Christian discipleship. We know of many tracts setting forth the scheme of salvation, but we do not recall a single popular and full statement of the kind of conduct imposed by Christ upon his followers.

Yet the need of a bold and legible presentation of the Master's conception of righteousness has perhaps never been greater than today. It is needed for the church; for the modern Jews and Greeks are not asking for signs and wisdom as the credentials of the church, so much as for the fruits of a new life, for a conduct palpably different from any they are used to. It is needed for the world; for the great task of our epoch is the re-casting of social institutions, and it will depend largely on us how much of Christ's conceptions of social relations will be infused into the metal which is now glowing in the furnace of modern thought.

The teaching of Jesus was always fragmentary. He spoke as the needs of his hearers prompted. There is none of the rounded symmetry of an elaborate system, going back to the beginnings and working everything out to the details. On some matters he spoke frequently and at great length, others he never touched, not because he was indifferent to them, but because he could take the knowledge of them for granted with his hearers. He never dwelt on the wickedness of murder or the sinfulness of stealing. The ethical training of the Jewish people in the past had taken care of that part of his task. He accepted as his own the moral heritage of Israel, wrought out by Moses and the prophets. It was not his task to raze those gigantic foundation walls to the ground, but rather to build upon them the shining pillars which were to support the temple of a perfect humanity. He had not come to destroy but to fulfill. He set about his task where the Law stopped. The Law said: "Thou shalt not murder"; he said: "Yea, nor shalt thou be angry with thy brother." The Law said:

"Thou shalt not commit adultery"; he said: "Thou shalt not even lust." The Law said: "Thou shalt not send away thy wife without a legal document defining her status and permitting her to marry another"; he said: "Thou shalt not send away thy wife at all save for the cause of fornication." The Law said: "Thou shalt keep the word thou hast sworn to"; he said: "Thou shalt keep thy word without swearing to it." The Law said: "If a man smites out thine eye, thou shalt not smite out his two eyes, but only one"; he said: "Thou shalt smite out none at all." The Law drew a white circle of love around all men of Jewish faith and nationality and said: "Thou shalt hate none within this circle; what is beyond thou mayest hate"; he blotted out the circle and drew it again around all humanity and said: "Thou shalt hate none and love all." Thus he fulfilled the Law, as one fills a vase that has been but half full.

In systematizing the ethical principles of Jesus, we must not forget then that he presupposes the plain moral convictions of humanity, and that he will not allow his followers to drop back of the lines of righteousness drawn by the past experience of the race. On the other hand we must not forget that he refuses to stop with them. The moral maxims of the past are buoys to mark the channel as far as explored; they are not invitations to anchor, but to sail on.

There is a noble union of the conservative and the progressive element in this position, which constitutes a permanent principle of action for the builders of the Kingdom of God. They must not destroy; they must accept and reverently disentangle the convictions of right and wrong which the past thought of humanity has matured. But they must not stop there, they must fulfill and always keep on fulfilling. The Christian conceptions of righteousness are gradually saturating public opinion in the civilized nations. The regard for human life and the sympathy for suffering which were formerly distinctively Christian virtues have become matters of simple humanity. The righteousness of the scribes and Pharisees is moving forward. If the righteousness of the disciples of the Master is still to keep its pre-eminence, they must break camp and move forward into the untried regions of the future, though there be but a few blood-stained footprints to show the way, and though there are many barriers and pitfalls.

Of course the real obstacle is the fact that it will cost us a sacrifice in some part of our own life. If we are to save others, we cannot save ourselves. If we want others to live in comfort, we cannot live in luxury. If we would champion the despised, we must say farewell to our own reputation. This is the gift of the cross, and the cross is not sweet but exceedingly bitter. But without the cross there is no discipleship of Jesus. As he gave his life to ransom others, so we must give ours. The cross is the badge of the new humanity, the test of our heart's allegiance. We can see from the writings of his greatest discipleship what an ineffaceable impression the cross of Christ made on the world. Paul mentions few of the sayings or acts of Christ, but that he became poor to make us rich, that he died to give us life is mentioned again and again. To bear one another's burdens was to him the sum of Christian law. In the same way John insists that as he laid down his life for us, we ought also to lay down our lives for the brethren. The duty to save the lost and to do so if necessary with loss to ourselves was raised to the dignity of a sovereign principle by Jesus. The world knows what a "Christ-like action" means. Even those who utterly refuse to act on the principle acknowledge its imperial beauty by admiring it in others and show their intellectual acceptance of it by censuring Christians for their lack of obedience to it.

Most men do not deny the obligation to love and save perishing life, but they try to shirk the responsibility by drawing limits and restricting the obligation within them. "See that ye despise not one of these lowly ones," said Jesus when he spoke of causing others to stumble. The personal insignificance of those we deal with makes us inclined to over-ride their rights and forget how precious their interests are to them.

> Rattle his bones over the stones!
> He's only a pauper, whom nobody owns!

Another limit drawn is that of nationality and creed. "Who is my neighbor?" Jesus showed what answer he understood the man to expect by telling the story of the good Samaritan, who knocks down once and for all the barriers which creed and nationality have erected against the full sway of love. "Who is my neighbor?" The alien and the heretic. We fully understand this as regards the Jew and the Samaritan. We have all poured our vials of scorn on the narrow-hearted Jew. But the tendency to draw such limits is as strong as ever. The history of the Negro, the Indian, and the Chinese can tell how difference of color and race can warp the sense of justice and dull the fine perception of love. The scorn with which "Poles and Hungarians" are spoken of in our papers and the cynicism with which they are hunted and shot show the same thing. The limitation of love by difference of religion is not yet wiped out, as men engaged in charitable work know. There are very few charitable institutions that are not limited on the score of religion. There are few of us whose hearts do not warm more quickly to a fellow religionist or fellow infidel than to another in the same distress. The story is told that when a Negro was seized in Boston before the [Civil] War and carried back to the South, a man came to [William Lloyd] Garrison the next day to inquire if the Negro were really a Baptist; he had been unable to sleep because he heard that he was. He was deeply shocked when told that he was not only a Baptist, but a Baptist preacher. The fate of the Negro had left him indifferent, the fate of the Baptist touched him.

Another excuse had been found from the exercise of saving love in the duties of religion. The Sabbath must be kept holy, that poor back that had been bent for eighteen years must stay bent another day. The Sabbath must be kept holy, therefore the withered hand must be palsied still. (Matt. 12, 1-14.) The temple has need of a gift, therefore this money is corban and the aged parents must manage to do without it. (Matt. 7, 9-13.) Jesus makes beautifully clear to them the loveless character of this religion by reminding them that they pulled their ox out of a pit on the Sabbath if he fell in, and that the work of taking their oxen to the water was performed by them every Sabbath. And was not the suffering of a daughter of their people as worthy of relief as the thirst of a beast? But then you see, the oxen were their own and the woman was not. It makes all the difference in the world.

There is still another point in the teaching of Jesus and the impairment of life and our duty in view of this. Men came to him out of breath to tell him of an event which had shocked Jerusalem. A number of Galileans had been killed by Pilate's soldiers while preparing their sacrifice, so that their blood had mingled with the blood of the beasts. There was something particularly inhuman and irreligious in this. This was the sort of event that would be published with extra heavy headlines in modern papers. Jesus manifested comparatively little interest in this. He told them of another case of a tower in Siloam falling upon eighteen men and killing them, and in each case he had only the warning "except ye repent, ye shall all in like manner perish." He looked beyond a single striking catastrophe which caught the imagination of the people to a doom which was overhanging the whole nation, and he wanted men to pay attention to this. Men are always stirred by catastrophes and always oblivious of the silent growth and pressure of destructive conditions. Yet the former are important mainly as manifestations of the latter. So if a children's hospital were burned today and fifty babies stifled in the smoke, a cry of horror would go up from millions. But when not scores but hundreds of little children are killed off prematurely every summer in New York by the crowding of tenements, that leaves love passive and syrupy and dormant.

The meaning of this is, then, that we must redirect a reconstituted love toward vicious conditions in the community and by repentive action avert the disaster with which the present is always pregnant. Just as that embodied the life-work of Christ and called for his total sacrifice, so it embodies the life-work of Christianity. And the fidelity of Christ's followers will have to be measured by this standard in all our relations to our fellow-men, to ourselves, and to God. We shall take up the teachings of Jesus in that order, after stating the nature, program, resources, and power of Christian ethics. We shall conclude with an evaluation of present prospects.

In discussing our relations to our fellow-men, we shall speak first of our treatment of their life, their reputation, and their property, for these are common to all; then of the special relations existing between men and women; and finally of the relations of the individual to the state.

1
CHRISTIANITY IS REVOLUTIONARY

Christianity is in its nature revolutionary. Its revolutionary character is apparent from the spiritual ancestry to which it traces its lineage. Jesus was the successor of the Old Testament prophets. The common people of his day discerned this kinship and whispered that he must be Elijah or Jeremiah or some other of the prophets. (Lk. 9, 19.) Although he denied his identification with them, he himself repeatedly drew the parallel between the work and lot of the prophets and his own. Like the prophets he was rejected in his own country. (Matt. 13, 57.) Like the prophets he was to suffer at the hands of the wicked husbandmen. (Lk. 20, 4-18.) Like all the prophets he must perish at Jerusalem. (Lk. 13, 34-35.) His forerunner he calls a prophet, a second Elijah (Mk. 9, 11-13; Lk. 7, 26); and to his followers he predicts that like the prophets they will be slandered and persecuted (Matt. 5, 10-12), and at last like the prophets meet their death. (Matt. 23, 29-36.)

Now what were these prophets, to whose spirit and purpose Jesus felt so close a kinship, and whose lot he expected to share?

The prophets were the revolutionists of their age. They were dreamers of Utopias. They pictured an ideal state of society in which the poor should be judged with equity and the cry of the oppressed should no longer be heard; a time in which men would beat their idle swords into ploughshares and their spears into pruning hooks, for then the nations would learn war no more. (Isa. 2, 4.) No slight amelioration contented them, nothing but a change so radical that they dared to represent it as a repealing of the ancient and hallowed covenant and the construction of a new one. A proposal to abolish the Constitution of the United States would not seem so revolutionary to us as this proposal must have seemed to the contemporaries of the prophets.

They did not expect such a change to glide in without a struggle. A day of vengeance would have to precede it. It would be like a refiner's fire and like fullers' soap. (Mal. 3, 2.) The Lord would have a reckoning with those that oppressed the hireling in his wages, the widow, and the fatherless, and those that turned aside the stranger from his right. (Mal. 3, 5.) He would come upon the high ones and the kings of the earth, and gather them as prisoners are gathered in the dungeon, and shut them up in prison. (Isa. 24, 21-22.) For they had eaten up the vineyard, the spoil of the poor was in their houses; they had beaten God's people to pieces; they had ground the faces of the poor. (Isa. 3, 13-15.)

Nor were the prophets mere impractical dreamers and declaimers. They were men of action. They overthrew dynasties. They were popular agitators, tribunes of the people. They rebuked to their faces kings who had robbed the plain man of his wife or tricked him out of his ancestral holding.

These were the men whose successor Christ professed to be. This does not imply that he sanctioned all their actions or proposed to copy all their methods. But it does imply that of all the forces in the national history of Israel the prophets were the most worthy of his approval and most akin to his spirit.

The revolutionary character of Christ's work appears also from the elements in contemporary life to which he allied himself.

The Messianic hope, kindled and fanned by the prophets, was still glowing in the hearts of the people. When John the Baptist lifted up his voice by the Jordan, men were on the alert immediately, querying "whether haply he were the Messiah." (Lk. 3, 15.) The atmosphere of Palestine was surcharged with this electricity. When, in the synagogue at Nazareth, Jesus chose for his text that passage of Isaiah which tells of glad tidings to the poor, of release to the captives, of liberty to the bruised, and of the acceptable year of the Lord, "the eyes of all in the synagogue were fastened upon him." The passage was universally understood to refer to the Messianic era. They were breathlessly eager to hear what attitude he would assume. And what was his attitude? He told them the time had now come: "To-day hath this scripture been fulfilled in your ears." (Lk. 4, 16-21.)

It is plain that the people counted him as their own. They were waiting to see him raise the standard of revolt and were ready to follow him as their king. (John 6, 14-15.) And in spite of all apparent disappointments to which he subjected them, they had their eye on him still. When at the very end he entered Jerusalem with something of public state, all their hopes revived and they hailed him as the Messiah coming to claim the Kingdom of his father David.

It is true that Christ steadfastly refused to fulfill their expectations. We shall discuss later on his reasons for doing so. Yet the fact remains that he did appeal to the Messianic hope. He found his followers among those in whom that hope was liveliest. He came so near to fulfilling the people's idea of the Messiah that they were always on the verge of expectation. To the Sadducean enemies of the Messianic movement he seemed, even at the end of his ministry, so closely connected with the movement that they regarded it as only a question of time when he would lead the revolt and plunge the nation into war with Rome. (John 11, 47-50.)

The contents of the Messianic hope of course varied. With some it was dyed in blood, with others it was irradiated by heaven. But this element was common to all who entertained it: they were weary of present conditions; they were longing for a radically different state of affairs; and they were sure that it would come and were ready to help it on. In other words, the Messianic hope was a revolutionary hope.

That this revolutionary element existed even among the most

spiritually minded men and women is discernible from the recorded words of those choice souls among whom Jesus, by God's own appointment, spent his early years and by whom his thoughts were moulded. The hymns in the first two chapters of Luke, judged by internal evidence, express the Messianic hope before it had been modified by the teachings and the life of Jesus. Note the revolutionary tone:

> He hath shewed strength with his arm;
> He hath scattered the proud in the imagination of their heart.
> He hath put down princes from their thrones
> And hath exalted them of low degree.
> The hungry he hath filled with good things;
> And the rich he hath sent empty away. (Lk. 1, 51-53.)

Those were the thoughts of her whose blood ran in the veins of Jesus and who had the fashioning of his early years.

Zacharias blesses Jehovah for having raised up a horn of salvation,

> Salvation from our enemies, and from the hand of all that hate us;
> . . . That he would grant unto us,
> That we, being delivered out of the hands of our enemies
> Should serve him without fear
> In holiness and rightteousness before him all our days. (Lk. 1, 71, 74-75.)

In these two songs the thought of the Messianic victory predominates, and Simeon thinks more of the conflict which shall precede it and which will bring about the prostration of some and the elevation of others. "Behold this child is set for the falling and the rising of many in Israel; and for a sign which is spoken against; yea and a sword shall piece through thine own soul; that thoughts out of many hearts may be revealed." (Lk. 2, 34-35.) But in them all is the prophetic hope: a mighty uprising of Jehovah, a casting down of the powerful and wicked, and then peace and prosperity for the poor and righteous.

When finally we turn to the man whom Jesus himself has called the choicest fruit of all the past, we find the same revolutionary language.

> Make ye ready the way of the Lord!
> Make his paths straight!
> Every valley shall be filled
> And every mountain and hill shall be brought low;
> And the crooked shall become straight,
> And the rough way smooth. (Isa. 40, 3-4.)

Here is a general straightening out and leveling as a preparation for the coming of the Messiah. His advice to the people explains what he meant by straightening out the crooked ways and razing the high places: "He that hath two coats let him impart to him that hath none; and he that hath food let him do likewise." The abolition of social inequality, according to John, was the first step in the Messianic renewal. His conception of the Messiah's work is likewise expressed in flaming images of destruction and overthrow: a dusty threshing-floor, a sifting of wheat and chaff, a consuming fire, a crashing down of rotten trees. The baptism of John, in which his preaching found its dramatic expression, was a revolutionary symbol. It was the baptism of repentance; a turning away from old ways and a consecration to the new; it was the rite of initiation into "the remnant" which would be prepared for the coming of the Messiah and fit for the new order of things to be ushered in by the Messianic judgment.

The revolutionary character of his work is expressly asserted by Christ. He came to cast fire upon the earth, and he longed to see it kindled. He had come to hide a leaven in the world's trough of meal, and it would be in a ferment until the leaven had done its work.

He brought a new spirit and the new spirit would demand new forms of life. Men then as now had little discernment for the new spirit, but they raised a decided protest against the abolition of old forms and the evolution of new ones. He might bring new wine if he wished, but let him put it in the old vessels. But Jesus told them that they must not think that his young, bubbling wine could be bottled up in the old, cracked wine-skins, and that it would not suffice reverently to patch bits of new cloth on the most shameless rents of the tattered garment wherewith society was seeking to cover its nakedness. A new spirit plus new forms and customs and institutions —that means revolution.

The change he was inaugurating was so radical, that after its consummation it would be found that the first had become last and the last first. Ideas now dominant would then be smiled over. Institutions now regarded as existing *jure divino* would then be recognized as having existed *jure diabolico.* Men now on top in society and state and church would move to the bottom, and many now despised and neglected would then be honored and would reign over the tribes of Israel. Such a reversal of values presupposes sweeping changes in the general conceptions and judgments prevalent in human society, and necessarily also in the social and political institutions in which these conceptions and judgments find their embodiment.

Jesus knew very well the difficulties of the work he had undertaken. He knew that those who have seats at the banquet where the old wine is served have little taste for the new. He knew that those who hold the places of power and privilege will seldom resign them without a struggle. He foresaw a terrible conflict, a division of humanity into hostile camps. A man would be set at variance with his father, and a daughter with her mother. Two in a household would be ranged against the other three. The strongest ties in the world would snap when they encountered this new force.

Jesus foresaw all this. If ever a heart was tender, surely it was his. Yet he did not shrink from precipitating the world into such a conflict. His was the revolutionary spirit, loving and inflexible.

Moreover his attitude became more revolutionary as he went on; his language grew sterner, his opposition to the powers that were more unyielding, until it grew plain that the most moral community of that age, and perhaps the most religious society of any age, was engaged in irreconcilable conflict with Jesus Christ, a conflict which could end only with the overthrow of one of the conflicting forces. We know that it did end with the apparent overthrow of the one and the actual overthrow of the other.

This interpretation of the tendency of Christ's work is borne out by the attitude of his contemporaries. Those who had anything to gain by a change followed him and heard him gladly. Those who had anything to lose by a change feared him. They feared him enough to hate him. They hated him enough to kill him. Self-interest is short-sighted, but its sight is marvelously keen for all that come within the range of its vision. When the chief priests and scribes and elders, the dignitaries of society as it then existed, combined to put him down at all hazard, they were not stabbing at shadows. They were closing with a deadly foe and they knew it. It was either his life or their privileges. They had no mind to be placed at the bottom in any overturning process of his.

In fact, if we consider what Christ's work really consisted in, we shall perceive that it could not but be revolutionary. He was sent by God, with his Father's thoughts and will in his heart, to make those thoughts known on earth and to secure obedience to that will.

Now if the world were lovingly doing God's will to the extent of its knowledge, and anxiously seeking more knowledge in order better to obey God, then Christ's work would have been educational and not revolutionary. With words of love he would have led his willing flock to the richer pastures and purer waters prepared for them. But that is not the state of the world. The crucifixion of Jesus gives the lie to that theory of life, and he that has eyes to see can see along the track of history a long line of Calvaries, where successive generations have sought to choke the Word of God calling them to righteousness. It has ever been easy for man to obey his lusts and hard to resist them. And the evil of centuries has found its proper expression and manufactured its fitting tools in the laws, the customs, the opinions and traditions prevailing in human society, so that an old man, who had seen much of life and yet loved mankind, sadly summed up his thoughts in the judgment: "The whole world is embedded in wickedness."

Given such a world, and given a great Christ who comes to see God's will done on earth, and in the nature of the case, there must be a collision, an upheaval, a revolutionary movement which must last and be revolutionary until either the world is brought into submission or Christ is conquered and gives up his attempt.

It is not within the purpose of this chapter to trace the course of the revolutionary movement initiated by Jesus, but simply to point out that the historical antecedents of Christianity, the contemporary forces with which it was allied, the express statements of Christ himself, the attitude of his contemporaries to him, and the very nature of his work prove that it was really a revolutionary movement. But a glance at the history of Christianity, as we find it in the apostolic writings of the New Testament, may serve still further to establish this point.

One of the most significant and earliest books of the New Testament is the Apocalypse. In gleaming imagery it portrays the overthrow of the brutal world powers and the inauguration of the Kingdom of Christ. In veiled words the wickedness of Rome, its luxury, its rottenness, its oppression, is pictured. The Christians of that age knew what was meant by "the great city that reigns over the kings of the earth" and that "is drunk with the blood of the saints," and doubtless many hearts longed for the sounding of hallelujahs over her fall.

Another crucial expression of Christian thought as it prevailed among the Jewish Christians is found in the Letter of James. There is something of the sternness of the Old Testament prophets and of John the Baptist in its rebuke of the incipient corruption of the church by property distinctions. Read this and see whether it sounds like complacent justification of existing conditions:

> Go to now, ye rich, weep and howl for your miseries that are coming upon you. Your riches are corrupted, and your garments are moth-eaten. Your gold and your silver are rusted and their rust shall be for a testimony against you and shall eat your flesh as fire. Ye have laid up your treasure in the last days. Behold the hire of the laborers who mowed your fields, which is of you kept back by fraud, crieth out; and the cries of them that reaped have entered into the ears of the Lord of Sabaoth. (James 5, 1-4.)

Such thoughts were probably far more general in the early church than we now suppose. The force and the bulk of Paul's teaching have in our minds overshadowed everything else in the apostolic church.

With Paul the revolutionary element is not so dominant. His mind worked in other directions and elaborated the thoughts of his Master on another side. But the evil of the present state of things, the certainty of an approaching Messianic judgment, and the establishment of a new world era were among his fundamental teachings. In fact he did do revolutionary work. However much and truthfully he protested that he was establishing the law, he was really making it unnecessary; he was leveling the distinctive prerogatives of the Jews and subverting everything in which they put their trust and pride. They were not altogether wrong when they called him "the man that teacheth all men everywhere against the people, and the law, and this place," and when they repeated before Felix the charge they had raised against Christ before Pilate: "We have found this man a pestilent fellow and a mover of insurrections among all the Jews throughout the world." There was truth in it. So far as Judaism, the whole intertwined mass of its religion, its politics and society, was concerned, Paul's work was revolutionary. And in heathen civilization he dropped a living seed which in the course of its growth was to burst asunder the masonry of its edifice and make it totter and fall. Very early men felt that he was attacking the principle of unity which held the Roman world together. It was not a mere misunderstanding when men accused him of turning the world upside down and of opposing Caesar by proclaiming Jesus as king. (Acts 17, 7.) We pass lightly over the passages in which he speaks of Christ as superior to "all government and authority and power and lordship and every name that is named," and calls him "the blessed and only Potentate, the King of kings and Lord of lords." But in those days of abject servility to human power, when the statue of the emperor stood in every market-place and divine honor was paid to the lord of the earth, the Christians must have felt those words to be more than pious phrases. At any rate the emperors soon came to feel the subversive power of these religious thoughts.

2
THE KINGDOM OF GOD

What, now, is the aim of this revolutionary movement inaugurated by Jesus? What word is inscribed on the banner he raised?

The Kingdom of God! That is the phrase forever recurring in his teaching. About that his thoughts circle like a host of planets 'round a central sun.

And what is this "Kingdom of God"? Jesus discusses many aspects of it, its value, its laws of growth, its blessings, its obstacles; but for a definition of what he meant by the words we look in vain. Why? Because his hearers were familiar with the words and with the idea contained in them. Jesus did not create the conception. It was there, the heritage of his nation's past and the most living hope of its present. Therefore to understand Jesus we must put ourselves in the position of his contemporaries and realize in our own mind the ideas with which the past had stocked the common mind of the Jewish people.

a. The Messianic Theocracy

The conceptions which ruled the religious life of Israel were the idea of the covenant and the theocracy. Jehovah had chosen Israel as peculiarly his own. He fought its battles through the judges. He reigned through the kings. He gave the laws. He spoke through the prophets. He heard the prayers of his people and interfered against their oppressors. If the people walked in his law, his blessing was promised to be upon them; they would till the ground in peace; the harvests would not fail; sickness would not come nigh them; their children would multiply like the young lambs of the flock. That is the Jewish ideal of life: a righteous community ordered by divine laws, governed by God's ministers, having intercourse with the Most High, and being blessed by him with the good things of life.

But the realization lagged wearily behind the idea. The people were recreant to their obligations. The kings were more often creatures of the harem than vice-regents of God. We hear the passionate protests of the prophets against the venality of judges and the covetousness of the nobles, and in the psalms the poor and meek sob for redress of wrongs. The national independence was lost. The rivers of Babylon saw the mute grief of Jewish exiles. After their return Jerusalem was ground under the heels of successive oppressors.

But the faith of this wonderful nation rose triumphant above this contradiction between their faith in a sublime vocation and their actual wretchedness. Its spirit was not crushed. Its faith was not relinquished. It must have fulfillment, somewhere, sometime. The perfect reign of God in Israel would yet be. Above the failures of the present rose the image of a glorious future. It took its outlines from periods of prosperity in the past, and its colors were pressed from the woes of the present. Every prophet saw it darkly and prophesied in part, but every one added some touch, and its lineaments grew ever clearer, till all the nation fixed its eyes on that hope.

It is not possible to trace here the long development of the Messianic hope, and the various forms it assumed in the two parts of Isaiah, in Ezekiel, in Daniel, and in the abundant apocalyptic literature after the exile. Its historic continuity was never broken, and in the days of Jesus the nation was full of eager anticipation of the Messiah's coming who was to initiate the new era by a mighty display of power in the judgment of the wicked and the liberation of the people of God.

The Messianic hope, then, was the hope for the perfection of the theocracy. Its contents varied with the character of those who entertained it. The majority perhaps looked for national revenge and temporal enjoyment. Some hoped for spiritual quickening. But this was common to them all, including John the Baptist; this belongs to the essence of the Messianic hope: the theocratic idea was at last to have its perfect realization in a Kingdom of God on earth, with the Messiah as its head, Israel as its dwelling-place and organ, and all the world as the sphere of its manifestation.

What attitude did Jesus assume toward the Messianic hope of his day? Did he oppose it as wrong, foolish, and perilous? Was he indifferent to it as to something remote from his own work? Or did he accept it, elevate it, and strive to realize it?

Evidently the latter. He used the vocabulary of the Messianic movement. He selected his followers from the circle most imbued with Messianic ideas. His attitude and preaching could not have been, and indeed were not, understood by his hearers as referring to anything but the establishment of the perfect theocracy.

And how could it have been otherwise? Jesus was not the successor of Greek philosophers teaching a system of self-culture. He was the successor and heir of the great thoughts of Israel. These, he said, he had come to fulfill. And if he protested that not an iota of the law should perish until it had come to its full fruition, would he cast aside as useless that greatest of all the Old Testament ideas, the idea of the theocracy? Here, if anywhere, his mission must be to fulfill and not to destroy. And to fulfill surely does not mean to supplant, to substitute something in its place which to all intents is not the same thing nor a fuller development of the same thing. If Jesus had brushed aside the idea of the reign of God on earth, he would have brushed aside the entire Old Testament and the entire past of Israel. And if any of the professed followers of Christ teach a Christianity in which that same idea is not the core and center, then they may protest their belief in the Old Testament, in its inspiration, its inviolability by criticism, and its divine contents, but they belie their own words. In theory they call it holy and wise, in practice they call it foolish and impracticable.

The assertion that Jesus identified himself with the Messianic hope does not imply that he proposed to fulfill every hope of everyone of his contemporaries, not even that he agreed with the conceptions entertained by a majority of them. The Messianic hope was a growth of centuries and its end was not identical with its inception. It was a popular idea that shaded off in innumerable tints, and not a rigid formula or scheme that had to be accepted entire or rejected entire. So in agreeing with some, Jesus could not help disagreeing with others.

Surveying the development of the Messianic idea, we find that there is a steady movement in certain directions; not a movement in a straight line, but a progress like the flow of a river, turned aside at one point by the peculiarities of one powerful personality, doubling on itself for a while under a temporary reactionary movement, and yet on the whole moving forward. And comparison shows that, in contradicting some popular conceptions and developing others, Jesus was working in the same direction in which the spirit of God had been slowly leading the prophets.

1) *The Messianic idea developed in the direction of universality.*

Prophecy was like a man climbing the winding stairs of a tower and gaining a wider and more glorious outlook with every window reached. The prophets of the first period, Joel, Amos, Hosea, speak only of a national salvation. Isaiah and Micah (Isa. 2, 2-4; Micah 4, 1-4) tell of Gentiles coming to inquire of the God of Jacob, and of Assyria and Egypt forming with Israel a holy triad of nations. (Isa. 19, 18-25.) The more Israel came in contact with the great empires, the larger grew the Messianic hope. The isles of the heathen and men beyond the rivers of Ethiopia would become suppliants to Jehovah. (Zeph. 2, 11; 3, 10.) They would bless themselves with his name and recognize all their religion as lies and emptiness. (Jer. 4, 2; 16, 19.) Then Jehovah alone would be king on earth (Zach. 14, 9), and the knowledge of his glory would fill the earth as the waters cover the sea. (Hab. 2, 14.) Finally universality became so prominent a feature of its Messianic hope, that a few at least rose to the idea that it was for just this purpose of being a light to the Gentiles that Israel had been chosen. (Isa. 40–66.)

This conviction had, in the time of Christ, issued in a wide-spread Jewish missionary activity. As Jesus puts it, they were compassing sea and land to make one proselyte. They numbered their adherents in the highest circles, especially among the women at Rome, and some years later Paul finds "devout proselytes" in all the Jewish congregations of Asia Minor. But this tendency to universality was hampered by the extreme nationalism of Judaism. All might share in the Messianic blessings, but only by becoming Jews and taking upon them the yoke of the law. That the Gentiles as Gentiles were to have a share in the Messianic salvation was unthinkable. We know how hard it was even for the apostles to strip off this narrowness, and how Paul waged a life-long battle against its effort to re-enslave the church.

The position of Jesus appears to have developed gradually on this point as on all others. He began his work, as was natural, among his own people. He concentrated his efforts on winning them to own him and obey him. (Matt. 23, 34.) He commanded his disciples on their missionary journeys not to go into the way of the Gentiles, nor into the Samaritan cities, but to go to the lost sheep of the house of Israel. (Matt. 10, 5-6.) Yet wherever he comes in contact with heathen, the wall of partition crumbles at his touch. He talks freely to the Samaritan woman and stays several days in her village. He is won by the faith of the Syrophoenician woman to do that which he had refused. The fact that the centurion at Capernaum was a heathen did not conceal from him that in this man dwelt a faith surpassing any that he had found in Israel, and he was led to prophesy that many like this man would come from the East and the West to share in the Kingdom, while sons of the Kingdom would be cast forth into the darkness without. In this disregard for names and regard for fact, in this unfailing hold on inward realities, lay the guarantee that Christ would limit his work not by the bounds of nationality but by the bounds of humanity. Faith and not Judaism qualified for the Kingdom. Unbelief and not uncircumcision disqualified for it. Therefore when his efforts for Israel as a whole had been unavailing, he told them that "the Kingdom of God would be taken from them and given to a nation bringing forth the fruits thereof." And so at the end he sent out his disciples to proclaim the glad tidings to all the nations.

We find, then, that the Kingdom of God, as Christ saw it, was not outwardly limited by the boundaries of any one nation. We have already touched on the fact that this outward universality was the necessary consequence of its inward universality. But we must expand that thought.

2) *The conception of the Messianic salvation developed in the direction of spirituality.*

The circle within which it would be manifested was widened; but at the same time the nature of its blessings and consequently the character of those capable of receiving them were differently conceived.

The early prophets spoke mainly of national independence and supremacy, and of temporal prosperity. Every Israelite would have a share in the blessing by virtue of being a member of the chosen nation.

But in time national experience taught the prophets that no outward reconstruction and no enforced obedience to the law would suffice. Jeremiah had seen the people slip back as soon as the strong arm of Josiah which had forced them up was withdrawn. A spiritual renewal was necessary as the basis for the bestowal of outward blessings. But if that was true, then not all of Israel would share in it, for it was but too evident that there were hearts too hard to yield. They would have to be weeded out. A great judgment would have to precede the Messianic salvation, and only "the remnant" would be saved.

In the nature of the case this conception could not be shared by all. Only those who were spiritual could discern that the profoundest chasm is not between nation and nation, nor even between those who perform outward rites and those who do not, but between those who have the love and fear of God in their hearts and those who have not. The children of this world stick to outward lines of demarcation. Accordingly, in spite of the growing plainness of prophetic preaching on this point, we find the people in the days of Christ still convinced that every child of Abraham who was in outward conformity with the law was entitled to a share in the Messiah's blessings as his birthright. There were some who saw it differently. Simeon had watched ecclesiastical life in Jerusalem long enough to foresee that there would be a rising for some in Israel but a falling for others. John the Baptist foretold a terrible sweeping out of the chaff and a hewing down of evil trees. He bade those who were comforting themselves with their descent from Abraham to look to their hearts; repentance alone would qualify them for the Kingdom; as for children of Abraham, God could turn the Jordan pebbles into as many of them as he wanted.

Jesus took up the same message. In the synagogue at Nazareth he proclaimed that the Messianic visitation was at hand. Then he spoke of the conditions of participating in it. He pointed out that in the days of Elijah it was a Sidonian widow to whom alone the prophet was sent. And in the days of Elisha it was only a Syrian leper who was cleansed, while Israel remained unblessed. The inference was that in the day of the Messiah also it would be spiritual fitness and not nationality that would ensure the blessing. It was that which angered the people: that they were to be placed on the same insecure and conditional footing with the rest of mankind. In praising the faith of the heathen centurion and in denouncing Chorazin and Bethsaida as worthy of greater punishment than the accursed cities of Phoenicia, he likewise overthrows the prerogative of nationality and establishes spirituality as the qualification for citizenship in the Kingdom. "Except ye turn and become as little children, ye shall in no wise enter into the Kingdom." "Except a man be born anew, he cannot see the Kingdom of God."

The tendency of prophetic development, then, was toward the recognition of the spiritual nature of the Kingdom of God. And this tendency finds its consummation in Christ's own conception. He proposed to found his Kingdom on spirit and not on matter. He gathered as the material for its upbuilding the poor in spirit, the meek, the merciful, and not the men who possessed temporal power and wealth and the ability of wielding the forces of this world. By his entire life he showed that he regarded the spiritual nature of man, the religious and moral element, as the core of the individual life and the real formative force in the life of society.

History assents to his position. Ideas and convictions are the enduring revolutionary forces. Changed institutions without changed convictions to uphold them from beneath are likely to slump together. In nations where religion has decayed or stands as a propped-up skeleton in churchly robes, where the sobriety and morality of the common people are sapped and poisoned, where the body politic has gristle instead of bone, the flabby mass may indulge in contortions, but it cannot march to greatness. Righteous and God-fearing men and women are the material with which the progress of human society can be made enduring. The infusion of a new principle, a new conviction into the thought-life of humanity is the condition of every onward step in the organization of society. The perfect humanity must be a growth, building itself up by vital forces from within, like the chambered nautilus secreting its own shell.

But while Jesus begin his work on the inward and spiritual side of human life, he did not propose to let it end there. That is the falsity of the conception of the Kingdom current among Christians today. They have learned so thoroughly the lesson that the Kingdom of God is righteousness and peace and joy in the Holy Ghost, that they are ready to close the book there. Social reformers shrug their shoulders at religion and labor away at environment as the source of social regeneration. "Nay," says the church, "not from without, but from within," and the church is right, as social reformers have found out and will find out yet more. But when the church silently adds "*only* within," it brings down on itself the severest invective of its professed Master. There was nothing that Jesus resented so much as an attempt to divorce the inward from the outward; to be saying "Lord, Lord!" and then not to obey him; to parade as a good tree and yet bring no fruit or bitter fruit. There was a man who had two sons. And he said to the elder, "Go work to-day in my vineyard." And he answered: "Certainly, Father, my will is consecrated to thee," but he did not go but sat on the fence and rejoiced in the assurance of his sonship within. The father made the same request of the younger. He was surly and muttered as he sat still: "In the first place I am not at all sure that he is my father; in the second place I think I only imagined that he spoke to me; and in the third place I am not going anyway." But after a while he climbed over the fence into the vineyard and began hoeing away, assuring himself that he did not do it on his father's account, but because he liked it. And the father wished that he had a third son who would both say yes and do yes.

Prosperity unsustained by righteousness ends in rottenness. Therefore Jesus did not begin his work by creating prosperity. Righteousness, if it has its full course, produces all prosperity. Therefore Jesus did begin with making men know and do righteousness, knowing well that if they did that, all things would be added to them. But woe to him that seeks to shut up the Spirit of God in his own heart or in the hearts of others and forbids it from going out into the world to do its creative work there, that speaks of a spiritual kingdom and means a kingdom of feelings and words and air and intangible moonshine, that looks for a kingdom of earth in heaven, but neither hopes nor desires a kingdom of heaven on earth, that asks for a "pure gospel" and means a disembodied spirit that haunts churches but never ventures out into the market and the stock exchange and the real estate office.

Christ initiated his Kingdom on earth by establishing a community of spiritual men, in inward communion with God and in outward *obedience* to him. This was the living germ of the Kingdom. But it was not the purpose of this community merely to dismiss one after the other of its members into heaven and to leave the world as it was, nor was the increase of its membership the only method of extending its power. By the power of the spirit dwelling in it, it was to overcome the spirit dominant in the world and thus penetrate and transform the world. In place of cruel customs it was to establish merciful customs. It was to push up steadily the average standard of right, making it approximate to the absolute standard of God. It was to break the enslaving power of lies by the enfranchising power of truth. Every such step forward, every increase in mercy, every obedience to justice, every added brightness of truth would be an extension of the reign of God in humanity, an incoming of the Kingdom of God. The more men became saturated with the thoughts of Christ, the more they came to judge all actions from his point of view, the more they conformed the outward life of society to the advancing inward standard, the more would Christ be the dominant force in the world and all humanity become the true theocracy.

That this development would not be a peaceful one, he foretold and demonstrated in his life. But that the Spirit of God can overthrow the resisting spirit of this world and oust it from one position after another, he also asserted and demonstrated. He also promised that at all the important junctures of this process and especially at its consummation God would interfere with awful judgments and demonstrations of his power from on high, co-operating with the spiritual work of the church in securing the triumph of Christ.

3) *There was a progress in prophetic thought in the value ascribed to spiritual means as against external means in the establishment of the Messianic Kingdom.*

At first, force was the means which the Messiah was to use and which those had to use who would anticipate his work. The reforming kings of Israel and Judah, instigated and upheld by the prophets, used force in suppressing the enemies of God and in bringing his people into obedience to the law. The Messiah was to be a warrior king, crushing the heads of his enemies, breaking their forces like potsherds, and distributing their booty to his followers.

But with the growing strength of the prophetic order and the influence of their teaching on the life of the nation, the tremendous force contained in the weapons of the spirit was increasingly recognized. During the exile the national government was non-existent. If the life and unity of the nation had depended on that, it would have dropped asunder like a barrel when the hoops are cut. But the national unity was maintained. The sense of oneness was increased. Patriotism and ardor for the law had never burned with so steady and persistent a fire. Evidently it was not by might nor by power, but by the spirit of Jehovah that great things were to be done. The suffering steadfastness of the godly had proved to be a power with men and prevailing with God. The Messianic salvation would be achieved by the same means.

These thoughts were dimly perceived by the prophets and treasured in some hearts. Spiritual men discerned with more or less clearness that as the qualifications for the Messianic Kingdom and its blessings were spiritual, so the means for its establishment must be spiritual also. But the majority of men put their trust in outward means. They expected that the Messiah would drive out the Romans by force. They showed their trust in arms by their readiness to seize them. They were impatient with Jesus for delaying so long his summons to arms.

Christ's choice of means was made at the outset of his work and consistently adhered to until the end. In the lonely days following his baptism he faced the temptations that pressed upon him in his official capacity and settled on his course. He decided first that he would not use his official power for self-gratification, not even to save himself from pain; in the second place that he would not seek to attract men by miraculous display; and finally that he would not ally himself with that Messianic faction of his people which had hate for its motive and force for its means, even if by that means he might gain the kingdoms of the world and the glory thereof. The latter two refer to the means to be chosen for his work.

In declining to gain adherents by the display of power, he put aside the influence which would most readily have gained him the leadership of his nation. They were all on the alert for high-colored marvels. Paul mentions it as the distinguishing characteristic of Jewish religious life that they were ever asking for signs. "Master, we would see a sign from thee." (Matt. 12, 38.) "What then doest thou for a sign, that we may see and believe thee? What workest thou? Our fathers ate the manna in the wilderness." (John 6, 30-31.) Even to the cross that temptation followed him: "Let him now come down from the cross, and we will believe on him." (Matt. 27, 42.)

Jesus refused their request over and over again, to the distress of his disciples and the pleasure of his opponents. He called those who were clamoring for a sign, "an evil and adulterous generation." When he did perform works of power he shunned publicity as much as possible. He restrained those who had been healed from hawking the news about. He did regard his restoration of the wretched and stricken and his victorious conflict with the sinister forms of insanity as demonstrations that a power stronger than the Prince of this world, the power of the Kingdom of God, was present in the world. (Matt. 11, 2-5; 12, 22-29). If men could not perceive that fact in any other way, let these ocular demonstrations at least make them hesitate and think; let the signs be signs, beacon lights to show the way to him. He was willing to have his works serve this purpose after they had been wrought, but he did not work them in order to serve this purpose. He worked them in order to relieve definite cases of pain and sorrow then before him. But display he discarded. One of the evangelists in speaking of his unostentatious method of work was reminded of the passage in Isaiah 42 concerning the servant of Jehovah: "He shall not quarrel nor be loud voiced, neither shall anyone hear his voice in the streets."

Why did he refuse a means so ready, so effective for impressing the people? If it had been his aim to build up a strong organization, to attract money and influence, to gain great numbers, and to make them blindly obedient to his word, he could have chosen no better way than to do what they asked for, to let manna fall from heaven or do some other dazzling and awe-inspiring miracle. But if he wanted to make men know God and love one another, why should he work miracles? Would the sight of a miracle give a Sadducee the child-like spirit? Would it make a Pharisee love a publican as his brother? Would it not simply frighten people into that outward conformity to the commands of God which his soul loathed? No, display would not serve his purpose. To use the power of God for such ends as would be accomplished by leaping from the pinnacles of the temple would be tempting God and prostituting his power.

The second means which it would have been natural to use was force. Its use was expected by the disciples. It was almost forced on him by the people. It was feared by the Sadducean conservatives. Jesus refused to use it. He forbade his disciples from using it even in defense of what was the holiest on earth to them. (Matt. 26, 51-52.) Before Pilate he disavowed the use of force for his whole movement as something incompatible with its very nature. (John 18, 36.) It would have been an endeavor to set up the Kingdom of God by a compact of obedience to the Prince of this world. Imagine Christ raising an army! National bigotry and jealousy would have been enflamed. The cave of passions would have been unlocked and the world demonized. Fancy Jesus inspiring his troops before battle by a sermon on brotherly love, on love to their enemies, and on forgiving seventy times seven times.

Both the display of power and the use of force are essentially of this world. The children of this world are expert in their use. The kings of the earth have used them from time immemorial. They are effective on their own plane. But in the nature of the case they cannot achieve any results that are higher than their own plane. Display can inspire terror or admiration, but not love. Force can extort assent or compel submission; it cannot awaken faith or persuade to willing obedience. External means can work external and mechanical changes; they cannot change the spirit or purify the spring of life. The Kingdom of God was to be based on the spiritual life, therefore carnal means could not establish it.

The spiritual means adopted by Jesus was the preaching of the truth. The truth, and not the sword, makes free. It has a germinating, productive life, so that if it is sown into the hearts of men it will take root there and do its work. Not that all hearts will receive it alike or be equally fruitful, anymore than all soil will bring an equal harvest. Yet those who are the truth will perceive it and respond to it and follow him. On that response and adherence he founds his Kingdom. (John 18, 36-37.) He that has found with him the words of eternal life will not go away in spite of perplexities and disappointments. (John 6, 66-68.)

The power indwelling in truth itself was in his case multiplied by its exemplification in his life, by its attestation in his suffering, by the power of his personality, by the community of believers testifying to it, and by the influence of the Spirit of God on the minds of his hearers. But of these forces we shall speak in a subsequent chapter. We deal here with the means he proposed to use and did use. His means were simply the truth. With that he shook the self-confidence of the religious, aroused men and women hardened in open sin, and induced wealthy men to forsake their wealth. With that he reanimated a nation, frightened princes, attacked a system hoary with age, drove its defenders to bay, and single-handedly did battle with the learning, the wealth, and the influence of his times.

Few of the principles of Jesus are as often insisted on to-day as this one of the spiritual means of establishing the Kingdom. Whenever the church is invited to influence legislation for the abolition of wrong, it replies with a shrug of the shoulders that it is not its province to use legislation supported by force, because its weapons are spiritual. The words are true enough, but the spirit of them is frequently false. They are too often but a convenient excuse for inaction, for skulking from the arena of actual life and confining attention to "the soul" and its soarings and droopings.

It is true that, like Christ, we wield no sword but the truth. But mark well, that truth was a sword in his hands and not a yard-stick. It cut into the very marrow of his generation. It was mighty to the casting down of strongholds. So it has proved itself wherever it has been used in dead earnest. It reveals lies and their true nature, as when Satan was touched by the spear of Ithuriel. It makes injustice quail on its throne, chafe, sneer, abuse, hurl its spear, tenders its goal, and finally offer to serve as truth's vassal. But the truth that can do such things is not an old woman wrapped in the spangled robes of earthly authority, bedizened with golden ornaments, the marks of honor given by injustice in turn for services rendered, and muttering dead formulas of the past. The truth that can serve God as the mightiest of his archangels is robed only in love, her weighty limbs unfettered by needless weight, calm-browed, her eyes terrible with beholding God.

Verily, if the people of God loved not tradition, not accepted words but truth; if they had the discernment of God's will and thoughts, the clear eye for the real relation of things, the terrible precision of judgement which continued intercourse with truth and obedience are bound to give; if they had Christ's utter fearlessness in speaking the truth, in calling wrong wrong whoever did it, and right right wherever it was found; if wealth and honor and the favor of men which are all in the gift of the Prince of this world and his ministers were but as the froth of wine when weighed against the love of truth; then the church could exultingly strip off all other weapons and go forth in its naked strength with a sling and a few shining pebbles.

Jesus deliberately rejected force and chose truth. The Catholic Church did not follow his example when it used the rack and not the truth on Jew and heretic. The Reformers did not follow Christ's example when they leaned on princes and consented to have whole countries change their faith as monarchy directed. The ruling church in any country does not follow his example when it secures or even consents to laws that in any way hamper or put on an unequal footing other religious bodies. The established churches of all countries do not follow his example when they derive their support from tithes or taxes, if but one solitary man is thus compelled to pay an unwilling penny. Truth asks no odds. She will not ask that her antagonist's feet be put in shackles before she will cross swords with him. Christ's Kingdom needs not the spears of Roman legionaries to prop it, nor even the clubs of Galilean peasants. Whenever Christianity shows an inclination to use constraint in its own defense or support, it thereby furnishes presumptive evidence that it has become a thing of this world, for it finds the means of this world adapted to its ends.

Christ deliberately rejected display as a means and chose truth. Defenders of Christianity have done it an ill service when they made of Christ's miracles one of the great proofs of the truth of his words and the reality of his mission. They endeavor to give to the world the signs which Christ refused it. They have turned into a demonstration of the truth that which Christ at most pointed out as an indication of the source of truth, and they have been sent to the Caesar to whom they appealed. They have conceded that the Kingdom of God came with outward demonstration, that it could be seen with the eye, felt with the hand, and its presence or absence ascertained by the trained intellect. And so the keen eye, the sensitive hand, and the trained intellect have undertaken to sit as a tribunal on the Kingdom of God.

But the most serious departure from Christ's method is the general adoption of display as a means of attracting followers to Christ. Dazzling miracles, it is true, the Protestant churches at least do not undertake to work. They neither leap from the pinnacles of the temple to astonish the gaping crowd, nor do they cause manna to fall from heaven. But they get as near as they can in many cases. I am not speaking of the Catholic missionary whose retinue and mitred magnificence convinced the heathen Prussians that his must be the true church. Papal splendor, jewelled crucifixes, glittering processions, robes, incense—what is all that but the means which all the emperors of the world have used to fire the imagination, prostrate the judgment, and subdue the will? The Catholic Church has sought to use display, that potent instrument of the world, to build up the Kingdom of God. It has failed. It has built up an organization, a hierarchy, but it has failed to make the people among whom it exists spiritual, pure, just, independent, tenacious of purpose, children of light. The Catholic Church has done most good where it has been most devoid of splendor, in simple country parishes. Wherever its display is most perfected, it breeds superstitution and blind obedience with some, and unbelief and hypocrisy with others.

But Protestants, while condemning Rome, have too often tried to steal a feather from Rome's gay plumage. They erect stately churches on the finest avenues, they fit them with costly woods and soft cushions, mellow light fills them, organ tones surge through them, and trained voices warble in them. Why is all this? Partly from the luxury of the men and women who worship their Nazarene Christ there and are too accustomed to ease to miss it for an hour. But partly also from the feeling that this is necessary to draw men in. Are the pews empty? Do indifferent masses pass by the church? Come, let us build a new front and fresco the interior; then men will behold and say, "Verily, this church has influence and wealth; we will go there with our wives and daughters. As for the preacher, he must prophesy unto us smooth things."

Display in buildings, display in furnishings, display in music and liturgy, display in rhetoric, display if possible in the numbers attending—who that is familiar with modern church work will say that this is not a large part of its working capital, whereby we hope to attract and retain the multitude? And who on the other hand will point out anything parallel to it in the ways of Jesus? If some men to-day had the power to work miracles, would they not use them as a means of attraction? Is not something of that sort actually advertised as part of the program in some publc meetings?

When constraint is to be used on behalf of religion, or when men put trust in the attractive power of display for the upbuilding of the Kingdom, then Christian men should insist on the spiritual weapons of Christianity, and not when they are asked to express themselves in regard to injustice or sin. Such an expression is a declaration of the truth, the wielding of the one spiritual weapon entrusted to the church.

4) *Finally, with the development of prophetic thought came an increased recognition of the value of the individual personality.*

The covenant of God with Israel was a covenant with the nation. The individual shared in it as a member of the nation, not because of individual qualifications. The blessings were national blessings. The sins were dealt with as national sins, and the punishments were visited on the nation. The religious desires of the godly man had to seek God through the medium of the whole people. For his assurance of acceptance with God, he had to fall back on Jehovah's mighty deeds for his nation. In the temple he approached God through the priests, the representatives of all.

And yet there was that in the soul of the godly man which sought direct access to the heart of God. There was a sense of spiritual relationship to God which was nearer and surer than anything mediated by blood descent. There was a refusal to be classed merely as a unit of a mass in which there were many of a spirit totally alien. The personality demanded recognition as a separate ethical entity. The righteous man longed for forgiveness of sins for himself, and assurance of it to himself.

The growth of this personal element in Israel's religious life is traceable in the prophets. It received no full satisfaction. The national disasters culminating in the exile fell upon the just also who had not deserved them. Indeed they felt the blow most severely of all. But in the Messianic age that would be changed. A great deed of salvation would be wrought assuring them of forgiveness. That personal intercourse with God which had found its fullest demonstration in the prophets would become common to all. The spirit of God would be poured out on all. They would all be prophets, knowing the Lord and bearing his will in their hearts. The constraint of the old forms of worship would widen out. The glory of the Lord would dwell among all his people.

In Christ the demands of the human personality found full recognition.

He taught that every man was personally responsible for his acceptance of the Messianic salvation. It would not come to all alike. Every man must personally strive to enter the narrow gate. The men of violence only would not succeed. If a man loved property or family too well, he could have no share. There would be a great division, as when the shepherd parts the sheep and the goats. One would be taken, the other would be left. The wise virgins would enter into the joy of the marriage feast, the foolish would be left in the outer darkness. There was no salvation to the entire nation or to entire classes. He that turned, became as a child and was born from above, would enter the Kingdom, though this one were a publican or that one a harlot. He that refused would not enter, though this one be a teacher in Israel or that one a ruler endowed with all the virtues.

Christ taught the forgiveness of sins for the individual soul. He assured the palsied man, the great sinner, and the crucified malefactor of forgiveness and acceptance. He insisted that it was sufficient to have men saved in the bulk, but that even the stray sheep must be brought in and the lost coin found, because it was not the will of the Father that even one of the insignificant ones perish. All sins could now be forgiven, even blasphemy; the only thing that could put a man outside the pale of forgiveness was that condition of heart which called white black and black white and could not distinguish between the working of the Spirit of God and the working of Beelzebub. This assurance of the forgiving love of God found its ultimate expression in the death of Christ. If God so loved the world that he gave his only begotten Son, then we have surety that God desires not our death but our life.

Furthermore the Messianic salvation of Christ offers complete satisfaction for all the spiritual desires of the individual. They that mourn shall be comforted. They that hunger and thirst after righteousness shall be filled. They that labor and are heavy laden shall find rest. In him we shall have the light of life to guide us in darkness, the bread of life that we may hunger no more, the water of life that becomes a spring within us and makes us sources from which rivers of living water flow out. Peace in the midst of tribulation, joy made full, the sight of God and converse with the spiritual world—all these are promised to him who fulfills the conditions of the Kingdom of God.

Christ recognizes the separate value of the human personality. He makes it individually responsible. He assures it of personal forgiveness and offers it satisfaction for all its desires. He offers the perfection of personal life to those that receive him. In the old covenant the entire nation was called the Son of Jehovah; even when the name was applied to the king, it was in his official capacity. Now the humblest member of the Kingdom is to be a child of God and a brother of Christ. And these names are given because there is an underlying fact to which they correspond. These are no longer of this world. Their lives are not entirely derived from it. Their characters are not explainable on earthly grounds, their aims are not limited by the life of time. They share the life of Christ as the branches share the life of the vine. They feed on his life and hence shall live because of him as he lives because of the Father. (John 6, 57.) Because they believe on him who is the resurrection and the life, they shall live even though they die.

They shall be with Christ in the place prepared for them and shall see his glory and be honored by the Father.

In sum, we find that Jesus adopted the theocratic idea and professed himself to be the Messiah who was to bring it to its fulfillment. This adoption necessarily implied assent to the essential core of the theocratic idea: the idea of an ideal human society, constituted according to divine laws and governed by God.

We find, however, that Jesus differed from his contemporaries on various points and that in the divergence he was advancing along the lines already traced by the development of Old Testament prophecy: (1) He extended the limits of the Kingdom. For the idea of God's nation he substituted the idea of God's humanity. In place of a small Kingdom organized on rigid laws and by its smallness and homogeneity capable of uniformity, the theocracy was now to be a Kingship of God in all nations binding their diversity together by unity of spirit and oneness of sovereignty. (2) He changed the basis of citizenship in the Kingdom. He substituted spiritual descent and relationship for natural descent and outward coherence. (3) He repudiated external means, force and display, and relied upon truth and love and the powers of the spirit to overcome opposing forces and establish the Kingdom. (4) He recognized the human personality as a responsible unit, which stands or falls according to its personal deserts, and offered to it the full satisfaction of its highest desires and the ultimate perfection of its personal life.

b. Ideal Vindicated

We anticipate objections from various quarters.

Some will object that God's designs have changed since Christ. The theocracy of Israel has failed and a new theocracy is not a part of God's plans. All that he desires now is the salvation of many souls. Therefore we must bend our energies, awakened, justified, regenerated, sanctified, and finally saved in heaven.

This is practically the position of the great mass of evangelical Christians to-day. The indexes of most systematic theologies show at a glance that, far from having the contents arranged with the Kingdom of God as the starting point and center, there are only isolated references to it. The hymnology of the Christian Church shows the same striking fact; the bulk of the hymns relating to man focuses on the salvation of the individual and not the salvation of the world. And so far as my observation goes, the idea of the Kingdom of God on earth is a forgotten idea among the mass of Christian people, except among certain bodies where it is very much alive in a peculiar form.

We must object to this conception on the ground that it is unscriptural. It is untrue by defect. It is right in preaching the redemption and perfection of the individual life. It is wrong in not preaching the perfection of the collective life of humanity. How far traditional theology has departed from the teaching of Christ can be seen by comparing the table of contents of a "systematic theology" with that of a "biblical theology." It is the province of biblical theology simply to group and systematize the actual teachings of the scriptures, and as a result the books attempting that task all make the idea of the Kingdom the vertebral idea around which the other thoughts are grouped in a coherent organism.

In this discussion I have endeavored to follow the same method and have arrived at the same result. Christ does teach the perfection of the personal life, but he makes the salvation of the individual the subsidiary idea. A man is saved according as he enters or does not enter the Kingdom. Even in the passage where personal regeneration is taught in the most exact and emphatic language, it is spoken of as the condition of seeing the Kingdom of God and entering into it. (John 3, 3.)

It would be difficult and hazardous to say what has been the cause of this gradual swinging away from the teaching of Christ. Even in the writings of Paul less space is devoted to the Kingdom than to the church and the upbuilding of the individual. But Paul by no means lost sight of the Kingdom. It lay in the nature of the case that he was compelled to think out and discuss especially the practical questions of the new life as it was seeking to take shape in the personal lives and in the life of the churches.

The same causes continued to operate later, and under the powerful influence of Paul's writings the thought of the church continued to run in the grooves carved out by him. But while with him the perfection of the Kingdom was a near and living hope which easily subjugated all other thoughts and aims, that faith died out in the church later. The hope of the immediate coming of Christ faded out. The manly faith which started out to overcome the world shrank into a lean old age, rubbing itself to keep up its own vitality, and content to save itself. In place of a church invading the world and wrestling with it, spirit against spirit, we see a church fleeing out of the world and in solitude, with fastings, prayers, and flagellations, guarding the flickering rushlight of personal godliness from the mocking breath of the world.

Due to the same lack of faith, the church of the present day takes the defensive attitude against the world instead of the offensive. Or is it not a defensive attitude when the saving of one's soul in heaven is the sum of Christian hope to so many? In place of the parable of the mustard seed and the leaven we shall have to invent a new one: The Kingdom of God is like unto a burning ship, from which a few escape in a boat and rest on their oars at a distance in helpless contemplation.

The assertion that God has abandoned the theocratic idea is a misconstruction of the facts. Did Jehovah miscalculate when he attempted the up-building of a reign of God, and has he now corrected his plans? Or did he grow weary of one way and is now attempting another? God never fails nor grows weary. His human instruments may fail him and be cast aside for new ones, but his plans are not abandoned. He does not destroy but he fulfills. The smaller is lost sight of because it is merged in the greater. The outline of his plans changes constantly, but it is a change like the change in the contours of a beach when the tide is rising.

When the personal element was magnified in the New Testament, the collective element, with which the Old Testament dealt, was not abandoned. How could it be? If there was that in the nature of the Jewish nation which justified God in treating it as a composite personality that could be held responsible for moral actions and conditions, then the same personality and responsibility must still inhere in the nature of communities, nations, and races. And if God once regarded the collective life as a force to be dealt with in the erection of his Kingship on earth, has the increased importance attached to the individual life caused God to lose his interest in the forces he once valued so highly?

A second objection comes from those who acknowledge the permanence of the theocratic idea and the purpose of Christianity to bring about a perfect humanity on earth, but now hold that the only way to act on humanity is to act on individuals. Let the units of society be changed, they say, and society itself will be changed. The only way in which the Kingdom of God can be extended is to seek the conversion of as many persons as possible.

There is certainly much truth in this. Jesus began the establishment of the Kingom by gathering a few men who had the spirit of the Kingdom in them. Every man of that sort is a new light set in the darkness, a grain of salt in the corruption of the world. The hope of changing the world by a mere change of system was not shared by Christ. He wanted changed men; men who obeyed the spirit and not the flesh; men in whom the potent spell of the visible and temporal was broken and who beheld the power and felt the value of the invisible and eternal; men in whom the world's rules and judgments were no longer dominant, but in whom God's will and thoughts reigned supreme; men in whom profit and pleasure had been dethroned, and right and love enthroned. Without such men no Kingdom of God will be established on earth. Every such man is an advanced fulcrum on which God can rest his lever in overturning the world.

And yet we hold that the multiplication of such men is not the only service that we can render the Kingdom, nor is the extension of the Kingdom necessarily co-extensive with the multiplication of such. The principles and aims of an organization may be better or worse than the men constituting the organization. If the organization is better than the men, it is likely to be changed for the worse very quickly. If it is worse, a change for the better will be made only if it is taken in hand with all seriousness. For instance, it would be hard to prove that the people of the South had a higher moral or religious average in 1870 than in 1850; yet in 1850 men owned their fellowmen, and in 1870 they did not. The constitution of the community had become more righteous, though the number of righteous persons in it may not have increased greatly or at all. Again, there were only a few years intervening between the reign of Oliver Cromwell and the Restoration of the Stuarts; the number of godly men cannot have diminished so much during that interval. And yet what a difference between the England of the Commonwealth and the England of Charles the Second! Or once more, who will say that the businessmen of America are cruel and heartless men? Yet our business life is very nearly as cruel as the grindstones of a gristmill.

Evidently the collective life of a body of men is not quite equivalent to the sum of all its units when taken separately. By contact with others certain propensities, good or evil, as the case may be, are checked and sunk out of sight, while others are called forth and given a potency that they would never have in the man by himself. A railway director rises in prayer meeting and speaks of his desire to be a true follower of Christ and to have the same mind that was in him. Next day in the board of directors he advocates the smashing of a small rival line. "He is a hypocrite," says the world. Perhaps so; perhaps not. Human nature is subtle and capacious enough to contain both actions within itself. Perhaps the best aspirations that were in man were brought out by the spirit of the community in the one case, and he was lifted above his usual self. In the other case, by the traditions and customs and codes of railway management, he did worse things than he would do in a private capacity and perhaps never thought that they were bad. Indeed as our business life goes, it would not be inconceivable that all his fellow directors were in the prayer meeting as active participants.

It is not enough to christianize individuals; we must christianize societies, organizations, nations, for they too have a life of their own which may be made better or worse. Christ addressed Capernaum and

Bethsaida as responsible personalities. He lamented over Jerusalem as a whole. He told his disciples to leave communities refusing them to their fate. We find Paul acting on that principle repeatedly. Throughout the Old Testament God dealt with Israel as a whole, which could rise or fall. In the book of Revelation the spirit addressed whole churches with praise or blame, and the forces of evil are represented as corporate beings, the beast, the harlot, the false prophet. And on the other hand the church is constantly present to the mind of Paul, not as a sandheap of many grains, but as a great body with many members, all framed and knit together, growing up into unity and fullness of life, developing not into full-grown men but into a full-grown Man.

A corporate life is bound to develop in a body of men. Even a chance mass meeting will begin to be a unity after it has responded to the same thought for half an hour, and that unity will be good or bad according to the thoughts that have united it. Humor or passion will sweep over the multitudinous souls like the breath of bellows over the iron in the furnace, and they will begin to fuse. The individual loses himself in the whole. He finds himself applauding as the rest applaud, laughing at things he otherwise holds sacred, enthusiastic about that which was indifferent to him and may be so again when he is out of this crowd. The subsequent speakers, if they have the oratorical sensitiveness, will find themselves led by or wrestling with a kind of huge personality, a good or evil spirit, whose unity in consent or dissent they can feel.

If that is true of a random gathering, it is much more true of a stable organization, of a church, a club, a party, a nation. Every sorrow, every joy that has thrilled all unites all, as the many pieces of a violin vibrate into unity in constant use. There comes to be a common feeling, a common judgement, which can be forecast and wrought upon, and which yet at times surprizes its most expert manipulators by the elemental spontaneity of its uprising. Before our civil war there was a jangle of voices in the North, a big anthill of apparently confused and separate interests. But the jangling voices became the roar of a cataract. Before the eyes of a wondering world a huddle of states arose a nation. Indeed, what was that war of the

Union but the nation's assertion of its oneness, the refusal of a living being to be drawn and quartered? What were the struggles of Germany, Italy, Greece, Poland, Ireland but the struggles of personalities for a personal life, the efforts of nations to be nations and not aggregations of individuals?

And if the life of a body is so powerful and independent a factor in the life of humanity, shall it not find its independent recognition from those who would revolutionize the world? Shall only the children of this world become the children of God, and not the kingdoms of the world become the Kingdom of God and of his Christ?

There is a continuity of life in an organization. The men who unite in it create its laws and institutions according to their own nature and according to the aims they have in mind. But those laws and institutions, once established, confirm, strengthen, and perpetuate the nature from which they arose and give the organization the power of assimilating new elements to itself. Witness the marvelous continuity of life and uniformity of thought and feeling and purpose in the Jesuit Order. Its members have come and gone like the particles constituting a human body, but like a human body the Jesuit Order has remained the same. Their antagonists, the Port-Royalists, during a much shorter term of life have demonstrated the assimilative power of an organization in which a vigorous spirit lives. Schools and colleges have their peculiar genius and stamp their graduates with their various seals and superscriptions.

In short, the efforts for the extension of the Kingdom of God are insufficient if they address themselves to the individual alone. A world of regenerated individuals is not necessarily a regenerated world. The laws of nations, the customs of society, the institutions of corporate life, though indirectly affected by every personal change, may perpetuate wrong and warp the individuals, and a conscious effort must be made to reconstruct them, until they cease to be based on selfishness and force and begin to be based on love and justice. Every step toward such reconstruction, as well as every individual conversion, is an extension of the reign of God, for God reigns where his will is done.

The individual and collective life of humanity act and react on each other. Every changed individual life makes a changed society possible. Every change for the better in the construction of society makes a higher perfection of the individual possible. Each is an originating center of power. Each, therefore, is a citadel to be captured in the name of God.

c. What Is and Was and Is to Come

A third objection will come from those who believe in the speedy second coming of Christ. With them the Kingdom of God is really a living hope which inspires and sustains them. They do believe in a glorified humanity with Christ as King, and the rapid spread of their ideas in our own day proves that they actually regard the present world era as short, too short to amass property or to lay the foundations of an enduring family life. (I Cor. 7, 29-31.) Their faith seems to me far more worthy of respect and more apostolic than the attitude of the average Christian who tries to be prosperous before he dies and hopes to be prosperous after he dies, but who lets this world wag on its even way to that final collision which he has been told will come sometime, but which is too far off to disturb his digestion or influence his testamentary arrangements.

But though these believe in the Kingdom of God, many of them will not agree to what I have said. They hold that the Kingdom will come when Christ returns. Then the government of the world will fall to him and to his saints, and justice and peace will reign. But until then the Kingdom exists only in the church, its only increase is in the increase of the church, its only province is to snatch individuals from the mass of the world that they may be ready for the coming of the Lord. As for the world, it cannot be saved till Christ comes. The life of the world may be modified by the existence of the church in it, but radical changes are not to be expected. An endeavor on the part of the church to work radical changes would be a waste of energy; some think it would be a wicked and adulterous compact with Satan and his kingdom. The apostles made no effort to influence the social or political life of the world. They watched for the coming of Christ and expected it to be done then.

It is true that Christ promised the completion of the Kingdom at his coming again. Now the tares are still growing in the wheat field (Matt. 13, 24-30), and the useless sea creatures mingle with the fish in the dragnet. (Matt. 13, 47-50.) Then the separation will be made; the sheep will be parted from the goats (Matt. 25, 31-46); the wise virgins will be admitted to the joy of the marriage feast and the foolish left in the darkness (Matt. 25, 1-13); all false disciples will then be rejected (Matt. 7, 21-27; 22, 11-14), and the true followers will be gathered from all parts of the earth (Matt. 8, 11) to claim their inheritance in the Kingdom and share in its joy.

It is true also that the apostles expected the speedy return of Christ. James admonished the brethren to be patient of injuries until the coming of the Lord, who was already standing before the door. (James 5, 7-9.) Peter regarded the end of all things as at hand (I Peter 4, 7) and the salvation of Christ ready to be revealed. (1, 5.) Paul, till near the end of his life, hoped to be alive at the coming of the Lord. (I Thess. 4, 15-17.) The day of the Lord was very near at hand. (Rom. 13, 11-14.) This hope was so much alive in some of the churches that they felt seriously troubled about the few Christians who had already died and so seemed unable to have their share in the Kingdom. (I Thess. 4, 13-18.) With this expectation pressing upon them, it was natural that they attempted no change in existing conditions, even if they had had any means of influencing them. They were like travelers in an inn, sitting booted and cloaked, listening for the knock to call them to horse, and hence caring little if in their room of the inn the windows were draughty and the fire nearly out. And for those who really share their expectation, that attitude of mind is still the natural one. But if they claim the right to disregard the state of this world because its construction is so soon to pass away, we demand of them the proof of their sincerity. If they think the time is short, let them "have wives as though they had none; let them weep, as though they wept not; let them rejoice as though they rejoiced not; let them buy as though they possessed not." But if any man surfeits himself with the pleasure and wealth of this world and beats his fellow servants that are in his power and enlarges his barns and increases his investments and looks well to the securities thereof, then that man may protest a thousand times that he is looking for the coming of the Lord, and he may be ever so diligent in figuring over the times and half times of Daniel, yet his words are idle words, and his faith is a nut without a kernel.

But do Christians really hold that belief to-day? They say they do, but do they? Can they? Eighteen centuries have passed away, and the end has not yet come. There have been honest men at many periods in the history of the church who fervently believed in the immediate appearance of Christ; the Montanists believed it; about the year 1000 there was a very wide-spread belief that the end would come with that year; great numbers were in expectation at the time of the Reformation; the Fifth Monarchy men were a force in politics during the English Commonwealth. During this century men have had enough faith to set the day over and over again. The hope of them all has come to naught, it has lost itself in the sand. They are worthy of honor. But did God want them to believe what was not true?

We shall be reminded that Christ commands his servants to watch at all hours, because they never know when the Son of man will come. It is true, but in what does the watching consist? In expectation or in obedience? What steward is prepared for the coming of his master, the one that is peering out of the gable window all the day to spy the first dust cloud that signals his return, or the one that keeps the house in the order his master loves to see? If expectation were a preparation for Christ's return, surely the people of Jesus' day would have been prepared for his first coming; they were full of expectation; yet when he came they crucified him.

Christ appeared the first time when "the fullness of the time" had come. (Gal. 4, 4.) He will appear the second time when the fullness of the time shall have come. When that will be, depends largely on us. In all the dealings of God with men the human factor is the variable quantity. God has so conditioned himself that within certain limits he allows us free action, and the fulfillment of his counsel is hastened or retarded according to our obedience or disobedience. Paul saw in his day that the day of the Lord would not come till certain hindrances which he met in his work were removed, and until the missionary work of the world as he knew it were completed. (II Thess. 2, 1-12.) We, if we have eyes to see, can also see certain forces that are antagonistic to Christ and that must go down if he is to reign; and we can see work still to be done in the world to make it a fit habitation for our Lord. Is not then our duty plain?

Or shall we wail at the slightness of our forces and weapons and say that we can accomplish nothing till he comes with re-enforcements and artillery of heavier calibre? Have we not the flashing sword of truth which has grown keener with the using? Have we not the persevering faith that can cart a mountain away in wheelbarrow loads? What weapons shall Christ bring that we have not now? He can come in power and glory, the sword in his hand and his avenging angels with him. But then it will be to sift and scatter and punish, and not to convert and win and up-build. Or shall he at the end convince the world by force and display, the means he always discarded?

We have power if we will but use it, power to win stubborn hearts, power to uncover social lies, power to make injustice blush and skulk away, power to break the chains of Christ's enslaved brothers, power to shame immodesty into hiding places. Will it be no service to Christ to use such power? Will he be indifferent to it? Or does he care only for the conversion of men? Frederick William I of Prussia was always enlisting recruits for his giant battalion, but he never led it into battle. Recruits have been enlisted for Christ these sixty generations. Every one had but a short term in which he was on the battlefield, and then he passed away to another world. Is the only service a soldier can render that he enlists others who in turn will die without having seen battle?

This world is a battleground, not a gymnasium in which we punch inflated balls to increase our own muscle. Our work tells, if we make it tell. We can change the world. None of us knows how much. None can tell what a place this earth would be, if all the force that has been spent on spiritual gymnastics had been put into fighting wrong and seeing God's will done on earth, and we surmise that heaven would have been filled, if not with more, yet with stronger, braver souls.

The fact is that the experience of all these centuries has been a long commentary on one of the prominent doctrines of Jesus: the gradualness of the coming of the Kingdom. The prophets expected it suddenly. The coming of the Messiah, the judgement, the destruction of the wicked, the erection of the perfect reign of God, all this they saw as one event. John the Baptist expected it that way too. Christ emphasized the gradualness of it. It was a growth like the growth of a mustard plant. It was an organic process like the fermentation of yeast. "So is the Kingdom of God, as if a man should cast seed upon the earth and should sleep and rise, night and day, and the seed should spring up and grow, he knoweth not how. The earth beareth fruit of herself; first the blade, then the ear, then the full corn in the ear. But when the fruit is ripe, straightway he putteth forth the sickle, because the harvest is come." This gradualness follows from the nature of the case. If he had used compulsion, he could have achieved great results quickly. Because he wanted an organic growth, he had to bide his time. There is no saying how much the process might have been quickened and may yet be quickened by the energetic fidelity of his followers. But hitherto the process has been slow.

And yet we are to be on the alert for his coming. Though all experience tells us that it will not come immediately, yet we are to act as if it were coming immediately. How is that possible? How can we keep ourselves always in a state of tension? We can do it only by understanding the law of evolution in the Kingdom. It is always at hand. When Jesus taught, he said the Kingdom had come, signs of its actual presence were visible (Matt. 11, 3-5; 12, 28), some men were near it (Matt. 12, 34), some entering it (Matt. 21, 31), some in it (Matt. 11, 11). Yet on the other hand he bids his disciples seek it and pray for its coming. (Matt. 6, 10, 33.) It has come, it is coming. As God is in all three tenses, the God that was and is and shall be, so is the Kingdom behind which is the force of the living God. It is forever coming. Hence it is forever pressing. The time is always short. One era after the other passes away. The need is always desperate. The opportunities never return, and where we have failed to answer the call of God and to throw in our strength, history will always show a hiatus which is but slowly closed. Our missing effect in this era becomes a missing cause in the next era. In the days of Jesus was the time for the Jewish nation. If it had known in that day the things that made for peace, who will say what the splendor of that people might have been and what the effect on the world? As a nation, Israel failed, and the whirlwind of judgement swept the chaff from the threshing-floor. The prophetic discourse of Jesus can hardly be understood in any other way than that the destruction of the Jewish nation was a coming of Christ. And if that was a coming of Christ, was it the only one? Have there been no other judgements of God on cities and nations that failed in the hour of their trial? Has not our own generation seen "the glory of the coming of the Lord," seen him "treading out the wine-press where the grapes of wrath were stored"? The religious man believes that God did terrible things in the far past and that he will do great things in the far future. The spiritual man sees God doing terrible things *now*. He sees the great Avenger standing ever within the shadow of history. He feels the spirit of the living Christ working in the hearts of men that think they know him not. He feels his breath coming across the frozen fields of the earth, and new life blossoms. In the moanings of the nations, in their feverish stirring, in the shrill laugh of skepticism, in the gropings of fanatics he sees the working of him who, like his Father, is ever working without haste and without rest, and with beating heart he whispers to himself: "The Kingdom of God is at hand, arise!"

d. Sanctification of This Life

This then is the program of the Christian revolution: the Kingdom of God on earth. It includes a twofold aim: the regeneration of every individual to divine sonship and eternal life, and the victory of the spirit of Christ over the spirit of this world in every form of human society and a corresponding alteration in all the institutions formed by human society. These two are simultaneous aims. Every success in the one is a means for a new success in the other.

The aim is vast, we know, and we rejoice in it. In this all-embracing aim is found that unity of life for the want of which modern Christian life is crippled. What earnest man has not felt this division of his life? All the week he gives to his business, and on Sunday he serves God. How? By prayer and praise, by testifying, by an expression of his inward experience, by teaching children religious truths. This is all good, but is this all? Speak to him about doing something for God, and he will think you mean giving his money for religious purposes, speaking in prayer meeting, teaching Sunday school, or taking part in a mission. He will *not* think of his daily work to which he yet devotes ninetenths of his time and strength. If he is a shoemaker, he will not refer your question about serving God to making better shoes. If he is a plumber, he will not refer it to the sanitary washing of joints. That part of his life has nothing to do with serving God, except that he keeps from doing wrong in it. The serving of Christ, according to the average conception, lies in doing "religious" work, in working on people's souls. If you hear a young lawyer say that he means to give himself entirely to God's work, it is almost certain that he does not mean that henceforth he will be a champion of justice in human relations, that he will see the facts brought out and right done, that he will do his share to untangle that snarl of ancient precedents called the common law and make the word "legal" synonymous with the word "just"; no, he means that he is going to become a preacher. The religious ideal of the people is not an ideal embracing their whole life. The church has so long restricted religious effort to saving one's own soul and the souls of others, that only the time and effort given to that are supposed to be a service of God, and only those who give their whole time to that kind of work are understood to have devoted their lives completely to God's service. It is only when a man understands that this earth with all it contains is to become the habitation of God, that all the homely services and relations of human life if rightly done are a loving service of the brethren and hence of Christ, and that any improvement in the method and spirit of human relations is the perfection of God's will, only then can the whole life of the common man become a sacrifice and his plain daily toil a love-offering to God. The saving of souls has hallowed the work of the preacher. The saving of the world will hallow the life of the farmer who toils for humanity's daily bread, of the engineer who bridges chasms and holds back the seething river from the cottages of his brothers, of the teacher who unfolds the germs of talent created by God and destined by God to be unfolded, of the mason and carpenter and glazier and plumber who build safe and dry and sunny houses in which little children will not be strangled to death by poison germs, of preachers who unfold the principles of justice and mercy, of lawyers who apply the former and of doctors who apply the latter, and of legislators who find ways for incorporating both. Doubtless all these have been hallowed before. God has looked upon many a workman's work and many a housewife's ceaseless round of duties and seen in them the real sacrifice of their lives, even though they themselves may have looked for it in other things. Doubtless too there have always been noble souls in all stations of life that have well understood this truth of the possible sanctity of the whole life of man. But I affirm that it is not the common thing among religious people. An understanding of it would be a gospel to many a man who desires to serve God and thinks that he can do so now only by the scraps of his life. It would enlist the services of those who have no gift of introspection, of preaching, or of dealing with souls. If Christian people would begin to do their daily work in such a way as best to serve their brethren and therewith their King, if they would refuse to enter into occupations in which they saw no benefit to men and hence no benefit to the Kingdom of God, then we should all find our common life uplifted by a great thought and the industry of the world affected by a new spirit. Some lines of business would either cease or be transformed, for there are some occupations of which it would be hard to say how they serve the good of men. Of them perhaps it would be true that they could be sainted only by their death.

We reiterate: the religious ideal of the average Christian embraces only a small portion of his life; the larger portion of it is touched by the religious purpose only insofar as he aims not to let it get in conflict with his Christianity. His business life is Christian in what he refrains from doing, and not in what he does do. The ideal of the Kingdom of God on earth is an ideal capable of embracing every useful human activity, making it sublime. It can give unity to human life and abolish that frequent and fearful discrepancy between religious profession and business action which is the withering disease of modern Christianity.

This all-embracing aim is able also to enlist the abilities and interest of all men. There is a diversity of gifts. Not all have the gift of prophesying or teaching. Some have the gift of superintendence and management, some of mechanical dexterity, of making something out of nothing. Such men and women may have the love of God and man in their hearts, but how shall it find an outlet? The only way now appointed for them is with a feeble, stammering tongue to speak of inward experiences and to address themselves to inward needs. The known sincerity of such men makes their expressions effective, and yet that is not what they can do best. Get them to cut garments in a sewing school or nail up boards at a picnic and see with what ability and alacrity they do that. The church cannot furnish them many opportunities for these gifts as it now works; but if all life became an effort to realize the Kingdom of God, then we should see a blazing forth of these faculties. The religious life, now pent up and forced to find an outlet through one narrow channel, would flow out freely on all sides and carry its blessings.

We surmise that it is the untrue division of the Christian ideal which has brought about the unequal representation of the sexes in the churches. The proportion at present is usually three women to two men, and if men followed their own inclinations without the attractive constraint of those whom they love, there would probably be fewer men yet. Why is this? Surely not because one half of the human race is created better than the other. We do not expect to see the same preponderance of women in heaven. Men are more prone to the palpable sins of the flesh, but the women's subtler sins of the lust of the eye and the pride of life are perhaps even more destructive.

Men are not naturally more wicked, less sensitive to moral impulses, and less capable of sacrifice than women. The fault is that no religious ideal is offered them capable of enlisting to the full the masculine faculties. Woman has her office in life and man has his. They may overlap, but they are not the same. And their gifts correspond to the office they are to fill. Woman is endowed with a delicate sensibility, a faculty of divining emotions and of tenderly touching them and altering them which only the poets among men can equal. Her whole calling in life teaches her to deal with the inward life and to nurture its frailest efforts into strength. A religion of the perfection of the personal life is her religion. It concerns her brother also, but it does not satisfy him. The man's life is turned out upon the world. That is his domain. Whether he wills it or not, it captivates his interest. Why are political meetings crowded with men while the churches are empty of them? Why are countless men working with sacrifice of money, time, and strength in the labor and social movements, who have only a shrug of the shoulder for the church? Is it because they are worldly and the church spiritual? Let who will believe that that is the sole cause. It is because in spite of the rottenness of politics and the many evil concomitants of the labor movement they feel that here is an effort to carry righteousness into the life of mankind along the lines in which their interest and ability lie. Let a preacher in the course of his sermon make a reference to or take an illustration from politics or the social question, and he will see the eyes of the men brighten, their necks crane forward, and an interested look come over their faces. Is that a proof of their carnal mind? How is it that so many of the strongest and most virile ministers "cannot let politics alone"? We see in all this a groping of man for his share in the work of God, a reaching out for the neglected half of the Christian ideal. What they ignorantly worship, the church should declare unto them, in order that the vast amount of truly religious work which is now branded as secular and regarded as almost illegitimate may stand forth as truly a service of God and may enlist the love and enthusiasm of God-driven men.

The two aims of the Christian revolution, the perfection of the individual and the perfection of society, blend and pass into each other; so do the offices and faculties of man and woman. Yet the directions of the one aim corresponds to the bent of woman's genius, the other to the inclination of man's ability. The fact that religious work as it now stands is not enlisting the same proportion of men as of women, and that many of the noblest men find nothing to attract them in the church, furnishes another presumption that we have left out one term of the Christian synthesis and ventilated the rounded perfection of Christ's revolutionary aim.

And, finally, the combination of the two aims is necessary for the attainment of either. That the perfection of human society cannot be attained without changed lives to attain it, is plain enough. But it is equally true that the life of the individual cannot be perfected except by seeking the perfection of society. One of the fundamental teachings of Jesus is that by seeking our life we lose it, and by losing it we gain it. Avarice that gets no enjoyment out of its wealth, social selfishness that blights love and friendship and so destroys the pleasures it seeks, the life of pleasure that becomes blasé, the life of intellectual self-culture which turns on itself in doubt, gaining keenness and losing firmness, rich in perceptions and bankrupt in convictions—these are demonstrations of Christ's law of life. Wherever human life turns in upon itself and seeks its satisfaction and perfection in itself and not outside itself, it is distorted and foiled. And what holds of every other form of life, holds of the religious life also. He that seeketh his own religious life, shall lose it. Who is the most likely to be acknowledged before the judgment seat of Christ, he that has sought to save his own soul by penances, contemplations, exercises, by striving against faults and seeking after virtues, or he that forgets his states and feelings in the active work for the all-around welfare of his fellows? Where shall we seek the Christ? In the hermit's solitude or in the busy towns of Galilee?

"Activity" has become the motto of modern religious life. But when the newly awakened heart asks: "What shall I do?" it finds but few avenues for going forth into the world with blessing. Speaking in prayer meeting, visiting hospitals, teaching a Sunday school class, praying with inquirers, joining mission bands, above all giving money and attending church, these are the activities which we declare religious. And it is most admirable to see how moments of rest are utilized and strength is poured out in these efforts which are called dear to the Master. But again we assert, these lines of work are not fitted to the gifts of all, and still less are they fitted to the time and resources of all. Many of the activities recommended by modern church life are aristocratic activities. The average working man and his wife have no time to attend many meetings and to spend afternoons in hospitals and among the poor. They can give only the scraps of their time to such work, and it means a sacrifice of rest and recuperation. And the working people, remember that, are *the* people. They constitute human society and not the people who have leisure. If therefore we desire to teach the bulk of mankind how to attain the divine personal life, we must be able to show them how they can spend themselves for others in that which occupies all but a fraction of their lives, their daily work. If they can consciously spend themselves in that for love of God and men, then they have the exercise of their own spiritual life which will give them spiritual health and vigor. They will strengthen the eternal life in them by working for the Kingdom of God outside of them.

Practically there are numberless plain men and women who in the round of daily work are growing up into self-forgetful Christian characters. Many of them think they serve God in their meetings only, but their lives are more correct than their religious theorizing. They are spending themselves in their entire lives, and their characters show the effects. They, and not those who have time for all societies and meetings and religious self-culture, are the elect and beloved of God. What we desire is that they should do their daily work intelligently and consciously as a part in the maintenance and upbuilding of God's Kingdom on earth, so that the full force of the religious principle may be brought to bear on it, and that they may have the full conscious enjoyment of the religious life which they really possess.

3

THE REVOLUTIONARY POWER

It is worth much to perceive that things are not as they should be and to long for their betterment. It is worth more to have a clear and great ideal of how things ought to be. But unless there is a power to overcome the inertia of conservatism, to overthrow the angry resistance of selfishness, and to fashion the better ways of life, the ideal will remain a dream, a solace to the solitary thinker, a transient homesickness to him that hears it, and no more. It is pathetic to see how many longings and efforts have wasted themselves in the history of mankind, like the blossoms of the orange-tree in the hot-house that drop and leave no fruit. Noble souls have been pregnant with ideals, but there was no power to bring forth. Spirits have brooded over the chaos, but no creative word was spoken.

The Christian revolution is distinguished not only by the splendor and comprehensiveness of its ideal, but also by the power inhering in it and pushing toward realization. It was that which struck the observant eye of Paul, himself a restless mover among men. The Jews had an ideal in their law. They also had zeal, and yet they had no power to attain. On the other hand it was the power joyously to achieve what Judaism painfully strove for to which Paul pointed as the characteristic of the Christian life. It was the fleet-limbed strength, the hurling, earth-girding force in it of which he boasted and to which he opposed without shame all the pride of the antique world.

What are the forces which originated and sustain the Christian revolution?

Through three forces the Old Testament prophets expected the renewal of the world and the perfection of the theocracy: the Messiah as the perfect theocratic king; the general outpouring of the spirit of God; the purified and glorified nation as the seat of God's manifestation. In three forces within Christianity these three expectations have found their fulfillment: Christ, the Spirit, the church. These three are the revolutionary forces which are to realize the revolutionary program discussed in the preceding chapter.

a. Christ

Christ was the initiatory power of the Kingdom of God. With his coming the Kingdom began. All who had preceded him had their faces turned to the future and spoke of that which was to come. Even John did only a preparatory work; he was leveling the road for the entrance of the King, his baptism was but a cleansing with water to prepare for the baptism of spirit and fire. He himself claimed to be only a Voice, a solemn figure pointing toward the greater One that was to come.

On the other hand Jesus turned the future into the present tense. The Kingdom of God was a hope; he created the actual fact till he could call his disciples blessed for seeing and hearing what the prophets had desired in vain.

And as he initiated the movement, so he sustains it. He is still the compulsory power, the fashioning force.

It cannot be our task here to discuss the nature of Christ or to attempt to exhaust the eternal significance of his work. We have simply to state the historical fact that Jesus Christ is the prime force in the Christian revolution, and to make clear to ourselves the ways by which his force was exerted and still is exerted to change human society.

1) *Christ's teaching* is an expression of his view of the world. Taken by itself, his teaching would tend toward a reversal of values and a reconstruction of society.

The Prince of this world is also the father of lies. His power of the air is marvelously used in creating optical delusions. The great seems small and the small great; the serene face of goodness seems distorted into a grin, and the narrowest pride and selfishness is rounded out to the fullness of virtue, when seen in these curved mirrors of his. It was so in the times of Jesus, and one of his most pressing duties was to clear the air of delusions and bid this lying devil begone. He had to restore the spiritual eyesight of his people and teach them to see all things in their true proportions as God sees them. Men had persuaded themselves that God was a step-father, fiercely fond of one nation and making *Aschenbrödels* of all the others for the sake of that one nation. They were convinced that God was exceedingly pleased with having a large number of animals slaughtered and burned for him, and with having great performances of white-robed people with marches and counter-marches, with singing and trumpet-blaring. They imagined that he liked to have them recite long prayers at particular hours of the day, and to have them wear little leather boxes strapped on their arms and foreheads while doing so. Consequently those persons who were most exact in performing these things, who gave a tenth of their income to religion even down to the mint and cumin that grew in a corner of their backyard, who recited their prayers faithfully even if they happened to be standing on a street-corner when the hour arrived were considered the most holy people and the special darlings of God, while those who were too hard-worked to get all these little niceties by heart were lumped as a desperate and accursed lot. As for irreligious or profligate people, the chief duty of man was to keep away from them and let them go to destruction as fast as they could.

We know what a battle Jesus fought against these lies, and how he labored to set up the true standard of goodness. He chilled their ethnic conceit by stories of Samaritan generosity. He walked rough-shod over their elaborate piety of fastings and washings. Against the reverence of sacrifices he was always quoting the prophetic motto: "Mercy, not sacrifice." He passed by the learned theologians as incapable of receiving the knowledge of God and gathered the common people about him as capable of understanding the deep things of God. He told the pious people that the harlots and sinners were nearer the Kingdom of God than they. He knocked the mumbo-jumbo idol of Pharisaism from its pedestal and let all men see that there was nothing in it but wind, cobwebs, and dirt.

It is almost amusing for us today to watch the pillars of Jewish society from this distance and see how they took the knocking down of their houses of cards. At first they were piously horrified. "Why," they gasped, "why, he doesn't wash his hands before he eats! He misuses the blessed Sabbath for healing people! He eats and drinks as much as he wants to! He—yes, actually—sits down at the same table with publicans and sinners and lets harlots touch him! And he wants to be a Rabbi? A holy man? He is a glutton, a wine-bibber, a friend of sinners, a Samaritan, a demoniac! He is possessed by Beelzebub, the biggest devil of them all!" After a while their tone changed. They had surveyed him from the secure height of their established religious infallibility. They had discussed the question whether *he* was to stand or fall. Now they perceived that it was a question of their own standing or falling. The people heard him gladly. They were drinking in his words. His words carried a strange authority with them. He said a thing, and everybody said: "Of course, that's plain, there is nothing to be said against that." The people were swinging away from their old religious authorities. If this went on, they would be left high and dry as useless teachers and bad men. Society must be saved, the Law was attacked, religion itself was at stake, incidentally their own standing was in danger. We know the outcome.

This revolutionary influence of Christ's teaching is still felt. Society is much the same from age to age. We have our sham substitutes for godliness. We have our little lawyers' precedents and penny rules as to which actions are allowable for religious people and which are not. We have our brutal and lawless classes, and we have our respectable saviours of society. The gnat is still strained and the camel swallowed.

Mint, anise, and cummin are still tithed and justice, mercy, and faithfulness forgotten. And so we need Christ's teachings. If any man will train his judgement by laying it parallel to the judgement of Jesus, he will soon find himself hewing close to the mark. He will find his judgements diverging considerably from the standard judgements of contemporary society. In time he will find that he is himself a revolutionist.

We cannot overestimate the effect which the teachings of Jesus have had in the course of centuries in training men to see clearly and judge fearlessly. It is true that many of the most radical teachings of Christ are tacitly left on one side by the average religionist. Over others the scribes have spun that same mystifying web of tradition, explanations, and limitations by which in Christ's time they had made the law of God effective. And yet there are his sayings. They have to be proclaimed. They have to be explained to open-eyed children and young people. Something of their sharp edge is felt through all the silken wrappings. And occasionally some man falls to unwrapping them. He finds they were made to be used, and he uses them. He proclaims: "Christ meant what he said." He finds wise men maundering over some Gordian knot, some insoluble problem of humanity. A flash of Christ's word, an antithesis, a parable applied, and the knot falls, cut asunder. Then the wise men arise and cry: "Stop him, he is a crazy fanatic, a crank, crucify him." And so the revolutionary force of Christ's teaching goes on.

The wonderful thing about the teachings of Jesus is that they do not grow old. Rabbi Hillel said wise things before him, but we can easily spare the flower of Jerusalem's learning for the words of the Galilean carpenter's son. Philo of Alexandria was good, profound, eloquent, but his writings are a weariness to all except the student of history. Socrates has had the pens of Xenophon and Plato to record him and explain him, and his intellectual midwifery is always interesting and stimulating; but lives are not changed by Socrates today, brave men do not fight the battles against the nether powers with words of Socrates as their weapons. It was this young man of Nazareth who gave the final and satisfactory expression to many of the darkest truths of human life. We have not passed beyond his words, either in form or substance. Lassalle has been called the Messiah of socialism. He was a man of profound learning, of flashing and supple mind. He gave a powerful impetus to the social movement. His memory is reverenced, his speeches are still widely read. But the demands formulated by him, in which he saw all hope, have even now, a few decades after his death, become antiquated. They were carried for a while in the party platforms for his sake; now they have been dropped. His party has passed beyond him. The Messiah of socialism has been exhausted. Christ has not been exhausted. His party, the church, is charged with slowness and uselessness. But it is not because she has outstripped Christ and still insists on cumbering herself with his worn-out teachings. It is because she lags so far behind him and has cut the tendons of his teachings and lamed them by tradition and false interpretation. A church based absolutely on the teachings of Jesus would be the most revolutionary society on earth, and its platform would be further ahead of existing conditions than any party platform formulated in this age of platforms.

2) But the chief power of Christ does not lie in his teachings. His words were only a partial expression of himself; he is more than they. It is *the personality of Jesus Christ* in which the secret of his power lies. We have declined the task of discussing here the nature of Christ; but in surveying the velocity of the current originated by him, we cannot help trying to get some approximate estimate of the power that entered human history in the person of Jesus.

He is himself the best witness concerning himself. Going back to the oldest and safest records of his sayings, we find high utterances concerning himself. He calls himself the desire of prophets and kings, the culmination of Old Testament history, greater than Jonah, greater than Solomon, more than the temple, the Lord of David, the Lord of the Sabbath. He claims the right to forgive sins; he promises to confess before the Father those who confess him; he that receives him, receives Him that sent him; blasphemy against him is a sin so serious, that he especially asserts that it can be forgiven. All things have been delivered to him of the Father; he will be the judge of all the nations of the earth. He calls himself the Son of man, a name that he adapted for himself; it asserts his humanity and yet implies that he is Man in a unique sense. He calls himself the Son of God in a manner and in a sense different from those whom he taught to call God their Father. He was conscious of a unique intimacy with God, knowing him and known of him in a way which could not be asserted of others. (Matt. 11, 27.) All this shows that he was conscious of a relation both to God and to humanity in which he stood solitary, of a personality which transcended that of all other historical persons in value, and of a power to fulfill the entire past, to initiate a new era, and to give the ultimate realization to the aspirations of humanity.

The same impression of an immeasurably great personality grows on us if we study the records of his life simply as candid students of history and watch the impression he made on his contemporaries. Here was a man who without the easy pedestal of birth, rank, wealth, or learning yet attracted all eyes. The people hung upon him, wondering, doubting, guessing, willing to believe him if he proclaimed himself the Messiah, insisting even against the potent authority of the hierarchy that he must be a prophet, Elijah, Jeremiah, or someone of the greatest. Here was a man of the people who could meet the learned and exceedingly able lawyers and theologians of his day with their own weapons and disarm them with easy superiority, till they took their refuge first in slander, then in violence. And, what seems to us one of the strongest historical proofs of the greatness of Jesus, here was a man who walked in simplicity, in poverty, homeless, weary sometimes and hungry, not withdrawing from men in austere loneliness, but mingling with them in the disenchanting smallness of daily life; and yet those who knew him best exalted him most. At a time when his popularity was waning, when he was wandering as a fugitive in northern Galilee, when the immense intellectual and moral weight of the teachers and leaders of the people, so calculated to shake the judgment of the simple, was thrown dead against him; at a time when all the popular glory of the first days of his ministry was veiled by adversity and lack of success, his disciples leaped beyond the average impression of the people, repudiated the judgement of the hierarchy, broke with all the Jewish standards of Messianic greatness and asserted as the result of their maturing conviction that he was the Messiah, the Son of the living God. How great was this personality that in spite of the paralyzing pressure of outward disappointment could call forth such a confession!

It would be easy to leap at once to the theological dogmas of the later church and assert the very highest things concerning the person of Christ. But we prefer the slower method of historical study to build up in our minds some approximate conception of the greatness of Jesus. We know how Paul conceived him. To him Christ was the second Adam, the center of a new humanity, the source of a current of life greater than the current of death which had swept in through the first Adam; he was the Lord through whom are all things, the head of the church and its life-giving spirit, the coming judge, the restorer even of the travailing creation. Now it is true that Paul confessedly takes no interest in narrating the facts of Christ's life and quoting his sayings. He refuses to know Christ merely after the flesh. His Christ was the risen, glorified, spiritual Christ, present in the church with palpable power. Yet he built up his conceptions on historical facts. From the few instances in which the need of others compelled him to step down and demonstrate the stability of his foundations, we see that he knew the facts of Christ's life and that his knowledge was the result of extensive, scrutinizing, even doubting inquiry. He was a reasoner by nature, and he had been convinced in spite of doubt and denial. Therefore we can conclude from the loftiness of the speculative structure erected by him that he fully trusted the strength of its historical foundation. Again we ask, what must this personality of Jesus have been, if very shortly after his plain life, when his memory was still spotted with the fresh blood of an accursed criminal execution, Paul could put his foot on that cross which to many Jews was the insuperable stumbling-block, and proclaim Jesus as the glorified Lord of the world for whose exaltation the highest Messianic theology and the wealth of Alexandrian philosophy scarcely furnished him adequate expressions?

The same argument holds in qualified form concerning the conception of Jesus expressed in the Apocalypse, one of the earliest writings of the Christian church, and in the Fourth Gospel, one of the latest. It was because the glory of the man Jesus in grace and truth was so great, that the spiritual eye discerned in him the eternal Word made flesh. The portrayal of the Christ of the Fourth Gospel is distinct from the words, the gait, the look of the Jesus of the other three Gospels. And yet for all these centuries the church, though always feeling the diversity, has not necessarily felt any incongruity between the one figure and the other. The Galilean Jesus of Matthew, Mark, and Luke is able to bear the exceeding weight of glory of the incarnate Word and Life. So great was he.

The larger perspective of later ages has not reversed the verdict of his first followers. Not only have countless sincere hearts found in him the way, the truth, the life; they see and have confessed the name of Jesus to be above every name known to them. Even those who have refused their consent to the doctrines of the church concerning him have testified frankly to the immeasurable greatness of his personality. From his pantheistic stand-point Spinoza said as much as he could when he called Christ "the temple of God, because God has given the greatest manifestation of himself in Christ." Goethe says: "Let culture progress, let natural science expand and deepen, let the human intellect grow as it will; it will never get beyond the elevation and ethical culture of Christianity as it shines in the gospels." Strauss, the great negative critic, whose attacks on the old guarantees of faith have been so terrible because there was so much powerful historical work in them, has repeatedly conceded the possibility of proving that it will be forever impossible to pass beyond Christ in religion, and that in the highest department of life he stands in the first rank among those who have educated humanity to higher ideals; that all religious life finds its full development in him, and that all our extension and elaboration, making the best use of what he has given, can only furnish grains of sand to the eternal structure for which Jesus laid the mighty corner-stone.

We hear many bitter words against the church in these days, but seldom do we hear a word against Christ. The church is hissed, Christ is cheered. And the accursers of the church pay an involuntary tribute to Christ when they condemn the church by comparing it with its founder. Judged by comparison with any other organization, the church stands high enough; judged by Jesus as the standard, its deficiency is painfully evident.

This great personality, Jesus Christ, has entered humanity as a force. He threw himself with all his strength into the history of our race. And we assert that he is now a revolutionary force, changing individuals and revolutionizing nations. We assert that the personality of Christ has in a few nations overcome the inertia and retrogression everywhere else visible and has started them upon that series of revolutionary eras by which they are hewing their way toward the perfect society. There was force enough in him to do what we have said concerning the power of his personality. It remains to make clear to ourselves how his personality exerts this force.

We have spoken of the force of his teachings. But the difference between moral and religious teaching in the abstract and the same teaching personified and realized is vital. Jesus embodied his teaching, and Christianity is built up, not so much on the doctrine, as on the person of its founder.

In the first place teaching merely in words is never intelligible beyond a certain circle. It requires some intellectual ability and training to grasp the profounder truths of life when put in words. Religions not founded on persons have usually been esoteric religions; they have been the property of a limited circle of intellects, while the mass of the people caught only the drippings of truth that leaked out in simple precepts of morality, or found embodiment in ritual which spoke in action. There was perhaps never a community so saturated with religious thought as the Jewish people; yet the Rabbis called the common people accursed "because they knew not the law." If Jesus was to establish a religion of the common people, a religion of which fishermen could be the teachers and which could in its perfection become the possession of the meanest slave on a Roman latifundium, then a doctrine in words would not do. A doctrine in a man would; for there is that in us all which understands a human nature. It is the most incomprehensible and the most comprehensible thing in the world to us. Watch a child looking at a stranger with the wide, searching eye and bestowing its confidence or dislike as the result of its scrutiny. If truth can find expression in human nature, then it has found expression in the most perspicacious, the most universal, and the most elastic language. It is the language common to the rich and the lowly. It is the language that holds good though the boundaries of many nations be traversed. It is the language which does not become fossilized with the lapse of time. The words of the Nicene Creed, its distinctions of person and substance, though recited so often in many churches, are meaningless babble to ninety-nine percent of those who hear it. Christ is just as intelligible to a church sexton to-day as he was to the porter that swept out the hall in Nicea after the Council adjourned. "The Word made flesh" is the necessary condition of a truly universal religion, for no other expression of truth can serve for all classes, all nations, all times, and all grades of spiritual development. In Jesus we find all these requirements, and therefore his personality has that power over humanity which a luminous Shechina of God, dwelling in the midst of us, must have.

In the next place, the embodiment of truth lends it a compulsory power which the clearest statement in words cannot give it. The attempt has frequently been made, and with some success, to parallel the sayings of Jesus by similar sayings of the Rabbis, of the Shastras, and of Greek and Roman philosophers. Why should they not have said similar things? It would be no guarantee of the correctness of Christ's thoughts, if no one had ever sought the solution of life's problems in the same direction. But if such collections of similarities are to prove that there was no difference between Christ and other wise men, they skip lightly across the immense chasm that yawns between dreams and realities. What noble words Seneca spoke, and what a mean man he was! Those Stoic dreams of the brave, wise man were partly rhetorical coruscations, partly longings. They were moral intoxications, followed often by weariness, despair, and suicide. Cicero sadly confesses the non-existence of the ideal of wisdom and virtue that he portrayed. (Tusc. Disp. 2.22: *in quo vero erit perfecta sapientia—quem adhuc nos quidem vidimus neminem, sed philosophorum sententiis, qualis futurus sit, si modo aliquando fuerit, exponitur.*) Goodness which is known never to have existed and to be unattainable, is not only without power, it is enervating. It substitutes the shrug of skepticism for the enthusiasm of faith. It benumbs self-forgetfulness even in the honest and makes them seek satisfaction in the appearances of virtue, which at least bring the admiration of others, rather than in virtue itself. On the other hand, the fact that truth and goodness are realized immediately lays them upon all consciences with compulsory power. They are possible, are they? Well, then they are necessary. Preachers can speak all they please about the beauty of humility, of surrendering privileges, and of becoming brothers to the lowly—men yield a ready assent and live as they lived before. But let some man voluntarily strip off his purple and fine linen and work as a Connecticut factory operative or as a Russian moujik, and the world is moved. Consciences are stricken, minds become restless. In a greater or lesser degree imitation follows.

It is thus that Jesus has lent to the moral conceptions of humanity a force which the clearest perception of them and the most lucid statement never did lend them and never could have lent them. He has furnished us with the demonstration of a life completely filled with God and absolutely mastered by goodness. Henceforth none of us can be satisfied with anything less. And as a matter of fact there is no impulse which even approaches the force which Jesus Christ exerts upon those who lay themselves open to his influence, in perpetually raising their ideal and driving them toward it.

But we have pointed out that the thoughts of Jesus are revolutionary thoughts, and his activity was a revolutionary activity. His judgements did not coincide with the judgements current in his day; in many cases they directly contravened them. He did not admire what others admired. He scorned their models of virtue and found goodness where they felt only contempt. His whole life incarnated those principles which contradict the ruling principles of existing human society. Hence, wherever his personality gains influence over a human soul, the result will be that that soul will go forth to live a revolutionary life. And the abiding power of the personality of Jesus is seen in the fact that, although elements of society really hostile to Christ have so often and so generally obtained control of the church and turned Christianity into a conservative and reactionary force, yet somehow his true character is forever bursting forth and impelling new men to revolutionary efforts.

Furthermore, the personality of Jesus is so powerful a force by the sanity and harmony of its qualities. Any student of history knows that there is no impulse comparing in power with that of a living religion. The trouble is that religion has so often spent its force by tearing its possessor loose from human society, setting him to lacerate his back with lashes, laming his joints by standing on a pillar, wasting his time on reciting prayers, or grimly locking him up on the Sabbath to examine his inward states and to torture his children with devotions for which they have no taste. It is wonderful. The energy and persistence developed is worthy of admiration. But it is force wasted. It is pounding the sea, which closes again on the blow. If all the force spent in the deserts of the East and the monasteries of the West had been exerted upon the world instead of spending itself upon tearing men loose from their friends, stifling their love, and choking down their longings, the world might by this time be a very different world.

But again, when religion has been brought to bear on practical life, it has often bruised itself to death by the wild onset of fanaticism. The Jews rising under false Messiahs, the Anabaptists erecting a spiritual Kingdom at Münster, Quakers running naked through London with pans of brimstone on their heads and calling for repentance, the dervishes of the Mahdi storming against a fire that no European discipline would face—is there nothing admirable in these to the thoughtful man? And yet how often have men discarded all religious enthusiasm because the fire-cracker enthusiasm of these hotheads has sputtered itself out, leaving nothing but smoke and perhaps a conflagration.

Now compare with these two extremes the equipoise of the life of Jesus. Here was quiet patience with heroic bravery, the most daring innovation with the most loving conservatism. It is he who has demonstrated the possibility of resting in God without leaving the world, and of living in the world without forgetting God; of obeying the spirit without asceticism, and of eating and drinking without serving the flesh. He was both the Son of God and the Son of man and showed that he did not cease to be the one by becoming the other. He alone has fully married the real and the ideal, the life here and the life beyond, the inward perfection and its steady reconstruction of the outward imperfection. No spirit soared so high, and none was more sensible and sane.

And just this combination is the most difficult thing to teach by verbal instruction. Tell a man to have neither pride toward God nor servile fear of him, and how shall he do it? Tell him that mere external performances are nothing in the sight of God, and that mere ecstatic raptures of the spirit are equally nothing, and see whether he will hit on something that does avail. The efforts of theology to find a reconciliation between the holiness of God and his love in the abstract are very perplexing. But let these apparent contradictions be actually united in a person whose life is not yet contradictory but consistent and lovely, and we draw a sigh of relief; we draw near that person, we come under his influence, and we feel the same harmonious wholeness of life developing in us.

Such men as John the Baptist knock more rudely at the door of the world and demand admission for heaven. But Jesus brought heaven into the world and commended it to the love of men, and so, even though they killed him, the Kingdom of heaven is here and has gained its habitation through the influence of his personality. But where heaven is, sin leaves, and if sin leaves, this world is revolutionized. It will be only a question of time when the new force shall have penetrated everything.

The Kingdom of God presupposes a reconstruction of the life of this world, till in spirit and form it shall be the doing of the will of God. Jesus bore the Kingship of God within him. He saw things as God views them, and his actions were done in entire obedience to the will of his Father. Hence the words in which he expressed his views of the world contradicted the lying views of society, and his actions likewise disobeyed the rules of propriety and right set up by society. In his words and in his actions we have the manifestations of his personality. His personality therefore was in opposition to the existing life of humanity. But this opposition did not remain confined to his person. By that inalienable influence which every human being for good or evil exerts upon all others that come in contact with it, his thought and action would attract others. That influence increases in geometrical ratio with the greatness of the personality exerting it. The personality of Jesus was immeasurably great, and even without any exertion on his part he would have drawn men out of their grooves into his. But Jesus deliberately exerted all his power to that end. His teaching came over men with all the inherent force of truth against which there is no appeal except denial. The teaching was made directly intelligible by being incarnated in his life. It thereby also gained the compulsory power which truth in action always has, and at the same time his life commended his radical teaching by showing the healthful balance which was possible along with all its forward push.

Thus Jesus won those to him who loved the light. They opened their hearts to his influences and put themselves under his guidance. His power became the supreme power in their lives.

The same influence still continues from the historical Christ across all these centuries. Men still absorb his words and reconstruct their lives more or less to accord with them. His personality also acts upon all who put themselves in contact with it. There are many who have vowed loyalty to the Man of Galilee and are satisfied if they can in any way execute the desires of him they call Master. They love him with a unique love. And upon all who have courage to pass by the false Christ whom men with the spirit of this world have set up to deceive us, upon all who push on to behold the sad, earnest face of the Son of man, comes the spirit of battle. If the Master fought, so must we. If his battle was against the great ones of the earth on behalf of the people, we know who is our enemy, too. If he found the bitterest enemy of his Father's will in religious bigotry and Pharisaism, we know where we shall find it to-day. He shows us the direction and lends us the impulse. The cross of the MacGregors had to be carried on.* So must the cross of the Christ. And if fear and loneliness come upon us, we gain renewal of strength from him who also wrestled with fear and darkness and then went forth in calmness and strength.

The center of the Messianic hope was the Messiah, the perfect King of his people. Jesus did not fulfill all the conceptions of the Jewish nation concerning the Messiah. He wielded no rod of iron, he piled up no heaps of the slain, he did not robe himself in magnificence like Solomon. His nation saw no regal power in him. Pilate, the Roman, knew the aspects of royalty, and when he saw that pale and forsaken figure before him, he asked in scornful surprise: "Thou—art thou a king?"

"Thou sayest it; I am a king," was the answer. And thousands of quivering lips have since echoed it: "Thou sayest it, O Pilate; he is a king." Royal not by gorgeous trappings bought with the sweat of his people, imperial not by the glint of bayonets; but the King of men, glorious by the sweetness and strength of his life, powerful by the attraction of love and gratitude and by the compulsion of truth and right. The Jews expected the Messiah as an Oriental autocrat. But despotisms are passing away. The greatness won by force is gaining less and less of admiration. The discernment of humanity is growing clearer. Men love heroism, self-sacrifice, love. Jesus has himself been the foremost force in bringing about this change, and in turn he reaps the reward of his work. The less men acknowledge the sovereignty of brute force and the more they yield their willing loyalty to the spiritual power of character, the more will Jesus become King of humanity.

b. The Spirit of God

The second force by which the Old Testament prophets expected the perfection of the theocracy was the Spirit of God. That Spirit which had been the exclusive privilege of a few chosen men, of

* [Probably a reference to the burden carried by the MacGregor clan during and after the Cromwellian revolution due to the execution of MacGregor of Glenstral in 1604. Many of the later portions of this story are recaptured in Sir Walter Scott's *Rob Roy*. M. L. S.]

kings and prophets and priests, would be poured out on all, on old and young, on the great and the lowly (Joel 2, 28-29), and thus that knowledge of God's will which had hitherto been imparted by the few to the many would become the common property of all. (Jer. 31, 31-34; Isa. 54, 13.) This inward knowledge of God, this writing of the law on the hearts by the Spirit of God, would make it possible to abrogate the old covenant of outward law and compulsion and to institute the new covenant of loving obedience. Where the Spirit was poured out upon the people, it would be like water upon the thirsty and like floods upon the dry ground; there would be a glad life like the sprouting of young grass, like the luxuriance of the willow withes along the water-courses. (Isa. 44, 3-4.)

At the beginning of the Messianic era this prophecy was renewed by John. He depreciated himself in comparison with the greater one that was to come, and his own baptism in comparison with that which was to be administered by the Messiah. He said the two would compare as water with fire. His ministry was the ministry of repentance, his baptism was the baptism of repentance. He had power to call men to cut loose from the old and to wash off the former life. He had no power to inaugurate the new era and to implant the principle of a new life. That remained for the Messiah and the baptism in spirit.

Jesus adopted the very words of John and renewed the promise. (Acts 1, 4-8.) It would be a misconstruction of his words and the subsequent facts to regard this gift of the Spirit either as the natural reason of man, or as that enlightening influence which God exerts upon all men, or as elevation of character, or as mere enthusiasm. It was not natural reason; at least Paul perceived a very profound difference between the clear-sightedness and intellectual ability which distinguished the leaders of existing society, and the insight resulting from the possession of the Spirit. (I Cor. 2, 6-16.) It was not the general enlightening influence of God; the Fourth Gospel evidently distinguishes between the Logos which is the light of men and illuminates every man, and the Paraclete that was to complete the work of Christ. It was not synonymous with elevation of character; the apostles had been undergoing a process of spiritual education under

Christ in faith, love, obedience, and knowledge, yet Christ bids them wait for something additional. It was not a boiling up of enthusiasm over the fire of opposition; it lasted too long and was apparently too objective a reality in the church to admit of that explanation. It was a gift, an impartation from God, not a product from within. The church in Jerusalem (Acts 2), the converts at Samaria (Acts 8, 14), the household of Cornelius (Acts 10, 44), the men at Ephesus (Acts 19, 1), had at one time not had the Spirit, and then they had received it. The power of that Spirit was a solid fact in the experience of the churches. (I Thess. 1, 5.) In writing to the Galatians, Paul assumed their recollection of the coming of the Holy Spirit as a matter of course and simply questions whether they at that time received it by the performance of Jewish rites or by the preaching of Christ's glad tidings. (Gal. 3, 1.) It was so universal in the church that Paul denied the title of Christian to all that did not have it and did not feel its guiding activity. (Rom. 8, 9, 14.) It was so palpable a possession that he calls it the earnest, the tangible pledge, the first part payment of the redemption for which the early church was so anxiously waiting in suffering. If the epistles of Paul are taken simply as historical evidence concerning the life and condition of the early churches, they demonstrate the existence of a new spiritual force in the world, which Paul found only in connection with the gospel of Christ, and which he regarded as neither the product of environment, nor as the evolution of personal character, but as an abiding contact between the spirit of man and the Spirit of the living God.

This new force is a revolutionary force. It must be, because it is of God and must unceasingly protest against the saying and doing of lies, against impurity and meanness, against injustice and oppression; it must work toward truth, right, and love.

And examining its historical effect we find that it is indeed a revolutionary force.

1) First of all, it frees man from that slavery which comes closest home to all of us, *the enslavement of our ethical and spiritual nature under the cravings of our animal nature.* We all feel that the moral demands within us are the higher and ought to rule, and we all know

that in most men they are overpowered by the brutal instincts and do not rule. Every man feels at least an occasional pang of sorrow at this fact. And the more earnest writhe under the consciousness of their impotence and cry out for some power to deliver them from the body of this death in life. Paul asserts that such a power exists. He asserts that what man cannot do even under the stimulus of a high moral law is accomplished by the indwelling of the Spirit of God. (Rom. 7, 15–8, 11.) There is an enfranchising power in it. A man who is born from above (John 3, 3-6), and in whom the Spirit of God dwells (Rom. 8, 9), no longer has the same purposes and desires that he had before. (Rom. 8, 5.) Not that the old desires have been annihilated, but the center of gravity in the man is shifted from the brutal to the spiritual, and the desire to eat and to drink what he pleases is held in check by the love and tenderness for others who may be injured thereby. (Rom. 14, 14-15.) The chief good becomes not to fill his stomach at any cost, but to be conscious of a right life, to be at peace with himself and his brothers, and to have the glad and quickening contact with the Holy Spirit. That fellowship and oneness with God is a prophylactic against any debasement of body and soul. (I Cor. 6, 15-20.) As long as the Spirit is kept supreme, the fruits of a man's life will not be a rank growth of lasciviousness and angry jealousy, but a harvest of peace, kindness, gentleness, and self-control. (Gal. 5, 16-24.) In place of the excitement of revelling he has the healthy stimulus of a glad and thankful frame of mind, filled with services of helpfulness. (Eph. 5, 18-21.)

In short, that first and worst servitude, the slavery of man to his own baser desires which compel him to do what he hates and degrade him in his own sight if not in the opinion of others, that slavery can be broken by the revolutionary power of the renewing and indwelling Spirit of God. Through that a man can become a freeman, lifting up his head before God and men. It makes him sane, sound, strong, a well-grained stone in the living temple of humanity.

2) In the second place, the Spirit is a revolutionary force by emancipating men from *the thraldom of superstition.* Religious superstition has doubtless been one of the most paralyzing, benumbing

forces in the world. It makes the African shiver at a black stump. It drives hundreds of thousands of people annually to the shores of Holy Ganges and to the grave of the Prophet, wasting them with the fatigues of travel and making them bearers of disease for themselves and others. Even in enlightened Europe there is Rome with its relics and Lourdes with its water, and as we write, the city authorities of Trier are building three railway stations, laying double streetcar tracks, and granting hundreds of saloon licences in view of the multitudes that are expected to visit the alleged garment of Christ which is to be exposed to the sight of the faithful.

One way of combatting superstition is by exposure. It examines the bones of the 11,000 virgins at Cologne and declares that in the first place, there are not enough bones there to supply 11,000 virgins with their necessary anatomy, and in the second place, many of those that are there never belonged to female skeletons. It watches the liquefaction of the blood of St. Januarius, and discovers that the miracle times itself by the church clock and not by solar time. The effect of this method of reasoning is twofold. Some, especially women, shut their eyes very tight and insist that they take all the more satisfaction in believing it because science calls it absurd. Others, especially men, say: "We have been fooled, have we? Well then, the whole thing is rot. Away with priests, away with God, away with moral obligations! Henceforth we believe what we see and do what we dare." If they succeed, they produce atrophy of their higher nature, they lose all reverence, their moral fibre gradually grows flabby, they become what they desire to be, intellectual animals. If the suppressed part of their nature asserts itself in spite of them, their superstition merely changes its form; they are frightened by black cats and falling salt-cellars and the number thirteen and follow as blindly their favorite form of skepticism as their wives follow the priests and their church. One devil has gone out but another has come in, and it is a moot question in demonology which of the two is the worse. The Latin nations of Europe will afford pathological cases enough to anyone who desires to investigate the question.

True Christianity applies a different method. It recognizes in superstition the helpless groping of a legitimate but undeveloped instinct. It sees the caged bird flutter when the time comes for the southward flight, and it does not cut off the fluttering wings, but it opens the cage, lets the air and sunshine stream into the room, and says: "Now fly!"

Does the Samaritan woman reverence places, balancing the sanctity of Mount Gerizim against the holiness of Jerusalem? The answer is not that there is no use in worshipping God at all, but that he who approaches the Father in spirit and truth can draw nigh to him anywhere and find him. Have men been accustomed to enter temples with awe because God is there, and to bow before altars with reverence because of the Real Presence in the host? Their true emancipation is not in thinking that God is nowhere near, not even in temples, but in experiencing the contact and presence of the Eternal One in their own souls. Then they will know that the Shechina is in no temple so palpable and near as in the temple of a God-conquered body (I Cor. 6, 19), and in a community of spiritual men. (I Cor. 3, 16; Eph. 2, 22.) If they seek God, they will not travel hither or thither to get near him but will withdraw into the silent solitude of their own hearts, and there God will meet them. He that knows God within him is free from the superstition of holy places.

He is free also from the superstition of ritual and sacred actions. Judaism was full of that; sacrifices, circumcision, ceremonial washings, the Tephillin on arm and forehead in prayer, the performance of the Paschal ritual, the reciting of the Shema, the punctilious observance of the Sabbath—all these were actions in themselves holy. God was pleased when they were performed and displeased if they were not. This also was a bondage from which it was hard indeed to free men. And here again the possession of the Spirit is the enfranchising power. Paul compares the ritualists in their slavish piety and the children of the Spirit in their free service to the son of Hagar the bondmaid and the child of Sara the freewoman. (Gal. 4, 21–5, 1.) The Spirit was everywhere working out a free and truthful life that was not chained to set words and fixed actions but sought its own natural expression. It is the undying merit of Paul that he cut the Jewish fetters by which the young church was bound, protested against the bondage of antiquated forms (Gal. 5, 1), refused the "weak and beggarly rudiments" (Gal. 4, 9), and insisted on liberty for the Spirit of God to do its transforming work. (II Cor. 3, 6-18.) But a mere refusal of the old forms would have availed nothing unless there were a new and creative spirit. It is not: "where the old forms are abolished, there is liberty"; but "where the Spirit of the Lord is there is liberty." Unless that Spirit is present, there will always be forms to which men cling. Men have made a form of Christianity itself. The Jews strapped on the Tephillin for prayer, Christians dip their finger in water and make the sign of the cross. The Jews substituted another word whenever the dread name of Yahweh occurred in the reading of the Scriptures; Christians bow their backs whenever the name of Christ occurs in the litugy. The Jews thought circumcision a saving performance; Christians sprinkle a child with water and mutter a formula and expect that to alter God's feelings toward that child. How Paul would cry out against these modern Galatians who have indeed forsaken the old Jewish yoke that galled his shoulder, but have constructed a like fabric out of Christian observances, still trusting in saving performances and formulas, turning his own passionate appeals for freedom into a new law of Moses which they may read with veils over their faces! Are we saved by faith or by manipulations? Does the Spirit create its forms or the forms conjure up the Spirit?

Set rites and creeds and forms are the grave clothes of a dead faith. The living Spirit alone is strong and daring enough to strip them off and stand forth in the strength of life. Where the veneration for sacred forms increases, it is an almost certain sign that the Spirit is departing and that hence a substitute has to be found. The form of godliness is most exalted where the power of godliness is vanishing. On the other hand, where the living Spirit grows dominant, forms become of slight account. They are used or not, as occasion teaches, but there is not compulsory holiness in them. The holiness is in the Spirit which uses the forms, and beside that wonderful presence all dead things seem as naught.

3) In the third place, the Spirit is revolutionary force because,

where it comes, *it breaks the power of priestcraft.* This also is one of the evil forces that has kept humanity in bondage. The medicine-man of South America, the rainmaker of Africa, the augur and haruspex of ancient Rome, the priests in Egypt, the scribes of Judea that laid heavy burdens upon the people, these all have wielded a power over men more tyrannical than the violence of kings and more blighting to the free development of human society. Almost universally has religion been bound up with the domination of priests, and some honest students of history have identified the two and cast them overboard together. We feel under no compulsion to do so. Enemies of popular liberty have quoted the sad words of Madame Roland when she was led to the guillotine: "O Liberty, what crimes are committed in thy name," and have reasoned that liberty is evil because evil things are done in its name. We hold that just because liberty is one of the sublimest possessions of man, some will commit atrocities to gain it, and others will use it to cloak their own selfishness. The same thing is true of religion. Because religion is one of the potent forces of human life, it has been used by designing men to fasten their power over their fellow-men. What noble aspiration is there which has not been thus misused? Sexual love, patriotism, the faculty of self-sacrifice—they are all used to bit and bridle the people.

The power of priests lies in their claim to some exclusive knowledge of the will of God and some exclusive right of approach to him. The Sudanese rainmaker alone knows the proper incantations to break the drought. The priest of Benares is the one that knows just how to beat the tom-tom and offer the sacrifice in the way that will please the terrible Goddess of Disease and cause her to depart from the Hindu's favorite child. The Judean scribe had the knowledge of the Law in the doing of which lay salvation, and therefore he had to be held in reverence.

Men want to approach God to know his will and be assured of his favor. They do not know how and feel unfit for it. They will submit to the direction of those who profess to know, and who claim by some title of caste or initiation to be qualified for approaching God.

How shall men be emancipated from this bondage of ignorance?

Here also we deny that the liberation can be a merely negative one. The human heart demands truth, it demands God. Demolish the power of one sort of priesthood but leave the people as they are, and they will run after some other sort. It will be a change of manner, not of things. The only true emancipation is for a man to have the truth and the voice of God within him by the Spirit of God. The prophets hoped for that: "This is the new covenant that I will make with the house of Israel; I will put my laws into their mind, and on their heart also will I write them. And they shall not teach every man his fellow-citizen, and every man his brother, saying: 'Know the Lord!' for all shall know me, from the least to the greatest of them." (Jer. 31, 34.) Christ promised the fulfillment of this in the sending of the Paraclete, the Spirit of Truth, who would dwell in his disciples, teach them all things, remind them of what they had heard, make clear to them what they had seen but not understood, and guide them into the truths too great for them as yet. (John 14, 17, 25; 16, 12-14.) This Spirit did come. It proved to be a Spirit of "wisdom and revelation in the knowledge of God," an "enlightening of the eyes of the heart." As Jesus foretold, it made of his unlettered followers "prophets and wise men and scribes" (Matt. 23, 34), stewards over a treasure of knowledge from which they could bring out new and old. Paul claimed for those who had the Spirit a great and general knowledge of moral and spiritual truth (I Cor. 2), an open-eyed vision of God, which far transcended what the painful scrutiny of the Rabbis could discern in their sacred writings. (II Cor. 3.) John distinctly declares that the Christians are of age; he himself has no desire to treat them as if they were still in tutelage, but simply offers his thoughts and counsels for their aid: "Ye have an anointing from the Holy One, and ye know all things. I have not written unto you because ye know not the truth, but because ye know it." "These things have I written unto you concerning them that would lead you astray. And as for you, the anointing which ye received of him abideth in you, and ye need not that any one teach you." (I John 2, 20-21, 26-27.) This is not the language of hierarchy but of a mutually helpful fraternal society. Similarly, the Epistle to the Hebrews is the record of a struggle for freedom, for a universal priesthood, for the right to do without priests and approach God directly.

It is no argument against what we have said that Christianity soon developed a finely graded hierarchy, evolved its "means of grace" which only an ordained clergy could administer, substituted the absolution of the priest for the free approach to God, and made the hierarchy the sole stewards of the truth and possessor of the Spirit. It simply proves what we assert, that no change of forms can emancipate but only the possession of the Spirit. He that has its witness in his heart needs no churchly sacraments to assure him that he is a child of God. He needs neither "the Holy Church" nor a "historic episcopate" to mediate between him and the God who is so near to him. He needs no infallible church, no flawless system of theology, and no arbiter of the faith in the editorial chair of a denominational newspaper to tell him what he will have to believe if he wishes to please God. There is a Comforter and Admonisher within him that opens his eyes and gives him a lively relish for the truth in the Bible or wherever he may find it in the thoughts of the great congregation of the faithful in all ages. "The truth makes free," says Christ: free from Pharisaic infallibility too; free from fear of the Jerusalem hierarchy. The "spirit of truth" is the emancipating power. He that truly possesses it can smile at excommunications, laugh at interdicts, shrug his shoulders at the devil's cry of heresy, for, like Stephen who was full of the Holy Ghost, he sees his Lord present while the Sanhedrin gnash their teeth at him. He is free from priestcraft. The Spirit has made him free.

4) The Spirit is a revolutionary power because *it is the constructive power of a new society.* Mere protests against existing conditions are not enough to evolve better conditions. It may be worth much to knock down the walls of an old and useless building; but those who can do that are not always able also to make the nobler edifice rise from the debris. There are tremendous destructive forces now at work in all the civilized nations, trampling on superstitions, protesting against unjust laws, bending like Samson against the pillars that support modern society. We cherish the confidence that in the long range

of history these forces also will be seen to have been God's ministers. Superstitions ought to be killed; unjust laws ought to be abolished; existing society is rotten and ought to be buried. But the question which we anxiously put to ourselves again and again is this: Have these forces the power to do anything more than destroy? Have they creative power?

In the arraignments of existing religion and politics and social order we always notice that the protests are much stronger than the positive propositions for something better. It is nearly all criticism, very little construction. Naturally a man grumbles at the bad food before he calls for something that he would like better; and yet, when he proposes to us to reject our entire bill of fare and our whole system of cooking, we must insist that he prove his ability to suggest something better, before we allow him to toss our menu out the window.

We ask not for a detailed plan of the new society. Such a demand is unreasonable. But we do ask to see those qualities of mind and heart which can cement men together into a better social structure. Peacefulness, self-control, love of right, and mutual forbearance are some of the virtues the diffusion of which makes a happy social life possible, but they are not virtues that grow in any superabundance among men. The number of people who feel the cravings of other people's stomachs as keenly as their own is small. The men who will not oust a rival in love if they can do it are also few. Selfishness is the primary force of human life, and selfishness is only to a very limited extent a unitive force. It unites men under the pressure of need. Even wolves unite to hunt when they are famished, but they snarl and bite at one another when they have run down their prey. Every higher form of society demands a surrender of selfishness under the impulse of larger thoughts and ideals. The lower form cannot be safely abandoned until that higher principle is present in the people, which is to underlie and fashion the better form of society.

While the destructive power of the modern iconoclasts is evidently very great, their constructive power, I fear, will be feeble. The average liberal in religion can destroy a nation's reverence for the Bible, but can he give the people a book in its place which will better educate the young, comfort the weary, and nerve the strong man to renewed fortitude? I confess that the system of ethics colored with current philosophy, which is usually offered us in place of the old faiths, looks very slender to me. It may serve as a staff on ground smoothed out by the labor of ages, but I fear it would snap like a reed in the hour of a man's passion, or when a nation descends into the valley of the shadow of death, as nations sometimes must.

The same thing is true of the political and social revolutionists. They destroy; can they upbuild? Will the men who so wonderfully hold together during their fight hold together when the victory is won and peacefully and gladly cooperate in building up the details of the new structure? History does not make us very sanguine. The French Revolution is a noble chapter in history. Its aims were admirable. Many of the laws passed were ideally just. But they did not stick. It was like modeling a statue of soft butter. Men passed resolutions like angels and hated one another like demons. And this glorious movement of freedom ended in feverish spasms. The gospel according to Jean Jacques Rousseau brought no millennium. "The Rights of Man" was a good cry to knock down with; but to build up we need a people that will respond to the cry of "The Duties of Man," and that is not a cry to which the average man lends a ready ear. I fear, too, that the anger, distrust, and hate which some social reformers are systematically infusing into the people do not make the people better fitted for the future work of upbuilding. It is an excellent method of evoking cheers from a meeting, of gaining a temporary advantage from an employer, and of hastening the overthrow of society. But what material will the men thus trained be for the positive work afterward? The armed men that sprang from the dragon's teeth sown by Jason slew one another. Make the beast that lurks in man sullen and snarling, and one day it will turn and rend you.

The assertion that Christianity is a constructive power containing the creative principle of a new society will doubtless draw a mocking smile from some. I need not tell those who have read the preceding pages that I do not call everything Christianity which calls itself so. I mean neither the Christianity of princes nor of well-fed priests;

neither that of the benevolent bourgeois who gives alms to keep the people contented and respectful, nor that of the tradesman who tries to make his ledger balance well both for this life and the life to come. I mean the Christianity of Jesus, which under the power of his Spirit has existed through the centuries, in various forms, always more or less despised, but always vital and energetic. That Christianity has in it the constructive power, because it has in it the Spirit of God.

The Christianity of the early church did knock down the wall of partition separating Jews from Gentiles. It did undermine the old principle of coherence which makes the Jews to this day a separate people. But the common possession of the Spirit was the bond of a new unity, by which Jews and Greeks grew into one body. (I Cor. 12, 13.) And only those who know the strength of the prejudices that kept them apart can estimate the strength of the force that drew them together, however imperfectly, in the Christian churches. Christianity at that time proved able to abolish the old forms of national coherence, without however leaving the individual isolated, because it united Jew and Greek and barbarian into a new society. The small patriotisms by which men have hitherto been united are also giving way to-day to the larger patriotism of humanity. This is well if there is a new principle of unity strong enough to bind together so large a mass. The only such principle that I can see is the idea of the brotherhood of humanity, which was first asserted by Christianity as an actuality, and for which Christianity is still the most powerful feeder as soon as the brotherhood gets beyond phrases and selfishness. Christian missions with all their shortcomings are after all the only force which drives men from their own kinsmen into strange nations in order to carry the seed of a nobler life to them. Traders and emigrants may carry civilization incidentally, but they go for their own sakes. Even the unselfish explorer and man of science go out in order to carry at least knowledge back with them. It is the Spirit of Christ alone which breaks down national barriers in order to lift up the low members of humanity to the same level with the rest of the family.

Again, the Spirit of God has proved itself the power to establish a form of society not only more comprehensive in its scope but higher in its nature. The church in Jerusalem was a social body that "walked in the fear of the Lord and in the admonition of the Holy Spirit." (Acts 9, 31.) And of this body we read that "they were together and had all things in common; they sold their possessions and goods and divided them to all, according as any man had need. And day by day, continuing steadfastly with one accord in the temple, and breaking bread at home, they did take their food with gladness and singleness of heart, praising God and having favor with all the people." We do not discuss here the question whether this life was meant to be permanent and universal in the churches, nor whether this was a rational and scientific polity or not. But this is plain, that under the first powerful impulse of the Spirit men united in a new society in which the divisive force of selfishness was broken, where love and generosity were the rule and men lived a glad, thankful, and single-hearted life. Suppose the experiment did fail. Most first experiments fail. But if the Spirit is present, it will impel to ever new efforts to incorporate it. That Spirit has remained, though by no means co-extensive with so-called Christendom. There was love among the early Christians, love so earnest that heathen writers ridiculed it, imposters abused it, and dark suspicions were current that so unheard of affection must be based on a sinister community of crime. That Spirit of God has given, as the Belgian economist de Laveleye says, the most powerful impulses toward liberty and an ideal society up to the present day.

Even its enemies must acknowledge that a true Christian morality and religion are a strong conservative and cohesive force. It gives stability to what it has once undertaken to support. For centuries England had more and purer Christianity in it than the other European nations. Since the Reformation, it has been the birth-place of all the progressive religious movements. England has also been the nation which has kept up the steadiest march toward civil liberty. It has been the nation which gained reforms and kept them. It has been the nation that has planted colonies which have the faculty of making free institutions work, while heathen nations plant despotisms, and European nations with a more paganized Christianity have planted colonies which are republics in name and often despotisms in fact.

Christianity has been the most fertile parent of advanced social experiments. We shall speak of them later. It has experimented with communism before science touched it. And it can be demonstrated that of all the communistic colonies the only ones that have maintained permanent inward peace and prosperity are those which were held together by religion. Of course the maintenance of a socialist colony is a difficult task, but these experiments show that Christianity has a greater unitive and organizing force than secularism. The unity of the Spirit is the bond of peace. The fellowship of the Spirit was Paul's basis of appeal for mutual forbearance and service. (Phil. 2, 1.) Jealousy and strife were to him a demonstration of a lack of the Spirit. (I Cor. 3, 1, 3.) The Spirit gives and stimulates the faculties of mutual service which serve for the organic upbuilding of a new society. (I Cor. 12, 4-11.) It seems to me that the diversity of organizations in religious life, the fertility of Christianity in creating new forms of life even today, is far greater than that of secular society.

Therefore, in the face of all the appalling sloth of so-called Christians, I assert that the Spirit of Christ is a revolutionary power for constructing a more perfect society. It is subversive of national and class distinctions and contains the principle of a race unity. It stimulates to endeavor after more just and merciful forms of social life and produces that responsiveness to duty, that love and forbearance and peace which are the necessary conditions of making more perfect social institutions stick and work. If sweeping changes are to come, the Christian people will probably be found to be the stable element in the new society, and it will fall to them to give shape and permanence to those of the modern revolutionary ideas which shall stand the trial of fire.

5) Once more, the Spirit of God is a revolutionary force because *it creates the temper, wisdom, and power of the revolutionary propagandist.*

Of this we have the authoritative example in Jesus himself. Before he entered on his active work he was, as Peter expresses it, "anointed with the Holy Spirit and with power." (Acts 10, 38.) Under the impulse of that Spirit he was led into the wilderness to settle the great questions of the work before him. (Lk. 4, 1.) In the power of that Spirit he began to preach "good tidings to the poor, release to the captives, and liberty to the oppressed." (Lk. 4, 14, 18.) Through the force of that Spirit he grappled with the sinister malevolence of lost souls, spirit to spirit, and overcame it. (Matt. 12, 28.)

He promised to his disciples the same power for the progaganda before them (Acts 1, 8; John 14, 12), and the same God-given wisdom. (Lk. 12, 11-12; 21, 12-15.) History shows that they received both. We find these plain country-people speaking to the cultured inhabitants of the metropolis with great boldness, and with entire fearlessness facing and accusing the great council of their nation, which to their minds must have seemed more august than any tribunal on earth would seem to us. And this boldness is given as the very consequence of their possession of the Spirit of God. (Acts 4, 31.) By their own sense of right, they defied judicial injunctions (Acts 4, 19), and rejoiced in suffering for their cause. (Acts 5, 41.) Such a choice man as Stephen is an almost ideal revolutionary character (Acts 6-7), and he was a man "full of faith and of the Holy Spirit." (Acts 6, 5.)

As for wisdom, we find that also with the men upon whose untried shoulders rested the burden of guiding a great international movement with all the forms of a new society to find and the most difficult questions to settle. They claim to have been guided by the Holy Spirit singly and as a body, not only on general questions but about single practical points. (Acts 8, 29; 13, 2-4; 15, 28; I Cor. 7, 40.)

It seems to me that to possess this Spirit is the most effective revolutionary equipment. He that has it, is independent above anyone in the world. He has the great Companion ever with him, whose presence Jesus declared to be better than his own visible companionship. (John 14, 14.) He can at any time lean back and feel the Eternal Rock supporting him. He stands among his neighbors in state and church, sharing with them, serving them, but not mastered by them. He does not draw his notions of right from public opinion nor limit them by existing laws; he has a higher canon within him by which he judges what he sees (I Cor. 2, 15), and where necessary strives to change it. The feeble aspirations of his fluttering human spirit are borne up on the eagle wings of that mightier Spirit. (Rom. 8, 26.) His conscience is quickened and steadied by reference to that inward guide. (Rom. 9, 1.) Who has undertaken the work of a true herald of righteousness and mercy without growing disheartened in time at the dead weight of selfishness to be removed? Who has not felt the leaden heaviness of polite scorn, trembled at the angry mutter of the multitude, and "battled with a dreadful ache at heart," as he saw before him "that loneliest solitude, the silent desert of a great new thought"? The true revolutionist, the pilgrim of this world, the child of eternity need that abiding Presence if they would have wisdom not to stumble at the critical movement, boldness not to flinch, strength to seize the opportunity, and a serene and hopeful faith that even a desert wind cannot scorch. (Eph. 3, 14-21.)

And finally we must call attention to the fact that the two, Christ and the Spirit, are not two distinct forces, different perhaps in character and demands and dividing our alliance. Jesus speaks now of himself being with and dwelling in the disciples, and now of the Comforter abiding in them. (Matt. 28, 20; John 14, 16-19; 15, 5.) In the seven epistles in the book of Revelation it is always the "Son of God," he that "was dead and lived again," that speaks, and yet every epistle closes with the words: "He that hath an ear, let him hear what the Spirit saith." Paul speaks interchangeably of Christ living in him (Gal. 2, 20), and the Spirit dwelling in him (Rom. 8, 9), of Christ in us as the ground of our hope of glory, and of the Spirit as the earnest and the firstfruits of our inheritance. (Eph. 1, 13; Rom. 8, 23.) Luke speaks in one breath of the Holy Spirit forbidding Paul to preach in Asia, and the spirit of Jesus not suffering him to go into Bithynia. (Acts 16, 6-7.)

I have no desire to dogmatize about this. But this easy interchange of expression certainly shows that the idea of the glorified Christ and that of the Holy Spirit were for all practical purposes nearly identical to the early Christians. Those who have a living sense of being acted upon by the Spirit of God—do they ever conceive of him as anything but the Christ whose words they have heard and whose person they have loved as they have seen him in the Gospels? Do they not feel the personal nearness and guidance and love of their Friend and Master? If so, we may unite the discussion of these two forces and regard it as the discussion of the twofold influence of the one force, the Logos of God, first by the perennial influence of his historical manifestation in humanity, and then by his abiding personal influence upon and in our own hearts. It is one electric current, here kindling the resisting medium of the carbon point into illuminating splendor, and there running with silent power through the coils of wire, turning dead bars of iron into irresistible magnets.

c. The Church

The third power by which the Old Testament prophets expected to see the glorious future realized was the purified and glorified nation as the seat of God's manifestation. This expectation finds its fulfillment in the church. The historic personality of Jesus, the all-pervading Spirit of God touching the spirits of men, and living men in whom these two other forces have wrought a change and found a dwelling-place—these are the revolutionary forces working in humanity toward the reign of God on earth.

Jesus sought to duplicate himself in his disciples. He singled out among the multitude of people with whom he came in contact those who by repentance had put away the evil deeds which would otherwise have made them recoil from him (John 3, 20), and who by faith in him had opened their souls to all impressions coming from him. By every holy bond he attached them to himself. He walked with them and talked with them. Patiently he planted his ideas in their minds, utilizing every moment of sorrow, of wonder, of sin, of hearty admiration to bring them to look at things in his way. He made them his companions, called them his friends (John 15, 14), ranked their nearness to him above that of kinship. (Matt. 12, 46-50.) He wanted to be their shepherd whose voice they would know and respond to. (John 14, 4, 14.) He wanted to be as meat and drink to their spiritual natures. (John 6, 35; Matt. 26, 26-29.) He wanted his life to be in them as the sap of the vine courses in the branches. (John 15.)

In a great measure he succeeded. Their hearts were plastic to his touch. They loved him. They found the chief good of their lives in him. His thoughts became their thoughts. His sympathies and antipathies were theirs. Christ was formed in them. Paul in surveying his life saw the Paul-life all merged in the Christ-life; it was no longer he that lived, it was Christ. Both during Christ's life on earth and after, it was true in greater or lesser degree, as Paul says: "We all, with unveiled face reflecting as a mirror the glory of the Lord, are transformed into the same image from glory to glory." They lived over again the life of Christ.

And as they lived over again his life, so they could continue his work, every one according to the measure of Christ's life in him. As he was the light of the world, so they could be lights shining in the darkness. As he was the saving power, so they could be salt preserving the world from putrefaction.

As they repeated his life and his work, they would re-experience his sorrows and sufferings. If the world had hated him, it would hate them in the measure that they were like him. (Matt. 10, 24-25.) Many of them drank the same cup that he drank and were baptized with his baptism. It was not Paul alone who carried in his body the dying of the Lord Jesus and made up what was left of the suffering of Christ for men.

Since then there has been a long, long series of Christ-like lives on earth, of men and women in whom Christ has taken form. History has recorded some of them; but history itself is but slowly being christianized; it is only gradually learning to apply Christ's standards of greatness. It has wrapped the saint's robe about many a cloven hoof. It has left many a saint's aureole hidden under the felon's cap. Many it has forgotten forever. And yet they belonged to the assembly of the first-born who are enrolled in heaven. They fed the hungry, clothed the naked, and cooled the feverish brow with the touch of love. They resisted injustice and poured oil in the wounds of its victims. They sought for truth when men had to pass through torture chambers to find her. They resisted prejudice, flung their reputation aside to grapple with bigotry, and stepped down the marble stairs of privilege to make the cause of God's poor their own. What a history that would be, the history of all the truly Christian lives on earth! What a diversity there would be: the daring and the tender, the nurse-maid of babes and the ruler of states, all the shades of speculative opinion, men in the church and men out of the church; there would be first who would be last and last who would be first. But this would characterize them all: they were revolutionists whether they knew it or not; they tried in some way to overturn the throne of Satan and endeavored to make this world a habitation for God. A Christ-like life without putting forth Christ-like words and deeds is a delusion. And a putting forth of Christ-like words and deeds without checking evil and extending God's reign is inconceivable. Every such life furnished a fulcrum for God's lever, a conservative influence to preserve whatever purity and justice had already been gained, a source from which rivers of living water moistened the earth round about and prepared a place for whatever seeds of truth a future hand might drop.

But the scattering of isolated revolutionary personalities through society by no means exhausts Christ's conception concerning the human agencies in his revolutionary work. Christ established the church, and this formation of a revolutionary community is essential to his work.

Jesus not only bound men to himself, he bound them to one another. He founded a community, created a corporate feeling which differentiated them from the mass of men, gave them laws of their own, and established the rudiments of an internal organization. He prayed for their unity. He expected them to continue in this society after his own departure.

They did continue so. The interlacing fibres held true through the shocks of disappointment and persecution. After his death they naturally came together. After the resurrection they sought to perfect again their mutilated organization, showing thereby the sense of their unity and the consciousness of a united mission. (Acts 1, 15-26.) This organizing impulse continued. They instituted new offices when needed (Acts 6, 1-6), and they settled pressing questions in common. (Acts 11, 1-18; 15, 1-29.)

The expressions used by the apostles show that they regarded the church as the new theocratic society and as a coherent organism. Peter calls it the elect race, the holy nation, God's own people, a holy and royal priesthood, a flock, a brotherhood, a spiritual house built up of living stones. Paul speaks of it as of a temple of the Spirit, a habitation of God. With him the conception of the church as a body, an organism with various functions and differentiated organs and yet with a unity of life, is fundamental for all his thinking and decisive in the smallest practical questions.

Christianity therefore is not a new philosophy which a man may entertain in isolation. Christ's purpose was the establishment and extension of the Kingdom of God, the regeneration of human society. To this end he established an organization which was to be at the same time a realization of the Kingdom within its own limits and the instrument for its propagation. Within this society Christ reigns, here his laws prevail, and his Spirit is the governing force. And from this society in turn his assimilating and conquering forces go out to extend the territory of his dominion. If Christ's purpose had been merely the conversion of individuals, the formation of the church would have been useful but not essential. Because his purpose was the immediate establishment and extension of a Kingdom, a society was absolutely essential.

What are the functions of this society?

1. *The first function of every organism is to maintain and strengthen its own peculiar life.*

The first duty of the church, then, is to maintain in its entirety, in its various local branches, and in its individual members that life and spirit through which and for which it exists. It is constantly absorbing new individuals who have the principle of the new life in them, but whose thoughts and habits have not yet been penetrated by it. The church has to nurture and train them and to call forth the ripe fullness of the Christian virtues. It performs for the new-born spirit the same office which the family performs for the infant. It furnishes the warmth and shelter within which the young life can grow. Jesus spoke of his disciples as being like mother, brothers, and sisters to him. (Matt. 12, 46-50.) He promises those who have forsaken their property or been cast off by their family that they shall find compensation for it even in this life. Where there is a true Christian community this promise is realized in it, while on the other hand many a young faith has been snapped by the first storm of ridicule and opposition because it stood like a solitary sapling.

The church is to protect the growing faith until it is emancipated. There is strength in numbers. Few men can bear to stand entirely alone; certainly the young should not prematurely be exposed to so heavy a trial. When all the world counsels selfish prudence and worldly wisdom, a man may know in his soul that Christ is right against the world, and yet, in the hours of weariness and fear, it is a wonderful help to have others beside him who are one with him. Christ himself felt the need of the church in Gethsemane.

While he had been with the disciples, he had protected and encouraged them. Is it not as a substitute for his personal presence that at the same moment with the announcement of his departure he lays upon them the new commandment of brotherly love? (John 13, 33-34.) The visible brotherhood stands in the place of the visible Christ. We can watch this educational attitude of the church in Paul's letters. There were many in the churches who had not yet emancipated themselves from the old reverence for special forms, the observance of sacred days, and the habit of regarding some food as ceremonially impure. When these people tried to foist their baby jackets on the lusty limbs of the young church, Paul resisted them almost fiercely. But when it was a habit of mind which they were not yet able to strip off, he showed the utmost consideration for them and advised those who had attained a broader view voluntarily to descend to the lower position, as an elder brother shortens his steps that the younger may keep pace with him. (Rom. 14.)

But while the church protects the weak and gains for them free play to develop, it is not an institution to keep the weak brethren weak. It nurtures, but it also stimulates.

It makes it possible for the individual to obtain an insight into a truth which he would never reach unaided. We all draw our ideas from a great public treasury. In secular life we are "heirs of all the ages." In our language, our literature, our inventions, our current conceptions of life we have a capital to which we are heirs at birth and with which we are free to operate. Thus every new individual receives as a gift "a pair of seven-mile boots; he travels in twenty years a distance that humanity has traversed in twenty thousand." (Schäffle, *The Formation and Life of the Social Organism,* I, 397.) The same is true in religion. Peter alone rose high enough to declare Jesus to be the Messiah, but the declaration, once made, became the property of all. The church contains a certain quantity of truth in solution, with which he that moves in it becomes saturated almost without knowing it. The quantity varies in different Christian circles. But even where there is poverty of thought, it is safe to say that the church furnishes to the individual more than he could acquire by himself. The church does for the spiritual life of a young member what a cultured family circle does for the intellectual and aesthetic life of its young members. Therefore Jesus could say that the feeblest member of the new society stood higher than the greatest prophet of the old.

Again, the church creates for its members a higher ethical standard than they would attain if unaided. The church cherishes a high moral ideal, not as high as it should be, not always higher than that of individuals outside the church, but probably always higher than the ideal generally prevailing in the world about it. And it not only passes laws, but it has sanctions to enforce obedience to them. Every society cultivates certain virtues and succeeds in infusing these into its members. It is the power of society which makes these moral precepts operative. Bravery is the prime virtue cultivated by army life, and cowards are scarce among army officers; on the other hand chastity and temperance are not considered as peculiarly soldierly virtues and are not nearly so frequent. The Indians prize stolid endurance of pain, and their young braves attain it. The Jesuit Order and the Salvation Army require obedience, and obedience flourishes among them. In short, the demands made upon us by the society in which we move and whose good opinion we prize are for most of us the strongest incentives to right conduct.

Now here is a society which in most cases comprises for its members the best persons of their sphere of life. This society makes certain demands on the moral lives of its members. Those who respond to the demand are rewarded by the approval and respect of men and women whom they themselves approve and respect. Those who disobey feel themselves under a cloud of suspicion and disapproval and, what is hardest of all to bear, of sorrowing love. The effect of this cannot be overestimated. It rises with the intimacy existing in the brotherhood and with the holiness and discerning justice of its members. One of the communistic communities of America once had the custom of calling a periodical meeting in which the members were reproved by one another for faults shown. The practice was discontinued after a time, not because it failed of effect but because it was too painfully effective. Christ's rule of church discipline is based on this same principle. A reproof of three persons is more powerful than by one, and a reproof by the community is more powerful still and indeed the last recourse. (Matt. 18, 15-20.) In his promise to be present where two or three are gathered in his name, Christ likewise implies that he is present in a community in a manner different from his presence with an individual. He simply emphasizes that this peculiar state begins even with the smallest community, with but two or three. (Matt. 18, 20.) In the same way he invests the community with the power to forgive or retain sins, and a community does possess that power in the measure in which it has the Holy Spirit. (John 20, 22-23.) A striking instance of the moral force of a judgment passed by such a community is preserved in the case of Ananias and Sapphira.

The possibilities of moral impulsion inhering in the community have perhaps never yet been tried to the utmost. It is a power that must be reckoned with in the forecasts for the future development of humanity. Men doubt if it will be possible to relax the restraints of force and the driving power of hunger. Probably not, unless some other force is substituted. But such a force does exist in the social appetite, the hunger for approval, the natural faculty for imitation and emulation. In a bad society that appetite works toward the bad; both a young tough and a young "society" man are impelled to evil by the desire to stand well with their set. But in a healthily constructed society that appetite may do wonders. Here also it is true: "To him that hath is given, and from him that hath not is taken even that which he hath."

A true religious community, therefore, small enough for all to know everybody, homogeneous enough for the members to be intelligible to one another, and holy enough to represent God, exercises an immense influence upon the moral life of its members. It not only imparts an ideal to them; it lays that ideal with effective force upon their consciences. It makes virtue and self-sacrifice contagious. The zeal for martyrdom in the early church was due to the spirit of the community more than to the courage of the individuals. The church can create any virtue in its members that it undertakes to create. In America, it has in a high degree made the demand for chastity and temperance effective. On the other hand, the business morality of its members is extremely open to reproach, because the church has been sadly backward in setting up a true ideal of business honesty and in outlawing those who transgress it.

Thus the church maintains and strengthens its individual life in the members of its body. It brings them into direct contact with a large quantity of truth and wisdom, which they absorb and then carry out into the world. It replenishes in them that warmth of faith in the invisible realities, which the chilling contact of the world steadily withdraws. It lays upon their conscience a code of morals higher than that of the average humanity about them, and enforces its performance. It thus makes possible that revolutionary influence which consecrated men exercise upon the world about them, and by keeping alive the revolutionary spirit in them it in turn ensures the assimilation of the newly entering members and thus its own enduring vitality. The church in maintaining its own life is the nursery of Christian revolutionists.

We are as conscious as anyone how far the church has practically fallen short of this ideal. Its shortcomings are great in the standard of truth and righteousness which it has in various ages laid upon its members. They are great even in the bulk of true Christian communities. In some European countries there is no such thing as a body of people who gather in the consciousness that they are one in life, in order to build up that life in themselves. Frequently the church bitterly resists the formation of such circles. Yet the organizing instinct of Christianity, like the ideal aspirations of humanity, has never been absolutely repressed by human tyranny. The danger to the churches in America lies perhaps in two directions: first, that the ethical standard of the church is kept so little above the standard of the world, that "joining the church" implies no cross to be taken up, no profit to be abandoned but rather a social function to be performed, so that worldly people flood the church under churchly forms, and the church loses its integrity and vitality; second, that the churches, especially in the cities are swelled to an abnormal size, mainly for pecuniary and aesthetic reasons. Their members are unknown to one another. They can go and come, do right or wrong, and no one knows. They are like young people afloat in a big city with no eye upon them. A church suffering with hypertrophy of that sort may present a glowing appearance, but it is a sick organism, unable to perform the functions of a true Christian community.

2. *The next function that the church, like every other organism, has to perform is that of growth.*

It seems as if it were a divinely implanted impulse in every man to make propaganda for the moral and religious truths that have taken hold of himself. The same Providence that has provided some seeds with wings and others with hooks to carry them abroad has taken care for the propagation of the truth.

In addition, the duty of making disciples is enjoined upon us by Christ himself. He sent the twelve into the wide harvest field of Galilee. (Matt. 9, 36–10, 1.) He sent them out at the end to make disciples of all nations. (Matt. 28, 19.) We see this discipling impulse at work in Peter's and Stephen's preaching, in Philip's conversation with the chance passer-by, in the church at Antioch's dismissal of its men, in Paul's laborious missionary journeys, and in the entire history of the centuries. Every man who holds, or thinks he holds, any truth which others do not possess feels that duty upon him. Every really living religious organization tries to multiply its members.

The danger in all this is that it will be proselytizing and not true discipling. Jesus says of the Pharisees that they were compassing sea and land to make one proselyte only to make him twofold more a son of hell than they themselves were. (Matt. 23, 15.) There is a difference between imparting to a man what one is conscious of possessing and what would be a blessing to him, and trying to draw him in to feed one's pride in the organization and to sustain one's own confidence by the increase in members. Proselytizing is a grave danger in our churches and denominations, and those who are always appealing to the love of the people for their church or their denomination are directly inciting to it. Yet as a general thing it is probably true that missionary zeal is an indication of life, and its absence an indication of decay. Heretical parties that make a vigorous propaganda usually treasure some vital truth amid all fantastic trappings, and thoughtful men would do well to stay their denunciation and lovingly inquire what truth of God is striving to get itself born there.

The church will always be fairly safe in its endeavors to increase its membership if it keeps its moral demands well above those prevailing in the world about it. If union with the church means a renouncing of reputation and profit, a selfish man will stay out, and the Christian who has become ambitious or avaricious will go out or be put out. If baptism, which Christ has placed at the door of the church, really means a putting off of many pleasant and luscious things and a joining possibly to the sufferings and the dying of Jesus (Rom. 6), then only he will ask for that initiation who has staked his all on Jesus Christ, as Israel staked their all on Moses at the Red Sea. (I Cor. 10, 2.) Christ showed no anxiety of not having enough followers but a great deal of not having the right sort. He warned men not to be like a man who begins to build a tower and has to stop when it is half-way up; or like a king that begins a war with an insufficient army. Let them count the cost before they join themselves to him. Let them remember that it may mean separation from family, loss of property, loss of life. (Lk. 14, 25-35.) Would they follow the Son of man? Then they must take the risk of being more homeless than the foxes and the birds of the air. (Matt. 8, 18-22.) Would they have eternal life? Let them sell all they have and give it away; a soldier in the skirmishline of battle cannot carry a Saratoga trunk on his back. (Lk. 18, 18-30.)

The church is a picked company of soldiers whose efficiency depends more on their quality than on their number. The Broad Church thinkers are entirely right in insisting that the church is to benefit not only a small circle of the elect but all men and the entire life of humanity. But they are wrong in thinking that this can best be accomplished by admitting everybody into the church by baptism at birth. Christ was wiser. The same error underlies the zeal of many evangelicals in multiplying their members. Because they have made of Christianity merely a system for saving individuals, they naturally try to multiply those individuals. But in point of fact they are in danger of repeating the error that has been committed ever since Constantine, of making the church co-extensive with the nation. It becomes almost a matter of course for the children of Christian parents to join the church when they reach a certain age. The churches are scooping in the world and they are in danger of being swamped. Like Gideon's army they are too many to rout the Midianites.

Christ commanded an unremitting propaganda. He himself has given the example of an unwearying proclamation of the truth. But he was very wary about receiving men into his community. He discouraged them rather than the reverse. And the loftiness of the duties that he imposed on them was a self-acting check. He was constantly applying the winnowing fan. Here as everywhere the Master is wiser than his prudent followers.

3. *No organism, however, is destined by God to live unto itself.* It has an office in God's world corresponding to its individuality and en-

dowment. Least of all was the church formed merely for its own sake.

The Christian church is not like the community on a Cunard steamer, shut off from the world and viewing a passing craft through opera glasses. Jesus did not join the Essene community that tried in solitude to live a pure and loving life. He founded a society which was to lead in the thick of the world a life higher than that of the world. Such a society must influence the general life about it, even if it should make no effort in that direction. It could not assert a system of ethics different from and superior to that of other men without influencing the standard of right everywhere. It could not cherish a supreme spiritual idealism without stimulating the ideal aspirations which God has implanted in every human being. The pillar of fire could not dwell in Israel and be invisible to others. The knowledge of God's love and righteousness could not burn within the church and yet no ray of it lighten the darkness without.

The church is distinctly forbidden to hide its light under a bushel. It was purposely mixed into the world, as a woman carefully kneads the leaven into the dough. Activity is made the duty of the church, it is a steward managing the master's property according to the master's purposes, a servant doing business with trust funds. Jesus expected the multitude of its fruits to work toward the knowledge and exaltation of God among men. (Matt. 4, 16; John 15, 8.) Paul trusted in the church, in spite of the weakness and lowliness of its members, to overcome the pride of Greek philosophy and Roman power. (I Cor. 1, 26-29.) He expected the manifold wisdom of God to be made known even to principalities and powers through the church. (Eph. 3, 10.) These expressions cannot be pressed to mean merely an extension of membership. They refer to the struggle of the church as a spiritual power with the spiritual forces ruling in the world as a whole, and its victory for them. As Neander says: "The aim toward which history is moving is that Christianity become the world-governing principle." (*Das Leben Jesu Christi,* pp. 136-37.) There are only three possibilities. It can flee out of the world; it can become like the world; it can make the world like itself. The first is asceticism, disobedience, and cowardice; the second is suicide; the third is ceaseless conflict till final victory. Which tallies with Christ's purpose? All his frequent sayings about taking up the cross, forsaking property and family, incurring suffering and death have no sense unless the church is to impinge upon the world and suffer from its angry reaction.

And such has in fact been the history of the church, and most so when it had most life. The Jews did not fully realize the conflict between the free spirit of Christ and ceremonialism till they saw it demonstrated in the life of the church, in the violation of Sabbath laws, and in the neglect of ceremonial washings by the disciples. (Matt. 15, 1-20; Mk. 2, 23-28.) The influence of Paul's continued preaching threatened trades that catered to superstition. (Acts 19.) Christianity is a force even in those who neither believe in it nor love it. James Russell Lowell has said with entire justice that the high morality maintained by those who have thrown off the dogmas of the church is yet due to the inherited purity and the moral atmosphere which generations of Christianity have created for them. It is the fashion at present to abuse the church for its conservative and reactionary influence on political and social progress. If by "the church" is meant the various ecclesiastical machines with titled and salaried hierarchies, then the church deserves much of the abuse that it gets. If, however, Christianity in fairness is taken as a spirit and life which has hovered like a tongue of fire over consecrated men and swayed the nations like a wind from heaven, then it must in fairness be conceded that the influence of Christianity on the race has been incalculable. Schäffle, speaking of it in his *Social Organism*, says: "The religious life has been a force of the first magnitude in the history of the world. It is as perceptible today as ever before, that history turns on the axis of religion." A. Lange, who will not be charged with undue favor to Christianity, says in his *Geschichte des Materialismus* (1st ed., p. 535): "In surveying history in its grand total, it seems to me hardly doubtful that we may ascribe not only our ethical, but even our intellectual progress in large part to the moral but continuous influence of the Christian ideas." He adds, not without truth as we shall see: "But . . . these ideas can develop their full effect only by breaking the ecclesiastical and dogmatic forms."

d. The Church and the World

How is the church to influence the world and overcome it? We grant that the church can withdraw individuals from the world. Can it do more? If so, how? What relation to secular society does the church demand for itself?

We can conceive of four diverging opinions.

First, that *church and state are co-extensive and synonymous.* This is the ideal aimed at in the union of church and state. Every child becomes by birth a member of the state, and almost at the same time a member of the church by baptism. The prince is head of the state and also summus episcopus and head of the church. But the practical difficulties of this conception are too great even for those who ought logically to be its supporters. It is too clamorous a fact that church and world are not circles with an equal radius and that they will not coincide. So the realization of this view is postponed to another world and in practice the second view is adopted.

The second view is that the organs of the church and the organs of the state are distinct, but that *the church is higher than the state and dominates it.* This is the Roman Catholic idea of the two arms, which caused the medieval struggles between the popes and the emperors. The Roman Catholic Church holds that all power is entrusted to it as to the vice-regent of Christ; princes hold their power by gift of the church. The church is independent of the state, but the state is dependent on the church. The church passes its own canonical laws, to which alone its ministers are subject. But the secular laws are subject to its revision, and the legal tribunals of the state are also the executors of the behests of the church. For instance, the church examines all literary publications, and the state destroys the books condemned by the Congregation of the Index. The church tries heretics and hands them over to the secular arm for execution of its sentence. That is the Catholic ideal of the theocracy.

The Catholic Church is right in asserting that the moral and spiritual life is superior to secular life and ought to govern it. It is wrong in binding up the moral and spiritual forces with a single organization and confounding the supremacy of the latter with the rule of the former. It makes the Kingdom of God synonymous with the Kingdom of the church. They are not necessarily synonymous. They have often been directly contradictory. Just as the Old Testament church withstood Christ, so not only the Catholic Church, but all the old and established churches have withstood him. Power has made them conservative. They have lost the revolutionary impulse. They have substituted the craftiness of politicians for the righteous zeal of prophets. The management of their affairs gradually entrusted not to the most Christlike of their members, but to the ambitious, wealthy, worldlywise and scheming among them. There are those who hold the age of a church and the unbroken continuity of its organization to be the first proof that it is really the church of Christ. The very reverse seems to us to be true. The older and more firmly established a church is, the less likely is it to be spiritual and progressive. Therefore to construct an ecclesiastical organization and entrust to that the supreme guidance of the entire machinery of secular society is not only paralyzing to secular government but destructive to the reign of God in that nation. The best service that can be rendered to the church is to keep it out of power.

This theocratic ideal, therefore, which confounds the reign of God with the supremacy of an ecclesiastical machine, is false and, indeed, contradictory to the teachings of Jesus. Church and state will each do its work best if the machinery of one is entirely unconnected with the machinery of the other. This has made the idea of religious interference in politics so odious that ecclesiastics interfere not for the sake of infusing righteousness but of getting power for their church. It is the sure mark of the ecclesiastic as against the Christian that he cannot distinguish between the progress and power of Christianity and the progress and power of his church.

Our reply to this second view, therefore, is that not only the supremacy of the church organization over the secular organization, but any mixture or inter-relation of the two is detrimental to the very work which the church is to do for secular life. It unchristianizes the church, and when the salt loses its savour, wherewith shall society be salted?

The third view of the relation of the church to secular society is that *the church should be indifferent to affairs of state.* Its business is to save souls. It is possible to live a Christian life in any form of society, therefore the forms are indifferent. This world is to pass away; it would be a waste of time to do anything for it. We must simply keep our lamps trimmed for the coming of the Master. If the world gets any indirect benefits from the life of the church, very well; but we need not aim to impart these benefits. A man may vote and do his duty as a citizen, but he does so as a citizen and not as a Christian. Christian morals are for regenerate men; it is an illusion to think of inducing the state to adopt them.

This position, so frequent in America, is the historical outcome of the protest against Catholicism. The Catholic church made the salvation of the individual dependent on the church and its means of grace; it exalted the church and depreciated the individual. Calvinism repudiated the church, exalted the individual by placing him solitary over against his God, and bent its energies to the salvation of individuals by personal experiences. In justly emphasizing this side of the truth, it lost sight of the importance of society and of the bearing of Christianity on the social organism. In addition to this, the type of Christianity prevailing with us is derived from the dissenters of England, who for generations had to battle for the right of simply being let alone by the state in doing their work of soul saving. They saw in the Established Church an evil union of church and state, and their thoughts on the relation of church and state were mostly limited to a protest against the Establishment. But both the religious value and independence of the individual, and the divorce of church and state are now with us recognized facts; it is time for us to examine candidly whether we have not burnt down the house to kill the rats when we abandoned the theocratic idea to protest against a false conception of it.

In the preceding chapter we have shown at length that the very idea of the Old Testament is the interest of God in the life of human society, and that this interest was not abandoned but adopted by Christ. Here is secular society, created by God, affecting us all, a power for good or evil, capable of being influenced by moral ideas. Is that to be indifferent to us? It is not. It is not indifferent to the most ardent believer in the speedy coming of Christ. He looks well to the plumbing of his house, to the social purity of the nurse that cares for his children, to the decency of their playmates, to the moral tone of the college to which he sends his boy, to the safety of the neighborhood in which he builds his house. Is not all that part of secular society? Is he selfish enough to look to the safety of his own family in these regards and not to the safety of the thousands of families more helpless than his, whose health and safety and happiness depend in vast degree on the good or evil actions of their town, their state, their nation? Common sense teaches us all to value highly the character of the society we ourselves live in. Christian sense ought to make us take the same interest in the character of the society in which others live. Shall it be indifferent to us whether the community of which we are part and on which we have influence legalizes oppression, encourages vice, and commits a perennial murder of the innocents? To have the power to stop evil and not to do it—what is that?

We are reminded of the non-interference of Jesus in affairs of government, and of the apostles' indifference to politics and to social questions. Three cases are especially pointed out in which Jesus refused to interfere: the case of Caesar's tribute money (Matt. 22, 15-22), of the Jewish tax (Matt. 17, 24-27), and of the division of an inheritance (Lk. 12, 13-21). It is argued from these cases that Jesus drew a sharp line through human life, dividing it into secular and religious affairs, and that he renounced all jurisdiction or interest in the former. This interpretation has been originated by people who did not believe in Christ's ethics and supposed that Jesus did not either. Suppose that a Roman or Jewish tax-collector would have come to Jesus and demanded the tax; suppose it had been an onerous and excessive tax; suppose that the collector had, after the manner of Oriental officials, added his own bakshish to the legal amount. What would Jesus have done? "If any man would go to law with thee and take away thy coat, let him have thy cloak also." (Matt. 5, 40.) He would quietly have payed the amount demanded, and then perhaps just as quietly told the man that he was endangering his soul through covetousness. He would reserve his right of judging whether the demand was just or not and of saying so, but he would not violently resist evil. That he preserved his inward freedom of judgment is evident from his conversation with Peter on the payment of the half-shekel. (Matt. 17, 24-27.) He felt that he was a child in his Father's house and free to go and come; yet he paid what people demanded "lest he cause them to stumble." In the third case (Lk. 12, 13-21), he refused to interfere for two reasons. First, it was not his business to be a judge or divider. The laying down of large principles and the investigation of specific instances are distinct functions. A pastor in a New England village might be very much interested in the labor question and yet wisely refuse to decide whether a firm could and should grant a particular rise in wages demanded by their men. His second reason for refusing is also apparent from the context. "Take heed, and keep yourselves from all covetousness." The whole request, to his mind, proceeded from covetousness, the vice that animated the rich fool of whom he goes on to speak, and that caused all this fretting and worrying over the future which frustrates the enjoyment of life and destroys man's trust in God. He took no interest in helping this man to squabble with his brother and to get a lot of money which would ruin his soul in the end. Jesus' attitude toward wealth in general makes his attitude in this case entirely natural and logical. But was he indifferent to social inequality? Read the parable of Dives and Lazarus. Was it nothing to him when widows were wronged out of their houses and oppressed by unjust judges? Read the parable of the unjust judge and the rebuke to the Pharisees. Verily it is the old blindness of the scribes over again, when men assert that *he* was indifferent to justice and mercy in daily life, who made such indifference the sufficient ground for condemnation on the day of judgment. (Matt. 25, 31-46.) The parable of the Good Samaritan is being re-enacted on a grand scale in our day. Entire classes of society are being stripped and beaten by robbers. Is it again the priest and Levite who pass by, busy in matters of religion, and the alien heretic who lend a hand? Or, if they come upon the robbers in the very act of their guilt, shall they assure the robbers of their divine right to rob and wait on one side till the victim is half dead and then begin their charitable care for him?

We are told that the apostles attempted no interference in politics and no leveling of social classes. It is true. Paul told Philemon to treat his run-away slave Onesimus kindly; he did not tell him that slavery was wrong. What a stock-in-trade that was for the advocates of slavery forty years ago! But, Paul notwithstanding, we have abolished slavery and hold it to be wrong. The same thing is going to be done with the social questions now before us, and those who hide behind Paul's non-interference are again going to bring shame upon Christianity. Their guilt lies in making of Christianity a set of rules instead of a living spirit. The question is not what Paul did then, but what he would do now. In his day he was a radical who made havoc of old laws and notions and cleared the deck for a new society. Thanks to his gallant fight, modern society has in some points passed leagues beyond the society in which he moved, and now his radicalism becomes our conservatism. He that adheres most strictly to Paul's rules of conduct will most fatally deny Paul's principles and spirit. His decisions on what was lawful and prudent to do are buoys which he anchored at the farthest points to which in his day the channel of the future had been explored. We shall use them best by keeping to the direction he marked out and passing beyond them, and not by padlocking our boat to his buoys. The early Christians did not try to ameliorate poverty by legislation, did they? How could they? Did Nero ask them for advice about his laws? Did Roman procurators invite them to vote on a constitutional amendment forbidding the persecution of Christians? They were glad if they could keep clear of politics and continue their hand-to-hand work in peace. It is different with us. We are now the citizen kings of our country, and it is as criminal for us to leave unjust laws on our statute books, as it would have been for a converted king in the first century any longer to oppress his subjects.

The idea that the followers of Christ can be indifferent to the conditions of society about them finds some show of defense in the letter of the Scriptures, but it is condemned by the spirit of Christ. Such indifference is sin. Its quiet diffusion increases with the spread of democracy which thrusts power upon us, and with power responsibility. It denies Christ's conception of religion, who taught us that there is no way of treating God right except by treating our fellow-men right, and that the only plane upon which Christianity can be exercised is the plane of social life.

We must find a fourth conception of the relation of the church to secular life which will avoid the evil of the others. Indifference is wrong. A union of organizations is dangerous. We want a separation of the organizations and an interpenetration of influences. The church must be independent of the state, neither oppressed by its commands nor bribed by its support. And it must as a body abstain from all attempts to control the machinery of government or to fill its offices. On the other hand, it is free to influence the ethical conceptions of the people and to stimulate the people to righteous actions. And under our form of government the convictions of the people are the final source of legislation. All influence exerted upon the mind of the people will finally issue in concrete form.

The church has the prophetic office in humanity. Because it is in contact with God, its conscience quickened, its ethical discernment clarified, its moral courage and energy strengthened, it is to be the teacher of society. It is to discern injustice where it is hidden to others by force of habit. It is to hear the sob of pain in the outcast classes whom others pass unheeded. It is to detect the sallow face of tyranny hiding behind the mask of patriotism and benevolence. Who is fit to do this if the church is not? Society rolls heavily on its way. What has always been so, seems divinely right to the mass, even if it is diabolically wrong. They must be made to see. Men feel their own pains acutely, but they are dull to the sorrows of others which they have never known. Men with the divining-rod of sympathy must pass through the nation and stop and say: "There is a deep well of tears here, hidden underground." Men must be made to feel. Men are slothful to self-sacrificing action. They see a wrong, they call it wrong, but they do not stop it. They must be made to act. They need leaders who will show the way and, if need be, break the way with spears on their chests.

There was a time when the life of a nation depended on the goodness of a monarch and his subordinates. Then it was proper for influential men to exert moral influence on the king and expect great things from his personal justice and benevolence. But with the rise of democracy the people have become the sovereign. The personal character of our chief magistrate means far less to us than the personal character of an absolute king means to his subjects. The moral education of the people is the formation of the future. That task is the rightful province of the church. The permanence of free institutions and the health of a nation depend on the general diffusion of intelligence and morality. The church can diffuse them. If in the swirling eddies of modern life a heap of ignorance and filth is swept together, and the cumbersome machinery of government is slow to reach it, the church is mobile and can invade it with light and cleanness. It can kindle the flame of patriotism and devotion to the public good in the hearts of the young.

Nations are moved by currents of thought and feeling that sweep through them. Sometimes these thoughts are just and noble and yet find but slight response. Often they are base, originated by demagogs and inciting evil passions, and they find a ready response. The nation is like the resonant body of a musical instrument, one side vibrates and the whole resounds. It is of utmost importance that just emotions should be passed on and bad emotions stopped. We can conceive of an enlightened, spiritual church, spread through all the nation, deaf to party cries, alive to the voice of right. A cry of angry passion is raised by a designing party leader, paid newspapers take it up, party followers declaim, newspapers in search of sensations respond, the people are roused and think there must be something in so much noise, their pride is stroked with nettles and there will be an outbreak. But now these emotions find everywhere points of resistance. The most respected people everywhere treat the matter calmly and with sense. They act as bits of non-conducting medium on an electric current, like the soft pedal of a piano on a sound. They frustrate an attempt on the welfare of the nation and discourage similar attempts for the future. But suppose that a just and true thought is uttered, which ought to receive public attention. It conflicts with established interests, no large party advocates it, some newspapers are studiously silent while others distort the matter, the people are not awake to the importance of it. Now again that wide-branching nervous apparatus of righteousness responds. It sends thrill upon thrill through the body politic. The people wake up. Newspapers find it profitable to discuss the cause. Finally selfishness itself takes it up. The social organism, like the human body, has its nervous apparatus. The nerves which look to the gratification of the lower and selfish instincts are always alive. They work almost by reflex action. But it is of the highest value to have a nervous system which finds its centre in the conscience and will respond to the nobler sensations. This function can be exercised by the church.

But if it is to exercise this function, the church must be enlightened enough not to be hood-winked by ecclesiasticism of any sort. Above all it must have a standard of public ethics superior to that prevailing in politics. It must be clear on the application of Christian principles to public affairs.

That clearness is lacking as yet. Men of refined moral sensibility in private life have a crude and rudimentary conscience for public life. This is an evil effect of the past. When the people had no power in the state, there was no instructing them how to use such power. Now the need has arisen. The people have public duties, and they should have public ethics. Steam and electricity are drawing society together and compacting it. The functions of the state are bound to increase. The welfare of the individual is becoming increasingly dependent on social action and construction. Who is to teach the people what public righteousness is? Shall they be left to the newspapers or to the tender mercies of the vote-hunting stump orator? A new need has arisen for Christian teachings, and the church is very slow to respond. On the whole Christian thinkers are discouraged from giving attention to social and political questions. There is a feeling that they are passing beyond their calling. Evangelistic and edifying preaching and writing are the only sort that finds real approval. But the very fact that the staid denominational papers and the wealthy men in the church discourage the handling of social questions is presumptive evidence that they ought to be handled and that this is the sore spot of our church life. Christianity has fairly penetrated the simpler relations of individual and family life with its ethical ideas. But the more complex relations of industrial and political affairs have not yet been so penetrated, and the church is so far from making a Christian public morality effective that it is not even approximately clear in its own mind what a Christian public morality would be. Schäffle says in his great work on *The Formation and Life of the Social Organism:*

> A true public morality has not yet come into effect. If not only a private morality for private citizens, but a public morality for public relations really prevailed today in the family of Christian nations, then entire classes of the people could not be abandoned to wretchedness and legally disinherited by the jobbing of the exchange, and whole nations could not be given over to military despotism. The chief source of social misery at present is not that our private ethics is not applicable to public affairs, but that a public morality for the more complex public affairs does not exist; morality has lagged behind the glorious progress of intellectual culture. (I, 417.)

If morality lags, it is because the morality-making organism lags, and that organism is the church. Christian people will do well to give all cheer to those who have bravely put their hand to this tremendous task and to ward off as enemies of the Kingdom of God those who would drug the body of Christ into stupor.

This we hold to be the duty of the church toward the collective life of humanity: by its keener sensibility it is to notice wrong and suffering where others do not see it and call attention thereto, by the guidance of the Spirit it is to have a clearer perception of ideal justice than others and impart this to society at large; by its superior moral daring it is to sustain the unpopular causes until they have become popular. It is to resist the materialistic and pessimistic tendencies of literature and philosophy by its pure spiritualism, and stimulate the idealism and the devotion to duty latent in men. Lotze says: "Only the single living spirits are the centers of force in the course of history; all general ideas which are to be realized and to become a power, must first be condensed in their living individualities, and then by action and reaction among them spread out and obtain general recognition." It is exactly this prophetic office which the church is to fulfill. It multiplies the number of such centers of power and stimulates them by association. Therefore its effect is not to be measured by the number of its converts only. It is well known that, judged by the converts, Christian missions are not gaining on heathenism, but the reverse. But the Christian ideas of God, Christian ethics, the duty of mercy and self-devotion, are spreading faster than the converts. Christ commanded to make disciples—not of all men but all nations—and it looks as if Japan, India, and China were to be brought under the actual sway of Christ faster in the bulk than in minute particles.

4. *Finally, it is a function of the church to lead society in action.* We have discussed the prophetic office of the church in leading the moral *thought* of humanity. But it is not to stop with thought. Philosophy is content to teach and to disseminate ideas, and for that reason philosophy is always the property of the few. As long as an idea remains abstract it will leave the mass of men indifferent; they see nothing in it. "Action is the word of the people," says Mazzini. "It would be false," says Schäffle, "to expect the progress of ethics merely from the extension of the circle of *ideas*. Great aims of *action*, of practical association, are the means of causing popular feeling to give birth to higher ethical norms."

Plato dreamed of an ideal republic, Christ instituted it. The Christian church immediately realized just those social principles with which humanity has been in travail for the last one hundred fifty years. If the church has back-slidden often it has repented often, and the ideal and impulse have never been totally lost.

The splendid parole of the French Revolution: "Liberty, equality, fraternity," contains the social principles of the church.

There is liberty in it. It knows no compulsion save that of love, and no command apart from the categorical imperative of duty.

There is equality in it. Again and again the apostles tried to carry the fashion of the rest of the world into their little society, and to have ranks and grades of honor. Jesus always rebuked them for it. "Ye know that the rulers of the nations lord it over them, and their great ones exercise authority over them. Not so shall it be among you; but whosoever would become great among you shall be your minister, and whosoever would be first among you shall be your servant; even as the Son of man came not to be ministered unto but to minister, and to give his life a ransom for many." The only title to greatness in the new society is service. The only way to honor is in stripping one's self of it. Is there any higher ideal than that? And yet the equality desired by Jesus is not the dead-level equality of the doctrinaire. He recognizes the difference of endowment and the aristocracy of character. He founds the apostleship. He singles out Peter as the solid man whom he can trust for yeoman's service. Not all are qualified for leadership. Setting the born leaders at work is no violation of equality but communism in the highest form of property—human ability.

There is fraternity in it. And on that score even its gainsayers must acknowledge the pre-eminence of the church. Fraternity was the weak point in the triad of the French Revolution. Men had far more to say about liberty and equality than about fraternity. But see the young church. They were "one heart and soul"; "they had all things in common"; there was "not among them any that lacked." No suffering or inequality was tolerated. (Acts 6, 1-6.) We see them gathered at night to pray for one of their number who was in prison. (Acts 12, 12.) We see them falling upon the neck of a parting brother, kissing him and weeping sorely. (Acts 20, 37.) What a spirit of tenderness, of mutual forbearance, of anxiety for one another's welfare breathes from their letters, their greetings, the little incidental remarks! That is the social spirit. Right is the chisel that smooths the stones; love is the mortar that holds them together. The society of the future is to be an edifice of wider arches and bolder curves than the present. But that will throw a greater pressure on every stone. Will they stand the strain? Will they hold together? It may be that the builders of the future will yet come to the church to learn what cements it so well. Churches quarrel, it is true; so do denominations. But observation seems to show that they are far more peaceful and compact than lodges, trade unions, and political associations.

Christ included those superb words in his idea of society. But he did not, like the revolutionary parties of today, wait with their realization for a distant future. He began straightway. He lived in a society that always extorted obedience by force. He asked for obedience, but only the obedience of freedom. He lived in a society organized throughout on the aristocratic plan and without even the idea of equality before the law. He abrogated rank and made the towel with which a slave washes the feet of the master a badge of distinction and the symbol of citizenship in his Kingdom. He lived in a society cleft and rent like volcanic ground after centuries of earthquakes; fissures made by nationality, by creed, by rank, by pride of learning. He laid the hand of the Jew in the hand of the Samaritan and said: You are brothers, love each other. He said to the man of wealth and rank: Leave your wealth, step down from your privileges that you may be a brother to us. Jesus anticipated the evolution of centuries, and by anticipating it brought it about. Sociology today has no image to represent a true society more perfect than that by which Paul expressed the nature of the Christian church: a body with many members. Paul formulated the theory, Christ created the fact.

The maintenance of a true Christian community is itself a prophetic action. It educates its members, it educates its beholders, just as the mere existence of the North American republic has influenced the political thought of the world.

But the idea of the church as Christ's body has another side to it. Paul uses the illustration mainly to teach the dependence of all the members on Christ, the Head, and their interdependence on one another. But, without in any way straining the simile, we may say, too, that Christ's body is Christ's means of action. As a man's hands carry out the will of his mind and his tongue speaks his thoughts, and as the mind is powerless without the body and hampered by a paralyzed body, so the spiritual Christ makes himself practically felt in human affairs through the church. It furnishes him with lips to speak his thoughts, with feet to go his errands, with hands to lift up the sick and to check the blow of cruelty. Generally speaking, if the church is paralyzed and irresponsive to the will of the Head, or if it has fallen to reveling and made itself drunk with the wine of Mammon, then the will of Christ will remain unperformed. Who will say how often that has happened?

But when the church performs the office of a sound body, it will not only speak Christ's thoughts but repeat his actions. He went about doing good, relieving suffering and drying tears. The church has done much in the same direction. Hospitals did not exist before the Christian era. There was some organized care for orphans in imperial Rome, but they were cared for not so much because they were destitute as because they were children of Roman citizens. Christian philanthropy has always carried the first torch into the dark subcellars of human society. In England, Christianity drove John Howard into prison reform. In Germany, Christianity moved Wichern to the institution of a school for indigent children (*Das Rauhe Haus*), and Bodelschwingh to the founding of homes for the epileptic at Bielefeld. The work which makes life tolerable to the blind and the deaf-mute is still mainly in Christian hands. The Catholic Sisters of Mercy and the Protestant deaconesses have carried mercy into war itself. The Red Cross shows the animating impulse by its form. Educational work for the colored people, for the Indians, for heathen nations, is almost entirely in the hands of the church. It furnishes the workers and it furnishes the bulk of support.

Revolutionary agitators often cry down this work of charity as having evil in it, especially if the causes producing wretchedness are left untouched and only the effects are being healed. And yet the church is truer in its instincts of humanity than those who would let misery pile up in order to use its stench as a means of agitation. Christian charities keep alive in society the tenderness for suffering and the indignation against the wrong that causes it, and that indignation gives the moral dignity to social-reform agitation, which would otherwise be a selfish clamoring for rights. The most effective protest against wrong is not raised by the man who paces up and down with folded arms and pours forth abuse, but by the man who pillows the victim's head on his breast and then says to him that struck him: "This is your work." When the Christian church, in caring for the suffering, begins to see who causes the suffering and boldly says what it sees, its protest will borrow a double force from its self-sacrifice.

Apart from its charitable work to alleviate or prevent suffering, the church serves a prophetic purpose. It serves to bring society generally to the same humane position. The charities begun by the church are taken up by the state. At first hospitals were maintained only by private charities; now it is part of the functions of a municipality to care for the sick. Institutions for the blind and deaf are established or subsidized by state or county appropriations. The care of the strong for the weak of the community, at first voluntary, becomes compulsory. It was religious; it has become civil. The ethical standard of society has been raised by Christian action as well as by Christian thought.

The historical Christ, the invisible Spirit, the visible church—these are the forces of God in human history. And they are revolutionary forces.

Christ initiated the revolution, marked out its direction, warned against the dangers, organized his army, carried the revolutionary standard before them, and consecrated the cause with his blood.

Through his Spirit he is still invisibly but powerfully present with his army. His Spirit strikes the shackles of baseness and superstition from their limbs and puts them on their feet as freemen. It removes old prejudices and infuses love and a common enthusiasm. It works among them a constant renewal of energy and sacrifice to carry the struggle to the end.

Every man who has promised allegiance to Christ and has his Spirit within him is a revolutionary element, carrying on a guerilla warfare, if no more. But in spite of apparent disjointedness there is a secret unity among them. Recruits are sought, filled with the enthusiasm of the army, and instructed in the warfare. The army resists the present Prince of this world by word and deed, levies the authority of his laws, refuses to submit to his officers, levels his entrenchments, and builds others where the flag of the true King is kept flying, and whence the conquered territory is maintained and extended.

The Kingdom of God is based not on material but on spiritual forces. Its advance columns are the invisible hosts of new hopes, new aspirations, new repentances, new convictions. The primary work of Christian propaganda consists in the propagation of Christ's ideas.

We must "preach the gospel." But preaching means to be a herald, and the gospel means Glad Tidings. To carry glad good news as a herald is not to drone over threadbare ideas dressed up in worn-out illustrations. Such a gospel is no news at all, and such preaching is no heralding.

We are told that we must preach "the old gospel." If men mean by that the everlasting verities of human life, of its slavery under sin, and its possible redemption by Jesus Christ, then we like "the old gospel" well. But if they mean—as in fact they mostly do—that we must express those eternal verities in the terminology of past ages and limit their application to those circumstances of life to which men in the past were by their historical condition compelled to limit them, then we object. We refuse to imprison the living Spirit even in its own words. We have no desire to play the part of the Judean religionists over again, who loved the past revelation of God so well that they would accept no present revelation of his.

The Spirit of God, the great Teacher, is no pedant that knows nothing beyond the once invented formulas and rules. The God who has adapted plant and animal life to the exigencies of climate and soil in such marvelous diversity will surely have as closely fitting a religious garment for the multiform spiritual life of humanity. Let every bird sing its own note. Let every man utter the word that God has spoken in his heart. And let every generation formulate in its own vernacular the eternal truths of Jesus. Only then will it be a "gospel" to preacher and hearer and not a study in dead languages.

And as the Spirit must be free to choose its manner of expression, it must be free to turn the point of its weapon where it will in the shifting battle of history. For the issues change. If the Reformation laid the stress of its preaching on dead works and a living faith, it may be that our age must spurn the dead faith and demand live works.

4

THE NEW LAW

The religion of Jesus is above all things a practical religion. It is life within, but not a life that stays within. Its source is from above; its manifestation is on earth. "Faith apart from works," says stern old James, "is dead." (James 2, 26.) Claiming to know Christ and yet not keeping his commandments is a lie, says tender John. (I John 2, 4.) This whole central doctrine of the Kingdom of God on earth gives the lie to any Christianity so spiritual or other-wordly that it does not change the manner of life of all who accept it.

Jesus founded a new and higher community on earth, and that implies new and higher laws. His community is revolutionary and in opposition to the existing state of things; to be in keeping with this character, the new laws must also differ from the existing rules of life.

Quite in accord with this supposition we find that, as soon as the tendencies of his teaching were clearly understood, Jesus was charged by the representatives of the old order with "destroying the law and the prophets." He emphatically denied the charge. He said that it was not his purpose to destroy but to fulfill and establish.

Yet there was a sense in which Jesus was breaking down the law. If the form of the legislation was confused with its essence and its interpretation with its spirit, he found himself in decided conflict with it. It is very possible that at the early stage of his work, when he preached the Sermon on the Mount, he was not yet fully conscious how much the law as the scribes held it differed from the law as it appeared to him. It is the privilege of a young man who is still in retirement, that he can gather from the ideas confronting him in society those which find him, and the detached thoughts which he expresses to older men may meet with their approval. But when he enters public life, he must think and say not what he loves to think but what is needful to be said. Other people may be intensely interested in questions to which he has given no thought because they seemed to him idle or indifferent. Jesus soon became conscious of the real divergence of thought between him and the people, and the interest of truth compelled him to take a controversial attitude more than he had ever expected.

Jesus also advanced in wisdom. He met questions one by one. The peculiarity of his knowledge was not that he knew all things at once, but that he knew each thing rightly when he met it. His tone toward the representatives of the old law became more controversial as he went on; it was because he perceived more and more clearly how far he and they were apart.

When he asserted his allegiance to the law, he was thinking of the law as he had it in his heart. When the Pharisees charged him with breaking down the law, they were thinking of the law as they had it in their minds. The law of Jesus and that of the Pharisees were different laws, just as the Christianity of the Quaker George Fox and that of the cardinal John Henry Newman were different Christianities.

Jesus found himself at variance with the Pharisees in the application of the law to single cases. They found a world of difference between swearing by the temple and by the gold of the temple, by the altar and by the gift on the altar. (Matt. 23, 16-22.) Catching water that fell from the sky on the Sabbath and catching water that fell from a wall made all the difference between righteousness and sin. With that sort of casuistry he had no patience. If that was their law, he had to knock it down because it obstructed the ways of God. They were forever setting up rules; he was forever getting at principles. And the man who has found a principle moves on different lines than the man who follows a rule. The man with a rule gives five cents to every beggar that asks. The man with a principle may give nothing to one, and a whole day's time and five dollars to the next. To the man with a rule he seems a very irresponsible and incomprehensible creature. It is a paradox when James calls the perfect law a law of liberty. (James 1, 25.) Law and liberty seem contradictions. Yet that law of liberty is the law of the Christian commonwealth. Its full-grown citizens have freely accepted it, and freely they follow it. They discern the real nature of every case and follow that and not the outward appearance. So they cross and re-cross the usual lines of conduct and seem to the staid planets of a wee solar system as eccentric as a comet; and yet the comet is as consistent as they, only in a wider orbit. Jesus was always puzzling the people. He preached purity and associated with the impure. He worked a miracle for a beggar and refused it to a king. He called men to come to him, and when they came he warned them off. He spoke with the utmost frankness and again refused to speak when it seemed most needed. (Matt. 21, 23-27.) Against that kind of men the cry of lawlessness will always be raised. And justly. They are a disturbing element. Their influence is revolutionary.

That was the specific attitude of Jesus to the law as he found it. In general he considered his influence to be conservative and not destructive. He established no new principles of morality. He accepted those which have their basis in the nature of man and have been expressed with greater or lesser clearness in all human societies. But he also regarded them as merely approximate, susceptible of extension in scope, of greater clearness in statement, and of more wisdom in application. And by changing the degree of emphasis, by grouping them about a central principle, by lending them a new impulse, and by endowing men with the Spirit as their interpreter, he has in effect established a new system of ethics.

The central principle of his system is the law of love. In that hangs the whole law. He that loves a man will not rob him. He that truly loves a woman will not wrong her. Love gives the quick discernment for the sorrows and joys of the loved one, and the readiness to keep sorrow away and bring joy near even at cost to one's self.

Christ loved. All the parts of his life open to that key. Even his anger, his denunciations, his prophecies of woe were due to his love. Therefore his follower must love. A lack of love gives the lie to all professions of attachment to God. (I John 4, 20-21.) It vitiates religious belief, knowledge, charity, martyrdom itself. (I Cor. 13, 1-3.) It turns the odor of sacrifice into a stench before God. (Matt. 5, 23.) Love covers faults and wakes all excuses that can be made; therefore cruel words and harsh judgments are sin, for they proceed from a lack of love. (James 3, 11.)

Love not only refrains from doing wrong. It implies doing good. Love is the unifying impulse. Love is the self-imparting impulse. To have seen another hungry, thirsty, naked, or in distress, and not to have shared with him, convicts a man of lovelessness and ranges him on the left side in the day of judgement. (Matt. 25, 31-46.) The law of Christ is not only to put no necessary burden on your fellows, but to take some of their burden on yourself. (Gal. 6, 2.) The law of Christ knows no limit of love either in its breadth or in its depth. In breadth it floods over the demarcation of family, kinship, nationality, race. It wipes out the line between Jew and Samaritan, Greek and barbarian, Saxon and Celt, orthodox and heretic. In depth it stops only where the fountain of life springs up. Jesus' laying down his life has both demonstrated the nature of his love to us and made the laying down of our own lives a duty. (I John 3, 16.) Negatively Christian love means abstinence from harm; positively it means the bestowal of good at cost to ourselves.

The kind of love on which Christ was compelled to dwell most was love unrequited. It is natural to love where we are loved. Even publicans and Gentiles do that. (Matt. 5, 43-48.) The real test of the divine love begins when love finds no response or the response of hatred. It is only when we are able to love our enemies, to do good to those who hate us, and to pray for those who despitefully use us, that we give proof of being sons of our Father in heaven. Christian love begins where natural love stops. Therefore Jesus has dwelt especially on that which lies beyond.

If we are wronged, Jesus commands us to forgive whenever he who has wronged us desires our forgiveness, even though it be seven times in one day. (Lk. 17, 4.) Not to forgive is to put ourselves outside the pale of God's forgiveness (Matt. 6, 14-15), for our debt to God is to our neighbor's debt to us as twelve million dollars is to thirty-five dollars. (Matt. 18, 21-35.) If the other has no sense of wrong, it is still not right for us to leave the matter as it is. The initiative of reconciliation lies with us (Matt. 5, 23-24), and we are not excused till we have tried all means to convince him of his wrong. (Matt. 18, 15-17.) The desire to forgive must always be present. Christ prayed the Father to forgive those who crucified him, although they asked for no forgiveness. He forgave Peter though we know of no request for forgiveness but only of tears. Love survives wrong.

And love overcomes wrong. It is natural to resent wrong. The resentment of wrong in others is the utterance of the same moral nature in us which, as the voice of conscience, protests against wrong in ourselves. We are right in resenting evil; we ought to resent it and stop it. But the question is, how? The old way is that of retribution. It turns back the evil upon him who has committed it. If he has robbed his neighbor of an eye, that neighbor or someone else in his stead must rob him of an eye also. Thus the protest of society against wrong is expressed, and future outbreaks of evil are checked by the fear of suffering oneself the pain which one inflicts. That is the old law: "an eye for an eye, and a tooth for a tooth." Jesus does not condemn this law any more than he condemns the law not to kill, not to swear falsely, and to love your neighbor. Like these others it is a good law as far as it goes, but it is not effective enough to satisfy him. He was more desirous of checking evil than anyone else, and yet he forbade his disciples to resist evil by returning it in kind. Why? Because he found that evil can best be checked by not returning it.

Suppose a man strikes you on the right cheek. You strike him back. Very likely you strike him harder than he struck you. He gets angry. He has quite forgotten that he was the aggressor and feels only the tingling of his own cheek. It is three to one that he will strike once more, and that you will part in a blaze of anger, and like Samson's foxes will carry the fire into all the neighborhood. You have not checked evil but sown it abroad. Or take the more favorable case; suppose that the matter rests after you have returned the first blow. Certainly there will be no love between you. The aggressor, if he is very impartial, will think you are quits, and if he is only an ordinary man, he will think himself hard used and pass his anger on to somebody else, his wife perhaps, or his children. There is no repentance in the matter, no recognition of the wrongness of wrong. The man may become more careful of his fists, especially toward you who have proved the possession of an equal pair. Otherwise nothing is altered. The chastised dog fears the whip but remains a dog. And the man, having been subjected to the same argument for righteousness as the dog, learns the same lesson of prudence; what else can he learn?

Now suppose Christ's way is adopted. The blow is given, but none is returned. The evil stops there. He that receives it certainly does not pass it on. And as for him that gave it, he is almost sure to feel regret very soon after. He will feel small and mean and long for a dark place in which to hide himself. Paul has compared the pain suffered by those who have thus had evil answered by kindness with the pain of burning coals tangled in the hair and burning through the scalp. (Rom. 12, 20.) It is an excruciating image and sounds as if Paul had gone through the experience. The return of the blow would have aroused pugnacity, wounded self-love, vanity, everything that blurs and confuses the moral judgement. The blow given and not returned stands in naked meanness and compels even the man who gave it to take the part of the innocent sufferer. The evil has been checked. It has been confined within the narrowest compass, and its repetition has been rendered unlikely all around. Evil has been overcome by good.

A brief survey would show how prominent this law was in Christian teaching. Jesus states the principle and explains it by three assumed cases; the command in every case is quietly to submit to the wrong and even to do more than is demanded. (Matt. 5, 38-42.)

When the disciples proposed after the fashion of Elijah to call down fire on a Samaritan village which had refused the simplest duty of hospitality, he rebuked them. An ancient gloss adds the words: "Ye know not what manner of spirit ye are of." Christ never used his power to harm. This became so well understood that men who were convinced of his miraculous power offered him affronts without fear. In Gethsemane he forbade his disciples to resist what surely was a great wrong, and before Pilate he declared that this non-resistance was deliberate and essential to the nature of his Kingdom. (Matt. 26, 50-53; John 18, 36.) Paul repeatedly warns against rendering evil for evil. (I Thess. 5, 15; Rom. 12, 17.) He calls it a defect to have a lawsuit at all and says the normal thing for a Christian would be to submit to wrong. (I Cor. 6, 7.) He begs his brethren not to let their minds be embittered by the persecutions they were suffering, but to bless their persecutors to do good to their enemies, and to leave vengeance to God. (Rom. 12, 12-21.) Peter speaks of the patient endurance of wrong as the chief way of following in the footsteps of him "who, when he was reviled, reviled not in return, and when he suffered, threatened not." (I Peter 2, 19-24; 3, 8-18.) There are few Christian teachings so frequently and emphatically stated, and few so little obeyed or even comprehended.

Perhaps it is because this law is distinctively Christian. Only a Christian can make it work. The man who submits to wrong must be a brave man, so that it will be apparent that his submission is not due to cowardice. He must also be a man who can discern the wrong and point it out, if necessary. Submission does not imply silence. When Jesus was struck in the high priest's court, he did not strike back but calmly pointed out the wrong. (John 18, 22-23.) In many cases no word at all will be necessary. The unconscious bearing of the man will show that he is neither too dull nor too cowardly to resist, but that in him the majesty of goodness has been insulted. Another thing needful is love for the offender. If the blow is taken with sullen bitterness or with proud scorn, it will have no softening and overcoming influence.

For a man with the righteousness, courage, and love of a true

Christian, submission is the most effective treatment of wrong. It stops it. Retribution does not. It is like the experiment in physics: a row of balls hang side by side; one is moved and swings against the next; that recoils and clashes against the first, and soon the whole row are battering against one another till finally the force is lost by friction. The law of the conservation of energy holds in the moral world too. But if a good man receives a shock and lets the vibrations of pain run through his own heart alone, the evil has been caught and extinguished. It is like the heroism of the soldier who climbed on the roof and rolled on the fire-brand that endangered the city. In fact it is the idea of the cross of Christ. Evil always brings suffering somewhere, to someone. The old method of retributive punishment is to turn it back on him who sent it out and let him feel the consequence. Christ's method is for the innocent to take its full force and lovingly to let the evil-doer go free. He trusted to suffering love in his own case; he expects us to trust in it too. Thus disciples will best prove their faith in the overcoming power of Christ's suffering by testing the power of voluntary suffering for sin themselves. If they have more faith in the restrictive power of violence than in suffering love, they profess themselves followers of Moses rather than of the Christ. There may be cases where the application of force is necessary by a Christian man, perhaps with children or with persons whose moral sense is too dull to be alive to anything but physical pain, if there be any such. But when a man undertakes to visit punishment, he takes upon himself the office of God to whom vengeance belongs. Let him look to it that he has the calm justice of God and the sorrowing love of God and that there is no personal anger in him, for the wrath of man worketh not the righteousness of God, not even the wrath of exasperated parents.

The central commandment of the Christian law is love. It excludes all wrong-doing as a matter of course. It demands in addition the relieving of suffering and the bestowing of good to the utmost limit of our strength.

The law is not abrogated by any conduct of others. If they sin and repent, we are to love and forgive. If they sin and repent not, we are to love and reprove. If they do wrong to us, we are to love and suffer, leaving the sin to God to requite if he will, but taking the sinner for us to soften and save if we can.

There are some applications of these principles which are not expressed in the New Testament, which yet ought to be made. We should debase Christianity into a mere set of rules if we drew only the inferences which the New Testament drew. Our times demand new applications of the eternal truth, and we are free to make them. Jesus spoke a profound truth when he put the same penalty on hate that former times had put on murder. There is an organic connection between hate and murder. Hate is murder in solution. Murder is hate crystallized.

But the connection does not end with actual cases of murder of which the courts take cognizance.

God has so ordered it that life originates through love, and the two everywhere stand and fall together. Love is the oxygen that feeds the flame of life, and when there is no love, life darkens and dies. This fact is most clearly discerned where life is feeblest and most dependent on love. Some years ago, statistics in Paris showed that of the children brought up by their parents only 18 percent died in their first year; of those given out to board after the French fashion 29 percent died; and of the children committed to foundling asylums 66 percent died in the first year. (This latter figure has decreased in later years.) In the great foundling asylum in Moscow, 367,788 children were received between 1763-1856, and of these 288,554 or 79 percent died in infancy. It must be taken into consideration that the parents of such children often transmit the germs of disease to them. But even then it is plain that, other things being equal, the child that lives under the care of love has better chances of life than the child under the sanitary care of doctors and nurses. Illegitimate children, whose coming is often hailed with less joy than their going, show a terrible rate of mortality. Of 1,000 legitimate children born in Berlin in 1878, 103 died in the first quarter and 65 in the second; while of the same number of illegitimate 261 died in the first and 113 in the second quarter. In some cases there may be purpose in it; in most cases it is simply lack of love.

Love gives a hold on life. On the whole, the cares of life rest more heavily on the married, yet, from the twenty-fifth year up, the death-rate of the unmarried is nearly double that of the married. The proportion of cases of insanity is similar.

An increase in Christianity in any country ought to show itself in a decrease of the death-rate, especially of the young and feeble. If there is a heavy mortality of the latter, it may be due to other causes; but the Christianity of that country is under indictment. True love does not wait for evil to be done before it sees it. Wise love will exert itself more in warding off evil than in curing it.

The Christian church has done most nobly in healing the wounds of humanity after they had been smitten. That was by precept and example taught in the New Testament. But there, on the whole, the church has stopped. It has considered the pound of cure better than the ounce of prevention. It is not justified in this by the absence of preventive measures in the New Testament period. The church then had no influence on legislation. Its hands were more than full with cases of suffering demanding immediate relief. Besides, it considered the period till the reconstruction of humanity through the second coming of Christ so brief that any efforts requiring time would have seemed foolish.

Affairs have changed. Christian men are a power in the world. They can prevent as well as cure. It must be plain to any candid observer that a very large share of the misery of men is not caused in the first place by the fault of individuals. Temperance reformers began by working on individuals, but experience has driven them more and more to seek social remedies first. They found that drunkards create saloons, but that saloons even more create drunkards. They have refused to go on merely curing the drunkard after he has been made. They see that the best way to cure him is to stop the making of him so far as society can. This is hard common sense, and Christian people may as well make up their minds to apply the same principle to other sources of evil and suffering.

For instance, the "fresh-air work" is annually growing in our cities, and it is a most Christian thing to color those pale cheeks with the flush of health. But why let the cheeks get pale? Why wait till the work of slow murder is half done? Is there nothing to prevent it? Of course there is. Land speculation is the chief cause of city crowding, as the saloon is the chief productive cause of drunkenness. Speculative land prices rise by the sufferings of women and children. Why should Christian men wear out their strength in curing the effects of the evil and have no word about the evil itself?

Society dumps its moral offal of pauperism and crime upon the church and says: "Here, take these and care for them." And the church works and moans about the unceasing flood of evil and the hopelessness of the task. What creates pauperism? Like diseased tissues it is self-perpetuating to some extent. But what creates it in the first place and maintains the conditions for its growth? Surely it takes only a slight acquaintance with history and economics to discern some of the chief causes. What has pauperized Ireland? Its land system. What has ruined the sturdy Italian stock ever since the days of Tacitus, and turns it loose on our shores hardy and laborious, but stunted and degraded? The Italian land system. What is the fertile source of our own idle, vicious, and criminal class? Vagrancy rises and falls with the price of grain. Industrial crises are marked by an increase in criminality. I have before me a table showing the criminal statistics of Massachusetts in 1860-79. In every category of crime there is an upward wave from 1872-75. The total number of cases was as follows: 1870: 39,705; 1871: 39,873; 1872: *45,303;* 1873: *46,137;* 1874: *43,691;* 1875: *40,411;* 1876: 33,113; 1877: 31,694. The years 1872-75 were years of industrial pressure.

Suppose an Italian city, supplied with water by an aqueduct, suddenly finds its supply failing. The people ascribe it to the devil, to the visitation of God, or to the nature of things. They catch rainwater in tubs, dig ugly cisterns, go for miles to the river to fetch water, and suffer terribly. The monks of the convent do all they can; they stint themselves of water, they care for the suffering, they moisten the parched lips of the babes with wine and make them drink rather than let them go thirsty. There is a heretical, red-bearded Englishman visiting in the place. He tries to make the people understand that there must be something the matter with the aqueduct. They look at him coldly. He speaks to the monks. They answer: "We are too busy with caring for the suffering to have time for masonry. Besides, God has sent this suffering to give Christian charity a chance to show its healing power." The Englishman shrugs his shoulders, hires men at his own expense, examines the aqueduct, locates the leak, and presses forward to work till the break is stopped. Meanwhile the townspeople shake their head at the crazy Englishman; the monks mutter at the lovelessness of the Protestant who scarcely stops on the way to give a fainting woman a drink from his flask and cares more for stone and mortar than for his fellow-men. At last the work is done. The water flows again. The people say: "We have had hard times; now the times are better again." The monks admonish the people to praise God for his goodness. God above knows whose love was warmest. But whose was wisest?

The apostolic church founded the order of deacons to avoid social inequality and to make sure that all want was relieved. Our deacons still care for the poor after they have become poor. Would it not be entirely in keeping with the spirit of Christ, if some of the nineteenth-century deacons should take it in hand to care for the poor before they have been made poor, by stopping the causes that pauperize society? Why should the church of Christ drive a one-horse cart, while the church of Mammon runs an express-train with all modern improvements? The devil and his servants are entirely willing to have the church take away their used-up victims and care for them, if only they can go on using them up.

Two things combine to produce sin; the outward opportunity and the inward inclination. The church tries to decrease the inward inclination, and it does well. But if at the same time the outward temptation is increased, the inward gain is neutralized and lost. Christ recognizes the force of this outward factor when he bids us pray: "Lead us not into temptation," and when he says that the man who causes one of the most insignificant of his fellow-beings to sin had better be sent to the bottom of the sea with a mill-stone round his neck. What an inarticulate moan is forever going up to God: "Lead us not into temptation!" Shopgirls who want to remain innocent; women who struggle to keep up a clean and decent home; men who desire to do an honest day's work. There are all grades of weakness among them. Increase the pressure by one ounce and some of them go down. Increase the industrial pressure, and thefts increase, divorces increase, suicides increase, youthful prostitution increases. Hear their cries as they go under, and the ruined homes, the blasted reputations, the broken hearts swirl by on the flood. Is there any help? Who does not by this time see that these "glutted markets," these "money stringencies," are due to the reckless covetousness of powerful men who coin money out of the sufferings of others? Verily Christ will have to take the rings of Saturn as mill-stones for the necks of some men now living, if the Christ on the throne views their guilt as the Galilean Jesus did. "Lead us not into temptation!" Hear that cry, church of Jesus, thou body of Christ! This too is a work for thy hands. Wait not till they have fallen, till shame has died, self-respect vanished, the blood been tinted, the imagination poisoned, the spring of life befouled, and hope has fled. Then the awful word of Christ takes effect: "From him that hath not is taken even that which he hath." Every loss prepares for the next. If rescue is still possible, it will be only as through fire; rescued and rescuer alike will come off with eye-brows singed. Christ takes the old morality for granted and sets in where it stops. Civil society can ask nothing more than: "Be just to one another." Christ adds: "Love one another." Civil society cannot demand more than: "Give thy neighbor *his* own." Christ says: "Give him *thine* own."

But mark well: Christ's commandment of love presupposes the world's commandment of justice. Justice is the foundation on which love can build its temple. Unless that foundation is there, the walls will crack.

It is necessary to say this because so many try to be loving without being just. Suppose a factory owner grinds down his men to starvation wages and pockets the increased profit. His wife and daughter are tenderhearted women. They find destitution, sickness, and ignorance all over the village. They spend their time and strength in helping cases of need. The husband and father is a church member and a generous man. He lets them have all they need for charity. He builds a chapel and endows a reading room. And yet the whole thing is false. He tries to make injustice and love pull in one harness. It will not work. Probably he will complain that his men are an ungrateful lot who never appreciate what his family does for them. The moral judgment of the men is more correct than his. They ought not to be thankful. He is giving them as a gift what belongs to them by right. Working men are fond of saying: "We want justice, not charity." It is a good saying. Perhaps it would be better yet to say: "First justice, then charity." After justice has been done, there will still be ample room for love, and then it will be love indeed and not "charity."

This demand the lower classes have a right to make of all who possess wealth, ability, or education, and who call themselves Christians. "First give us what is ours by justice; then if you wish to do anything for us from love, we shall appreciate your love. But if you do not love us enough to be just to us, do not call it love."

Stopping wrong by suffering it is certainly the method commanded by Christ. It is not to the credit of the church that only a few sects and individuals have accepted the commandment in earnest. Most Christians relegate this morality to the Millennium, on the ground that in existing society a man acting so would be stripped and beaten up. It is a question whether he would or not. There are those who have tried it and assert that they suffer fewer injuries than before, and that certainly they fret and fume less over those they do receive and therefore have a more severe and sweeter life of it. The man that beats about him most wildly will be stung most—by bees and men. There are always compensations in obedience to Christ which we discover only when we trust ourselves to him. A man taking upon himself this commandment might think that he was about to lose his life and find to his surprise that he has gained it.

But suppose he did suffer under it and was buffeted about more. What is that to the Christian? It is not the part of love to inquire about its own suffering but about the good of the loved one. Is it because, in spite of our praise of love, we think of our own welfare first that we refuse to let the blow rest on us but insist on passing it back to him who gave it? There are probably many young Christians who ardently desire some way to serve Christ and to suffer for him. This is a short road to the cross and open to all. We can all suffer for the sins of our friends and, by suffering without resentment, show both the sinfulness of the sin and the forgiving goodness of love. And this martyrdom has this advantage over other kinds that it brings no publicity and fame with it to poison the heart of the martyr with pride but acts quietly like oil on the angry waters of the sea of which but a very little will calm many breakers.

This is a perfect rule of Christian conduct, but we must remember that there are many approximations to it. As we have seen, Christ does not reject the old law of retribution as wrong but as imperfect and dangerous. He rejects it because it is likely to recoil on him that uses it (Matt. 26, 52), and because it belongs to those who love themselves more than the wrong-doer. Yet he that resents wrong done to himself is a better man than he who is too cowardly even to resent. And he that forcibly resists wrong done to others is far better than he who is indifferent to it. If a man cannot rise to the best and most effective way of treating wrong, then it is better for him to resist evil by force than to let it run its unhindered course.

It is necessary to remember this in our judgement of the actions of others. When we consider the stern Ironsides of Cromwell going into battle with prayer and psalms, or the soldiers of Young Italy striking for the unity of their country, we can render all praise and honor to their patriotism, their love of right, their self-sacrifice. Their actions are immeasurably above those who crouched by their hearth and mumbled piety. The question is whether there is not a way braver still and more effective.

Force has this evil about it, that it ranges the noblest virtues on the side of wrong and makes even wrong look noble. The bravery of the Parliament troups was met by the gallantry of the Cavaliers who rallied round poor King Charles. Charles the First and Louis the

Sixteenth were neither great nor good. If men are to die for treason at all, these two probably deserved it more than nineteen-twentieths of the men who have been executed for treason in England and France. But in executing them, the patriots furnished martyrs to a bad cause. Half of Europe wept at the sorrow of the kings. A hair from those poor heads became a treasure, an heir-loom, a spur to bravery. Tenderness, pity, chivalry pleaded for what was bad. Each execution was followed by the restoration of monarchy. If the cause of freedom gained through the two revolutions, it was in spite of, and not because of, the violence used. The influence of the French Revolution in loosening the shackles of the European nations has been immeasurable. But how much greater would it have been, if the Reign of Terror had never stained the cause of liberty with blood? At first all Europe sympathized with it; the reversal of feeling set in with the increase of violence, and to-day the majority of men know only of the terrors and not of the glories of that uprising.

It cannot be denied that forcible resistance to wrong has done good. But the good is so mixed with evil that often the social body is more prostrated by the effects of the medicine than by the sickness. Slavery has been overcome in our country by force. It had to be overcome somehow, and all honor is due to those who poured out life, happiness, property to overcome it. But who can survey the terrible cost of life to both sides, the resentful anger which is so slow to die out between North and South, and especially the present sad condition of those on whose behalf all the sacrifices were made, without wondering whether there was no other way?

There are painful struggles before the civilized nations now. There are vested wrongs that must be overthrown. If blood is spilt, it will be spilt as justly as any other that has flowed on earth. And yet the saddest day for the cause of the people will be the day when they begin to shed blood. While they *suffer* violence, they have all but the small self-interested minority on their side. As soon as they *use* violence, they will have on their side only the reckless and the most righteous men. All those that stand between will see the blood on their hands and see nothing else, and the cause of God and the people will have to wait for another era before it can recover from that defeat in victory. It will be well for the workingmen of America and all who lead them to think this out well before the time of need comes, because their enemies understand it well already and will not fail to provoke them to violence.

But those who warn the people against force and insist on a moral revolution should remember the responsibility they assume. Here are wrongs that God is calling on this generation to remove, if he ever called on any generation to act. There are hands outstretched to seize them and tear them, and feet ready to trample them into the dust. We Christians say: "Stop! Use no violence; trust to the power of truth and righteousness; agitate, persuade, protest, but do not strike." We have a right to say that only if our spiritual weapons are really more effective than powder and steel. And they will be more effective only if the blade of truth is ground sharp on the rough stone of suffering, and if they who wield it have cut loose from family and ambition and love of ease, and march against wrong like the black Brunswick hussars, who wore the skull and cross-bones on their helmet in token that they gave no quarter and asked for none. That was the spirit of Jesus. If we had men of that spirit, a revolution by force would be unnecessary; if we do not have them, it will be inevitable.

a. Social Rank

In surveying the ethical applications which Jesus made of his cardinal doctrine concerning the relation of man to man, we find first that he protested against all exalting of man over man in rank. It is not love that makes a man gather every little chip of wood under his feet to raise himself half an inch above his fellows and look down at them with condescension.

Jesus ridiculed the small ambition which scrambles for a high seat at a dinner-party, loves to be surveyed in a front pew in the synagogue, and takes the deferential greetings in the market-place as a rooster swallows a choice slug, with closing of eyes and side-ward cocking of head. (Matt. 23, 6-7; Lk. 14, 7-11.) He advised them as a mere matter of prudence to leave it to others to exalt them instead of doing it for themselves.

The system of giving and taking titles seemed to him born of the same spirit of self-exaltation. He forbade his disciples either to assume titles or to use them in addressing others. (Matt. 23, 8-12.)

The form which pride took in so religious a community as Judea was especially repulsive to Jesus. He saw the religionists stopping short on the streetcorners when the hours of prayer came and going through their devotions in the sight of all, and he knew that the beholders were by no means out of the thoughts of those who seemed so absorbed in talking to God. He saw them make a studied display of their benevolence to the beggars. He saw them assume sombre looks and a disheveled appearance to announce to all the world that they were fasting. "Ah, Jochanan is fasting again; how pious that man is." To the mind of Jesus, using the worship of the Father as stilts on which to mount above one's brethren was a vile prostitution of the body. (Matt. 6, 1-18; 23, 5.) In the parable of the Pharisee and publican he has given the classical portrayal of this religious ambition which fasts and gives tithes in order to have the satisfaction of thanking God for not being "as the rest of men." (Lk. 18, 9-14.) He forbade judging one another because the judging spirit is the spirit of pride. It warms the cockles of our heart to pat our brother on the back and say: "Brother, on the whole I approve of you, but—ahem—you have a mote in your eye which hinders it from being as clear and bright as you perceive mine to be."

Therefore in legislating for the new community, Jesus forbade his subjects from exalting themselves above one another. It was difficult to wean his disciples from that desire. Their hope of the speedy erection of a temporal kingdom fostered any latent ambition. They quarreled repeatedly about their future grades of rank. Once the mother of two of them tried by a bit of feminine diplomacy to preempt the chief positions for her sons. (Lk. 22, 24-27; Matt. 20, 20-28.)

Jesus unflinchingly resisted that tendency. When they wanted to know who was greatest in the Kingdom, he told them that, unless they turned and became like children, they would not get into the Kingdom, let alone be great in it. (Matt. 18, 1-4.) He often held up the childlike spirit as the untainted spirit of true humanity. For children with all their frank little egotisms are all democrats till they have been spoiled by their elders. A little prince would make mud-pies with a street-arab if he were let alone and consider himself in the best of company. As he condemned pride and ambition, so Jesus praised the qualities of meekness, purity, simplicity, and peacefulness as belonging especially to the Kingdom. (Matt. 5, 3-9.) He asked men to learn of him to be meek and lowly of heart, so that they might shake off the heavy yoke of ambition and resentment and find rest for their souls. (Matt. 11, 28-30.) John tells how, on the last evening of his intercourse with the disciples, he performed the menial office of washing their feet and drying them, in order to impress it on their minds that the greatness to be sought by them consisted not in exacting service from others but in serving them. (John 13, 1-17.) It is a sad example of the way men have distorted the teachings of Jesus that some have turned the foot-washing, which was meant as a typical case of a universal duty, into a sacrament and perform it even in latitudes where cow-hide boots, instead of dusty sandals, have to be taken off to permit it. If I am not mistaken, both the pope and the czar annually wash the feet of a fixed number of beggars to demonstrate to the Lord Christ that they are the humble and self-forgetful servants of their fellow-men.

In this respect the ethics of Jesus is distinctly opposed to that prevailing in the world. For in all the world men lord it and rule it and allow themselves to be called benefactors, highnesses, gracious majesties, and what not. (Matt. 20, 25; Lk. 22, 25.) Jesus says: "Be not like them. There are some who will stand higher than others in the sight of God and in the sight of men too. They are not those who try to stand higher, but those who abandon all thought of how they will stand and simply love and serve." That law has once for all been fixed by the example of the Son of man, who, if any, had a right to honor, but sought pre-eminence only in being everybody's helper and giving up his life as a ransom to free the lives of others. (Matt. 20, 28.)

We notice in the writings of the early church that this quality of Jesus and this precept especially impressed the apostles. Paul exhorts his friends at Philippi to do "nothing through self-seeking or vain glory, but in lowliness of mind each to count the other better than himself," and thus to "have the same mind in them which was in Christ Jesus," who surrendered every privilege and stepped down, step by step, till he reached the depth of poverty, ignominy, and suffering. (Phil. 2, 3-8.) So to James it seems painfully incongruous to introduce any difference in rank into the Christian church. The "faith of our Lord Jesus Christ" and "the respect of persons" have nothing in common. (James 2, 1-9.) And with the same purpose in mind both Peter and Paul beg the women not to load themselves with ornament or to take pride in the material and cut of their dress. In a society where women are uneducated and do not mingle on equal terms with the men, their social ambition goes mainly toward the quantity of their jewelry and the elaborateness of their dress. Perhaps that pride never quite leaves. We have all observed that a bit of gold or a few yards of shimmering stuff can serve its wearer as a satisfactory vantage ground and may disturb the fraternal equilibrium of an entire social circle. For a man to endeavor to outstrip others by his wealth, honor, or ability, or for a woman to take pains to outshine others by her beauty and social position, is the same ambition in different spheres, and its effect is equally disastrous in either case and equally destructive to Christ's society and the Kingdom of God.

We find, then, that Jesus bids us stand side by side as brethren of equal rank. Any attempt of an individual to raise himself above the rest by titles, social distinctions, or displays of religious superiority, he condemns as evil. He desires that we forget to consider what men think of us and how we stand compared with others, and give ourselves entirely to serve others and lift them up. And he who does that most fully, not with a Uriah Heep's conscious, self-congratulating humility but with unconscious sincerity, shall be the greatest in the Kingdom.

There is profound wisdom in the radical position taken by Jesus against pride and all its works.

Religious pride is self-sufficiency and independence of God, and that is isolation and death. At the root of Paul's speculative protests against salvation by works lay a very practical experience. He knew from experience that the close attention to religious performances, this keeping of a cash account with the Almighty and crediting one's self with so and so many good deeds, begot a pride which was spiritual death and made religious men be bad men. Therefore he insisted on including all under condemnation, that all might be dependent on the grace of God, "lest any man should boast." Paul was right. In Browning's "Paracelsus" we read:

> Man's weakness is his glory, for the strength which raises
> Him to heaven and near God's self, came spite of it. God's strength
> His glory is, for thence came with our weakness sympathy which brought
> God down to earth, a man like us.

Paul's protest was leveled against a religious aristocracy. He aimed to bring all men down on one plane before God, and to unite them in one great brotherhood of sin and redemption. Even for the work done by him and others he refused praise. They were but husbandmen, planting or watering; but it is not the husbandman who gives the seed the faculty and the means of growth, but God. "What hast thou, that thou hast not received?" he asks, and "If thou didst receive it, why dost thou glory, as if thou hadst not received it?" Modern science entirely confirms the major premise of Paul's syllogism, and from the ethical conclusion there is no escape.

Social sciences confirm the correctness of Christ's protest against the stratification of society in ranks and classes. What is the general tendency toward democracy and the gradual abolition of hereditary privileges but history's assent to the revolutionary dogmas of Christ?

Higher classes by their existence are a damage to themselves and to the body of a nation. They are exposed to special temptations and there is no force to exact from them obedience to the corresponding obligations. Those who should speak to them sternly, plead gently. They are up in a rarefied atmosphere whither the voice of truth sounds but faintly. It is painful to see how much more sedulous the church has always been in preaching the duty of the people to the princes than in pointing out the duty of the great toward the people. The upper classes appear to get the very best quality of preaching, but they are in fact suffering with a self-imposed famine of the Word of God to them. They would not tolerate it if they did hear it. There is an inward obstacle in the heart of those who are fed with honor against the plain truth of Christ. "How can ye believe, who receive glory one of another?" Jesus asks. (John 5, 44.) He seems to have had little hope for the upper classes. Those who did feel drawn to him had the usual timidity of the privileged classes and feared to side with him, "for they loved the glory that is of men more than the glory that is of God." (John 12, 42-43.)

No part of humanity can stand to be in any degree severed from the great body. The prisoners in Russian prisons suffer under their isolation, and the czar and his nobility suffer under it an another way. There is a moral obliquity about it which distorts the entire life and even cripples the intellectual faculties. The nobility of Europe has had the most extraordinary opportunities for producing at least intellectual work of value. They have had heredity, wealth, associations, familiarity with art, travel, everything in their favor. But considering these odds, what have they done in poetry, in art, in natural science, in the severer departments of philosophical research? In the list of soldiers and statesmen the names of ancient families occur more frequently; but then, these careers were almost closed to all but the nobility. And in how many cases did the titled general gain the royal praise, when the real work had been performed by men unknown to history? It is interesting, also, to notice that both in the English and the French revolutions, when a chance was given for the military talent of the common people, generals arose who stand head and shoulders above the average of those produced by an aristocratically graded military service. Free contact on terms of equality with the great body of humanity is the necessary condition of moral health, and hence indirectly of intellectual greatness.

Dividing off humanity into horizontal layers imposed one above the other is really equivalent to the formation of separate humanities. It is the devil's denial of God's doctrine that all men are of one blood and brothers. As Mrs. Browning says, there are more infidels to Adam than professed infidels to God. It is vain to comfort ourselves that Christianity bridges the chasms best by closing them. While they exist, it can signal across them, run baskets across them on pulley-lines, and show its good will; but that sort of engineering has its natural limits. Christian sympathy, it is true, works downward; but natural sympathy works sideways, in horizontal lines. Our real intelligence and love goes to those who are akin to us in manner of life, in education and views.

A businessman has a neighbor whom he has met in a friendly way off and on for twenty years. He also has a book-keeper who has been with him for twenty years, with whom he has been in contact for hours every day and whose probity he sincerely respects. The neighbor and the bookkeeper both die in one week, and our friend learns that in each case the family has been left in want. How will his sympathy go out in either case? He may do more for the book-keeper's widow, but will it be with the same feeling with which he offers his assistance to the widow of his friend? Will it not be pity in the one case and true sympathy in the other?

The differences of rank are real differences. Surely modern literature is sufficient evidence for that. In ancient Greek literature the will of the gods or Fate is the obstacle against which human freedom dashes; in modern literature it is the established difference in rank against which love or ambition beats its wings. And where sexual love, the most powerful passion of life, finds it hard to bring two persons together who are separate by rank, Christian love will find it hard too. For the Christian love of the upper classes cannot well manifest itself in anything but a mild benevolence; "love" is diluted into "charity."

A class inevitably substitutes a class code for Christ's morality. What is proper becomes of more importance than what is right. Kingsley has a neat touch in his *Yeast*. The game-keeper's ballad with the lament of the preacher's widow is read to the squire.

> A labourer in Christian England,
> Where they cant of a Saviour's name,
> And yet waste men's lives like the vermin's
> For a few more brace of game.
> There's blood on your new foreign shrubs, squire;
> There's blood on your pointer's feet,
> There's blood on the game you sell, squire,
> And there's blood on the game you eat.

"You villian," interposed the squire, "when did I ever sell a head of game?"

Killing men is inhuman; selling game is ungentlemanly. The squire resents the latter charge.

The life of a privileged class is an unsound life. It is less open to radical moral truths. It is subject to class prejudice rather than to justice. It struggles against very great obstacles in endeavoring to obey Christ's law of love. It is like a camel going through the eye of a needle.

It is not for us to say that men in the upper classes cannot be Christians. It may be possible to support life in a glass vessel from which the air is partly pumped out. It may be possible to balance one's self along the straight and narrow way with a tremendous burden on one shoulder and an empty bag on the other. But it is unnatural and unchristian. And it must be remembered that it is to some extent voluntary. It is possible to step down and become a man. That is what Christ advised a wealthy young aristocrat to do. He did not do it.

I have spoken of the effect of class isolation on the isolated class. But the condition of any part of the social body must affect the whole. It is only true to say that whatever good the upper classes generate, e.g., culture, refined taste, etc., has to be carried downward by force and purpose, as a balloon of gas has to be dragged down, while corruption trickles down of itself. The licentiousness of an idle class has to be fed by the working class. Their luxury and display generates the love of luxury in those who can afford it less. This love of pleasure, this wasting of substance on dress and ornament, this living beyond their means, which is justly deplored in working people at present, has been aroused by the luxurious living of the rich. You may preach simplicity and contentment all you please. As long as there are those who live in idleness and waste, you are telling men to resist or reverse the law of gravitation. God has planted the love of the beautiful and the desire of imitation into the heart of man. It is the faculty by which he progresses. In a true society the aesthetic faculty is incentive to a nobler life, and we praise those who give up some of their daily bread if necessary, in order to enjoy the higher life of art and literature. In a false and classified society this same love of the beautiful, and this same readiness to sacrifice the lower needs to the higher, become a cause of destruction. *Corruptio optimi pessima.* The daughter of the workingman too has a taste for natty bonnets and a woman's touch for soft and clinging stuffs. She too could lean back in an open carriage or enjoy a box at the opera. If she copies her "favored sister" so far as she can with cotton velvets and Bowery theaters, has her favored sister the right to lift up the first stone? How many young girls in our cities suffer always the tortures of Tantalus? They hunger for beauty and refinement, and beauty and refinement are dangled up and down, up and down, within an inch of their famishing life, in the stores, on the streets, in the novels they read, even in the churches they go to. And then the tempter shows them a shortcut to it all. Verily it is a marvel and cause to praise God that the bulk of our people are as pure and true and solid as they are in the face of such influences of corruption as are represented in the "higher classes" of city society. We fear that if Jesus should walk on Fourteenth Street in the afternoon and watch the women then, and walk there again in the evening and see the other women so like them in dress and gait and even perfume, only everything a little louder, he would place the mill-stone of this awful responsibility around many a neck covered with lace—or nothing. The stumbling blocks over which girls and men trip at night have been strewn there during the day.

It is idle to seek a remedy in begging wealthy women to dress more plainly. When will moralists cease to plaster cracked walls with untempered mortar? How long in this age of science will they try to do away with effects and leave the causes at work? Why try to conceal the appearances of inequality and leave the inequality in existence?

As long as there are upper classes, there will be men and women so near them that they may hope by effort to rise into them. And this hope will not generate noble qualities in them. It will drive the women to display, to petty scheming, to the wasting of their own lives and the lives of their children in the soul-pulverizing machine called "society." It will drive the men to race and tear in their business, to skim close to the precipice of dishonesty, to turn the screw tighter on their employees—all to furnish their wives and daughters with the necessary stepping stones to mount into these upper classes. Young men of ability and aspirations have to forsake the pride of rectitude and the strength of unselfish daring. They must curry favor, win influence; anyway, every way, they must rise. Rank, wherever it exists, is a devourer of youthful promise. Rank is the worst court of divorce; it divorces true love and pronounces its benediction over that most insidiously destructive form of prostitution, marriage for position or money.

It behooves Christian people to recognize that Christ is against inequality, and that he denounces the effort to create inequality as hostile to the nature of the Kingdom of God on earth. Therefore they should welcome and foster every effort to abolish the causes of inequality and thus remove the over-powerful temptations from the members of the upper classes and give them a fair chance to become good men and women. A follower of Christ should not wait till the slow change of society rectifies these evils. The command to depart from unrighteousness and to join the society of Christ lies upon him for immediate obedience. If he is on the house-top, let him come down and tread the solid earth. If he is on the earth, let him not try to get astraddle of a roof-beam. Christian young men in business should refuse to join in the chase for wealth, for wealth will infallibly carry them into the dangerous classes. Young men in intellectual pursuit should refuse to join in the chase for titles, offices, and distinctions, for if they strive to win the proud distinction of being called rabbi, they will have to fight shy of the Galilean heretic. Daudet's *L'Immortel* is a striking commentary on Christ's condemnation of titles. It shows how even so respected an institution as the French Academy exercises a baleful influence of temptation, awakens small ambition, fosters the meanest jealousies, straitlaces courageous utterance, and freezes love and friendship. Like all caricatures, the book exaggerates; but like all good caricatures it is an approximate portrait. The duty of resisting this ambition lies especially on the clergy. If they fix their eye on a title or on a bishop's chair, the locks of their strength are cut. They will not fight Jehovah's battles but grind the corn of the Philistines. "He that hates not titles, newspaper puffs, and his own promotion, cannot be my disciple."

The obligation to break the force of ambition lies especially on the women. It is probably fair to assert that the scrambling of men for place and money to a large extent is done under the conscious or unconscious impulse of the women they love. The better a man is, the more will he prostitute himself to give his wife the social station which she desires. It would be a stern and rare type of virtue in a man to be practically a brother of the poor if his wife desired to be a sister to the rich and he could satisfy her desire by a slight lowering of his moral aspirations. It will be a great day for humanity when Christian young women refuse to bestow their love on young men who are so hostile to the Kingdom of God as to desire to "rise in life," instead of desiring to raise life.

It may be necessary to add as the closing word on this subject that equality does not mean uniformity. Whenever a proposal is made for a more just construction of society, the cry is immediately raised: "You want to have a dead level of uniformity. God created inequality; you cannot abolish it by act of Congress." We ought to be beyond such objections, in America at least. The experience of the American republic ought to have demonstrated that an equality of political rights for all citizens does not mean an equality of political wisdom and power, but that in a nation in which Abraham Lincoln could cast but one ballot, he could sway millions of hearts and command their wealth and heart's blood. It is probably true that there will always be inequality of ability. The number of born leaders is always limited.

Society will always group itself about its leaders, and the process of finding these leaders and putting them into the position in which their ability will have full play is one of the most serious tasks of humanity. The old method has been to select the oldest sons of certain men, a method which had the advantage of stability but of very little else. An isolated class is least fit for true leadership, because it is out of contact with the people, has least comprehension for their true need, and least inclination to serve them. Men of the people are the true leaders of the people. But as long as there is a pseudo-aristocracy to dazzle the vulgar eye and deflect the popular judgement, it will be much harder for the true aristocracy of intellect and character to gain the positions belonging to them by divine right.

It is not those who ask for equality that desire a dead level; it is those who desire to perpetuate hereditary inequality that practically keep the mass of the people, with all its latent powers, down on the dead level of a scramble for bread. The family demonstrates the co-existence of equal rights with unequal powers. From the father down to the baby there is a long gradation of ability, but there is a single grade of dignity and no right to exploit the weak. What father would tolerate it if the older children, because they are stronger and know more, should set up claim of doing least, eating best, and occupying the parlor alone while the others crowd into a cubby-hole? And if we, being evil, desire to see equality among our children, how much more will our Heavenly Father desire equality among us!

b. Wealth and Poverty

Christ's law of love is violated as soon as we love others less than ourselves. One way in which this greater love for self manifests and satisfies itself is by seeking special honor for ourselves; of that we have just spoken. Another way is by acquiring property at the expense of others, or keeping it for ourselves when others need it more. On this section of the law Christ's commands are especially full and emphatic.

Of course Jesus recognized that we have need of property. As we have life, so we need food to preserve it and clothing to shelter it, and our Father in Heaven, who has given us life, desires that we shall have all that is needful and has made most ample provision for us. (Matt. 6, 25-34.) So we are to do our work, cheerfully garner its produce, and eat of our Father's bounty with thankfulness of heart. It is foolish to worry and fret about the morrow, saying: "What shall we eat? What shall we drink? Wherewithal shall we be clothed?" All our fretting will accomplish little. The wisest way is to bear the burden of every day as it comes and let the morrow be anxious for itself. If God finds food for the birds of the heaven that sow not, reap not, and have no barns into which to gather their surplus, how much more is our life assured, who are of more account than they, in that we can sow, reap, and gather into barns? And if God clothes the lilies with beauty, though they toil and spin not, why should we fret about our clothing, to whom he has given deft hands to take the material of all creation and fit it to our wants? (Lk. 12, 22-31.)

Above all we are to remember that our material needs are only the foundation for the higher and real life. If like Martha of Bethany we are so absorbed in setting a good table that we let the choicest spiritual food pass by untasted, we are not choosing the good part. A body cannot well have two centres of gravity; and a life cannot well be devoted to the anxious care for material things and have much time and strength left for thought and for converse with the unseen. We cannot serve God and Mammon.

If another is in need and we have what he needs, of course we should give it to him. We should consider his needs and not our profit. We should not be carefully calculating the help we give our brother and wonder whether we shall get it all back. Any man will lend to another on good security; he need not be a Christian for that. (Lk. 6, 30-34.)

This seems to be Christ's ideal: every man working cheerfully, eating contentedly the fruit of his labor, making the life of the body the foundation for the spiritual life, and sharing with his brother who happens to be in need. The same conception was in John's mind when he advised men to live simply and honestly and to share with the needy, as the best preparation for the new society of the Messianic era. (Lk. 3, 10-14.) For a short time the church at Jerusalem realized this ideal, where they shared according to their needs and took their food with gladness and singleness of heart. (Acts 2, 44-47; 4, 32-35.) Such a form of society would indeed be one in which gladness would spring up like a fountain to sweeten the air. Love would be easy and mutual service a pleasure.

Now Jesus saw men living far differently. He saw them fretting and worrying for mere food and drink. He saw them saving and stinting themselves to lay up treasures for the future, and when they had succeeded, leaning back with a sigh of satisfaction: "There, my soul, it is done now; thou hast much goods laid up for many years: take thine ease, eat, drink, be merry." He saw that this care and this love for wealth was in many choking down higher thoughts, as the luxuriant thorns of Palestine outstrip the slow-growing grain. (Matt. 13, 7-22.) He saw that when a man was once entangled in the meshes of wealth there was next to no hope that he would break loose and become a member of the Kingdom and a lover of the truer life. (Matt. 19, 23-26.) He saw that in this mad scramble to secure themselves, men could so far forget the love they owe their fellowmen, that one man could be carousing in purple and fine linen, while another lay at his gate day by day in rags and hunger. (Lk. 16, 19-21.)

Of course this is foolish and wicked. But what shall we do? Shall we say: A man must not be *too* absorbed in money-getting; he must not become *too* rich; he must not forget the poor entirely? In other words, shall we acknowledge the necessity and rightfulness of the scramble but try to dull the roughest edge and check the worst brutality of it?

Jesus was far more radical. His demands cannot be designated by any milder word than revolutionary. He forbids the hoarding up of unused property entirely. (Matt. 6, 19-20.) He ridicules a typical case of selfish thrift, calls the man a fool, and shows how God snuffed out the light of his life when it was just beginning to sputter in the richest fat. (Lk. 12, 13-21.) He tells the story of a man who made clever provision for the future by giving away right and left what happened to be in his power now; and he advises the possessors of the mammon of unrighteousness to do the same, because at the coming of the Messianic Kingdom its use will collapse, and their only chance then will be that they have made friends among the children of the Kingdom, who will mercifully receive them into their tabernacles. (Lk. 16, 1-13.) When some of the Pharisees "who were lovers of money" turned up their noses at this story (as the Greek has it, Lk. 16, 14), he told them another one of a rich man who failed to use his wealth thus and one day found himself in the torments of Hades. (Lk. 16, 19-31.) A rich man, who seemed really willing to join him, was advised to get rid of his wealth as a preliminary, but Jesus found to his sorrow that his love of property was too much for the man. (Matt. 19, 16-22.) One case is recorded in which a man of position and wealth, touched by the brotherly freedom of Christ's presence, determined to give away one half of his property outright, and with the other half to make good all moral claims against him by paying them fourfold. This was indeed a camel going through the needle's eye and coming out on the other side without its humps. The words with which Jesus received this announcement evince the liveliest satisfaction. (Lk. 19, 1-10.)

In short, Christ forbids the citizens of his Kingdom to pile up wealth, and where it is already piled up, he commands them to disperse it. It takes little imagination to picture the changes which obedience to his command would produce in society.

Of course, the representatives of things as they are take no delight in these teachings. They would very willingly exchange them for more teaching on the nature of God or on love in general. The treatment of Christ's teachings on property is one of the most interesting chapters in the history of morals. The critics get at it by criticism. They doubt the genuineness of the parables of the rich fool, and of Dives and Lazarus. Luke who reports most of these sayings seems to them tainted by Ebionite ideas and so far untrustworthy. Others who regard Jesus merely as a teacher like others—like themselves, for instance—frankly contradict him. He was "a good soul, but a limited intellect," and he knew nothing about political economy. The greater part of the church of course is more reverent. It carefully leaves the shell of his teachings intact and scrapes out the contents by a proper exegesis of this sort: It is true that Jesus called the rich farmer a fool, but that was because the man did not remember the shortness of life. It is true that Jesus sent Dives to Sheol, but that was not because he was rich, but because he did not look after Lazarus; moreover the chief point of interest in that parable is not its bearing on wealth, but its revelations concerning the future life. It is true that Jesus bade the young ruler give away his property, but that was because in this special case his heart loved wealth more than God; if he had said, "Yes, Lord, I will," he might have kept it with safety, for then his heart would have been free. As for the parable of the unjust steward—well, that is a very difficult passage, on which we are reluctant to venture an opinion. The communism of the church at Jerusalem was peculiar to it alone, and God seems to have expressed his disapproval of it, for a few years later the church at Jerusalem was poor, which was probably the result of that communism. The command to give to him that asks and to lend without expectation of return must be interpreted by sanctified common sense, which tells us that indiscriminate charity is a great evil. On the whole, the teaching of Jesus must be considered in its general balance, expecially with an eye on that notable text: "The poor ye have always with you." Moreover Abraham and Solomon were rich, the apostles had boats, and Paul bids the rich not be highminded, but he says nothing about giving away all their property. By all this we see that Christ expected rich and poor to dwell together that in their interchange of love Christianity might be exercised. The rich must keep within the civil law, not acquire *too* much, give away at least a tenth of their income, and not set their heart on their wealth.

As a consequence of this dulling off of Christ's teaching we have a state of things in the church of Christ which is doing more to make Christianity a by-word and a hissing among the civilized nations than all the higher criticism in the world. The salt has lost its savour, and men are trampling it under foot, as Jesus foresaw. The writings of the Old Testament prophets show that in their day drunkenness existed and lewdness was rampant; but the sin which they denounce over and over and over again is neither intemperance nor unchastity, but the covetousness of the powerful which results in the oppression of the weak. With Christ the same proportion holds. There is no other ethical topic to which the Gospels devote so much space as to questions of property. Even Paul calls the love of money the root of all evils. (I Tim. 6, 5-10.) On the other hand, in the modern church a man must deal very carefully with questions of property. He may speak as plainly as he pleases against intemperance, but let him weigh his words well if he deals with injustice. Is it not by the wincing of the patient that the physician detects the seat of disease? The New Testament puts lasciviousness and covetousness on an equal footing of guilt. Does the church do the same? I have heard of many exclusions from church fellowship for causes of impurity. But though I have made continued inquiry, I have so far heard of but three cases of exclusion for covetousness. They occurred in small and poor churches, and in two cases out of the three the proof of the covetousness was that the persons concerned contributed nothing to the church, though well capable of doing so. There are thousands of inquiries to be dealt with every year by Christian ministers and some of them are rich. Suppose we grant that the demand made of the young ruler was exceptional and not a general rule. Still his case must recur now and then. Has anyone ever heard of a Christian minister repeating Christ's demand? I know of one case where an able-bodied man, living "on his income," was refused admission to a little church till he should earn his living, because the Bible said: "He that will not work neither shall he eat." The man acknowledged that the point was well taken and was subsequently looking for work.

The church is, on the whole, more backward in this department of the ethics of Jesus than in any other. And yet it is exactly on this territory that the world is fighting its battle in this generation. The social question is confessedly the question of our age, and the social question deals primarily with property. If therefore we undertake to set forth the bearing of Christ's teaching more fully, we do so for the sake of the Kingdom, and not because we expect to reap any harvest of love or gain through it.

It seems to me that the teaching of Jesus on property is an entirely plain doctrine, coherent in itself and well backed by reason, so that there is no excuse for those who make it nebulous. When Jesus says that there is something in wealth which makes the entrance into the Kingdom next to impossible for its possessor, he must mean that the possession of wealth is very closely bound up with injustice and selfishness, which are the contradiction of the justice and love of the Kingdom. Let us examine why they are so closely bound up.

1. *It is not possible to get great wealth except by offending against justice.*

If we run over, in our mind, the large fortunes of our own country, we find that they are nearly all traceable to the following sources: city real estate, mineral lands, banking, monopoly of means of traffic, speculation in stock or produce, and patents. It can, I think, be demonstrated that there is an element of injustice and lovelessness in every one of these, and that it is this element of injustice and lovelessness which gives these lines of business their productive faculty. Without going into economic discussion or attempting to support these assertions by reasoning, I will indicate where the wrong seems to lie.

In the real estate of cities, growing as most of our American cities do, there is an increase in the value of the ground which is not traceable to the labor or expense of the owner, but which is due to the existence and industry of the entire community. It should therefore in justice return to the community to serve in defraying the expenses of the communal life. Instead, it goes to the private owners, and it is this and not personal exertion which has built up the estates of the Astors, Goelets, Rhinelanders, of Snug Harbor, Trinity Church, Grace Church, Collegiate Dutch Reformed Church, etc. It is the effort to appropriate this public product which causes speculation in city real estate, keeps city lots vacant, and causes the crowding of our cities. The price of the vacant land rises chiefly because the people are so crowded and suffer so, that they are willing to pay more to escape. Land value rises by the sweat of men and the suffering of women and children. Is it not injustice and lovelessness to accept wealth at that price? If Christ came to New York, would he approve of wealth drawn from city real estate?

A second source of wealth is the possession of land giving access to mineral wealth, e.g., to deposits of coal, silver, iron, oil, etc. Men need these minerals for their work or their comfort. Those who work these deposits and prepare the material for use are justly entitled to a return for their labor and expense. But it is well known that the price charged for these products in many cases includes not only a return for labor and expense, but a payment for the substance itself. This would be just only if the substance, the iron or coal, really belonged to the so-called owners. It does not. They did not make it or cause it to be buried there. It is part of the means of life which God has prepared for all his children. Individuals hold it only by right of appropriation. Suppose a mother were obliged to leave her children for a day. She leaves the pantry well stocked. The oldest boy in her absence makes a claim of owning the goodies, and the hungry little ones are obliged to surrender their playthings if they want any. That boy will be spanked when his mother comes home. He might perhaps have demanded a reward if the eatables were stored on the top shelf which only he could reach. But to ask pay for the food itself was injustice. It was also lovelessness, for he got the playthings only because his brothers and sisters suffered. The cost of anthracite coal in New York is said to be about twice the cost of production and transportation. That extra fifty percent creates the wealth of the mine owners, and in that fifty percent lies their injustice and their lovelessness; for men pay so much because cold hurts, rheumatism tortures, and pneumonia kills.

A third source of wealth is banking, the commercial management of money. In this also there is a legitimate service to be rewarded and an unjust privilege which is the chief source of profit. The subject is too intricate to be briefly stated. The people of the United States are rapidly coming to see that the medium of exchange, the commercial life-blood of the nation, has been manipulated in the interest of the banking business; legislation conferring unjust privileges has been served, artificial stringencies created, and times of national distress, like the Civil War, have been dexterously used to enrich those who had money and still further to deplete those who had none.

A fourth source of wealth is the ownership of the means of communication, railroads, street-cars, telegraphy, telephone, etc. All these are undertakings which cannot come into being unless public properties are granted for their use and public rights exercised on their behalf, and it is this public element in them which lifts their profit above that of ordinary business. There would be no injustice in the private working of railroads, if a profit were made only on that which the private persons really contribute to their working; but in that case the fortune of the Vanderbilts and Goulds would never have been made. The injustice consists in making private profit out of the monopoly feature, which is a contribution of the public. The lovelessness consists in making dearer than need be the cost of transporting the means of life, and of making difficult or impossible the visiting of friends or lovers, the change in climate for the sick, and all the intercourse of men in which the chief enjoyment of life consists.

A fifth source of wealth is speculation in stock on produce. Here also there is a legitimate foundation and an unjust superstructure. Brokerage is a necessary function of a complex commercial system. But by plain brokerage men do not grow rich. The fortunes made on exchange are not pay for work done, though we confess that the knowing done in the New York Stock Exchange or the Chicago Wheat Pit deserves a larger pay than most other physical labor. A railroad president once said to the writer: "These men who go up and down town on the L roads between eight and five, they really do something; they add value to what they work on. But we who go down town at ten create nothing; we only try to take things away from one another." It was good-humored self-ridicule and exaggeration, but it was also truth. The fortunes changing hands in the Produce Exchange must finally come from somewhere. The men who make them stand as middle-men between the farmers who raise the grain and the people who eat it. Whatever is lost in the transit between the farmer's hand and the laborer's mouth must be a loss to either of these or both. It will be difficult for the speculators to prove that their service in meditating between producers and consumers is worth the profit extracted by them out of the business. And if they artificially enhance the price of that by which the people live and without which they suffer, where are their justice and love?

The last source of large fortunes mentioned is the possession of patents. An inventor of anything useful to men ought to be rewarded. He ought in many cases to be rewarded more highly than many poor inventors are, who are compelled to part with their rights under pressure of need and see them exploited by others. There are only some patents which are, as it were, the padlocks which individuals have succeeded in fastening on the doors giving access to new forces or materials of nature; these can be made the source of immense profit, and this profit is due not so much to the invention as to the natural force which lies back of it and of which man stands in need. In that case our parable of the boy and the pantry is again to the point. It is hardly true to say that without the holder of the patent that force would not have become available. In the case of almost all great inventions a number of men reached the idea almost simultaneously, and, as the patent litigations show, it is often due only to the mildest haste that one man succeeds in putting in his claim before the other. Mankind needs that force of nature and mankind will get it, if not through one man, then through another. It is questionable justice that the man who has struck the last blow of the pick, at which the water gushed out, shall have the right to wave thirsting humanity back and for a long term retail the water at his own price. It is the greatness of the possible unearned gain which dazzles so many honest men, sets them to leave their trade to go inventing, and finally lose their family happiness and perhaps their minds over it. The lovelessness of those who exploit the monopoly in their inventions is even more apparent than the injustice. For instance, the company controlling the Westinghouse brake charges a heavy price for every car supplied with their brake. As a consequence, the freight-trains of most railroads are still provided only with the old hand-brake, the operating of which entails a steady annual loss of life by accidents and another steady loss of health by exposure. Of course the railway companies might introduce the brake in spite of its cost, but the cost certainly is deterrent. If the patent is finally introduced, it will be because the loss of life and consequent expense couple to it. So here again the wealth is made by the suffering of others.

To these sources most of the large American fortunes are traceable, and if businessmen are at present gaining wealth fast, they will most likely have tapped one or more of the aforementioned sources. But if our reasoning is only in a measure correct, it would be impossible to gain large fortunes in these ways without constantly setting justice and love aside.

Even in the common business life of to-day it is hard to see how a man may acquire wealth fast under ordinary circumstances and yet have a tender regard for justice and love. The golden rule of competitive industry is to buy in the cheapest market and sell in the dearest; that is, to give your neighbor as little as you can and to get as much from him as you can. That may be justice, but is it love? Would not love require that you should give the product of your work as cheaply as you can afford, and pay your brother for his work as much as you can afford? We are not so sanguine that we hope to see the law of the market reversed. Nor can a man at present entirely avoid acting according to it even in buying a loaf of bread. But is it not true that he who would gain wealth in a business life governed by that law must appropriate that law and act heartily according to it? And if he does, he will surely take advantage of the needs of his neighbor. He will watch for opportunities to buy when his neighbor is pressed for money and has to sell cheaply. He will try to sell what men most need, in order to get the highest price from it. It is all coining money out of your fellows' distress.

A party of travelers came to the camp of an Arab sheik, astray, footsore, and quite out of food. They asked for bread, for dates, for milk, for anything to eat. The sheik ordered his servants to bring out a tempting array of food, but when the strangers were about to fall to, he asked them first to pay him twenty pieces of gold. The indignant travelers exclaimed against such extortion, for the food was not worth a single piece. The Arab smiled benignly and said: "Allah, whose name be blessed, brought a stranger here a year ago who slept in my tent. Going, he left a foreign book which with the aid of an interpreter I have read. It is entitled *Political Economy*. From this book I have learned that the price of a thing is not what it cost me to produce it, but what I can get you to pay for it. I learned also that it is a law of heaven that every man buys in the cheapest market and sells in the dearest. You are my dearest market. I have not a complete monopoly of food in this desert, for there is another camp five miles from here. But you are weary, the night is falling, and you cannot expect me to show you the way. The price is high, but the food is worth more to you. You are free to buy or not to buy. The food is mine to sell or not to sell. This is a free contract." The travelers paid twenty pieces of gold and swore. The sheik blessed Allah for revealing to him the wisdom of the foreigners.

This extreme case displays the principle in its crudest form. But is it not true that he who pushes this principle to its farthest feasible limit avails himself of the needs of others, and that only he who pushes it with cleverness and determination can acquire wealth in modern business life?

Indeed, the entire wage system is a system of taking advantage of our fellow-men. An employer pays his men not according to what they produce, but according to what he can get them to work for. And he can get them to work for less than the net proceeds of their labor, because they are in need of food and shelter, and for some reason can find no chance to employ their labor in such a way as to get the whole proceeds. That is taking advantage of their necessity (for his own advantage), and that is not love.

It would be easy to extend this discussion indefinitely to show that it is hard for any man to engage in business today without being in constant temptation to close his heart to generosity and manly squareness, and that it is hard indeed for a man greatly to "prosper" in business without succumbing to the temptation.

I do not mean to deny that men who have gained wealth may be tender husbands and fathers and generous friends. Some of the most terrible men on Wall Street are known for their delightful family life. I do not mean to assert either that they are always conscious of doing wrong when they employ the means of money-making which all the world about them is employing. The guilt of social wrong lies on the entire society which permits it to exist. There is not a thinking man in America who is not to some extent responsible for every exploitation of human weakness under our business system. And yet we cannot, as some do, put the whole blame on the system. Within certain limits the individual is free to obey the system or not to obey it. And it would be hard to persuade me that, for instance, the directors of the New York Elevated Roads, when they united their lines and watered their joint stock to escape paying part of their profit over to the public according to law, were not conscious of doing wrong.

In short, it is hard for a rich man, who has gained his riches himself to enter the Kingdom, because money-getting is not well compatible with the justice and love of the Kingdom of Jesus. It is still true, as in Paul's day, that "they who desire to be rich fall into a temptation and a snare and many foolish and hurtful lusts, which drown men in destruction and perdition." (I Tim. 6, 6-10.) And yet men think themselves happy if they have a chance of falling into that temptation and think their lives well spent if they can see their children firmly caught in that snare.

2. *As a man cannot well gain wealth without sacrificing the Christian virtues, so he cannot well possess wealth without damage to his own soul.*

The common church doctrine is that it does not matter how much a man has, but how he uses what he has. People are fond of quoting Christ's explanation as reported by Mark (10, 23-24), "how hard it is for them that *trust* in riches to enter into the Kingdom of God." It is exactly the meaning of Christ that they who have riches are certain to put their faith and heart into them. Christ expressed a profound fact when, in connection with his commandment not to hoard wealth, he said, "for where thy treasure is, there will thy heart be also." It is a magnetic force, the sinister attraction of the *Hort* of the Nibelungen, to which even those are victims who think they are masters of it. Charles Dudley Warner in his *Little Journey in the World,* a novel of delightful delicacy and self-control, has told the story of the gradual crumbling of a noble character under the influence of wealth and society. Our fiction is full of such, and our real life fuller yet.

We frequently hear protests against the habit of denouncing the rich as a class and lauding the poor as a class. The assertion is that both have equal temptations and equal chances of being bad. I deny it. If the chances are equal, why does Christ make them unequal? Why does he say that it is hard for a rich man to enter the Kingdom, and not that it is hard for *any* man? Why does he pronounce blessings upon the poor, upon those that hunger now and weep now, and woes upon those who are rich, and upon those who are full now and laugh now? (Lk. 6, 20-26.) To explain this passage spiritually, by speaking of spiritual humility and weeping for sin and of religious self-satisfaction and carelessness, does violence to the text taken by itself. Matthew gives the beatitudes a more spiritual turn (5, 3-9); but unless we reject either account as unfaithful, we must suppose that the same class was poor, hungry, and crushed in temporal affairs and lowly, meek, and mourning in religious needs. If we picture to ourselves the Galilean peasants flocking about Christ, we can easily understand the union of bodily and spiritual needs. There were many, like the palsied man, who needed to hear the word of bodily and spiritual help. Those throngs who followed Christ into the desert places were so hungry for righteousness that they listened to him all day, and so inured to physical want that they had made no provision for a lunch-basket on leaving home, as a better-fed people is sure to do. In the psalms and prophets the "poor man" is also the weak and God-fearing man, who puts his trust in Jehovah in the face of the oppression of the mighty. Matthew and Luke have each given one side of the Old Testament *aniyim;* Matthew reports Jesus calling "the poor in spirit" blessed; Luke reads, blessed are "ye poor." Those who today side with the poor as a class against the rich as a class are quite in harmony with biblical conceptions.

The brightest virtues and the truest lives are with the common people, to-day as in Galilee; not with the pauper class, nor with the upper class, but with the great body of the people who earn their living in the sweat of their brow. They do not get a dollar without doing an ample dollar's worth of work for it, whatever others may do. They suffer wrong far oftener than they do it. Men call them discontented. They are not. They are not as impatient, or restless, as lustful for change, as blasè to the simple pleasures of life, as those who have all the appliances for happiness. Their patience is a marvel. It is no wonder that poets and artists, once they have come to know them, love them and pour the richest colors of their sunsets about the peasants' prayer and work. Christ loved them too.

The poor are brave; the rich are timid. The common people fought the Civil War, while the rich made money out of it. The wealthy classes of England sided with the slave-holders; the poor cotton-spinners of England, once they understood the bearings of the war, sided with the North and starved. The year 1848 was the revolutionary year of the European people. The general distrust of the future found its accurate barometer in the savings banks. They showed a general decrease in the number of accounts and a tendency of the people to keep their cash in hand or to hide it in old boots. But this timidity was greater in the larger accounts. In the savings banks of Saxony the number of accounts under 20 thaler actually increased from 1847-48 by 4.4 percent. Those between 20-50 thaler decreased 1.1 percent; 50-100 th. decreased 3.6 percent; 100-200 th. decreased 7.9 percent; over 200 th. decreased 11.3 percent. That is to say, the poorest people, to whom their few thaler meant most, were yet the most hopeful and stable element. The timidity and anxiety increased in rapid ratio with the wealth of the depositors. This timidity of wealth makes it a reactionary element in every reform.

The greatest generosity is not found with the rich. Their gifts are heralded and praised. They have all the incentives of ambition and public admiration to spur them to liberality. And yet it is not the rich who cast in much who get the praise of the just man sitting over against the treasury. It is the poor widow who gets his praise. It is rare that a rich man gives as much, proportionately, as many a laboring man gives habitually. Probably any pastor of a working class congregation has seen gifts which, according to Christ's method of book-keeping, would count for more than anything he has read about in the papers. Even if the rich man and the poor man give in the same proportion, their gifts are not equal. If a workingman earning $15 a week gives a tenth, he has $13.50 left to support himself and his family. If a rich man earning $150 a week gives a tenth, he has $135 left to support a family which is probably smaller. The amount needed for the absolute necessities of life is about the same for every man's stomach. Cut that out of the $13.50, and there is not much left; cut it out of the $135, and there is a great deal left which can go for the unnecessary. The man who gives $15 out of $150 is like a man on a cold day wrapped in warm clothing, fur-coat, fur-cap, fur mittens, and a light muffler about his throat. He meets a freezing child, takes off the muffler, gives it to the child, turns up his fur collar, and goes on about as comfortable as before. The man giving $1.50 out of $15 is like a man wearing a single thin over-coat and giving that to the child, while he goes on beating himself with his arms to keep warm. How much would the wife of a rich man have to put down as a charity subscription in order to equal the sacrifice of a woman who bends over the wash-tub all week and who, after finishing her day's stint, goes over to a sick neighbor to do up her week's washing? Such unpretentious deeds of love and heroism are being done all the time and without making a fuss about it.

The possession of wealth is the insidious destroyer of character. The children of the rich are exposed to sore temptations. It would be easy to find middle-class families who can trace their family back for generations of solid, clean, capable men of business or the professions, and the stock is still as good as new. Rich families deteriorate.

But more insidious is the deterioration of the finer faculties of the soul, of truthfulness, simplicity, generosity, daring. Wealth blights these. The social forms of high society are full of untruth. Life is artificial. The simple verities of life become nebulous themes for conversation, flints out of which to strike the sparks of wit. The perceptions are keen, but knowledge and obedience are divorced. Such society is the hot-bed of skepticism. It is sterile of high thinking and of courageous action. Young men of promise who marry rich wives seldom do anything great. A rich man cannot well fight the cause of the people which is the cause of God. London society is the undoing of popular reformers. Send a man to Parliament, let him be invited in a few social circles, let him get money enough to keep a horse of his own, and his politics will change. Poor people need their children for their support in old age, but they send them out as foreign missionaries. Rich people have enough to support themselves and to make life easy for their children on the foreign field. We hear occasionally of a wealthy man's daughter who desires to go, but she does not go. Her parents cannot spare her.

Was the case of the young ruler who turned away sorrowfully an isolated case? Did Christ mean anything less than he said when he called it hard for a rich man to enter the Kingdom? Is it not a solemn truth that a man's life consists not in the abundance of the things that he possesses? Why do Christian men desire to possess much? Why do they spur their children on to gain much? And why do Christian ministers not warn those who are about to slay their higher life on the altar of Mammon, as they would warn them if they saw them drifting into intemperance or licentiousness?

3. *In the getting and in the having of riches there is danger to their possessor.*

Therefore Christ warns against riches and commands the surrender of them. Besides, the owner of wealth is not qualified for citizenship in the Kingdom, because its citizens must build up, and not destroy, the perfect human society. The rich as a class do not make a true life easy for the rest of mankind, but hard.

It has come to be a proverb that the tramp is the corollary of the millionaire. Where Dives is, Lazarus must be too, if not at his gate, then on Blackwell's Island or in the East Side Tenement. If some have more than they earn, others must have less than they earn.

But neither wealth nor extreme poverty is conducive to the best life. Each is full of temptations, the subtle and gilded temptations for the rich, the sordid and brutal for the poor. But the guilt for both classes of temptation lies on the rich. No one compels the rich to be rich; the poor, on the contrary, though individually they may often be at fault, are not poor because they love to be so, but because they are compelled to be so.

The condition in which men are most secure against temptation and most useful as constituents of society prevails where they work steadily for their daily bread, without the immediate pressure of want or the haunting fear of it, with a comfortable home, and leisure enough to read a good book, to see their friends, and to take an interest in public affairs. That used to be the condition of life in America. A nation consisting of such men is a great nation. The English yeomen were the material for England's greatness and freedom. With the growth of a wealthy class, this middle class is cut into, at once from the top and the bottom. There are districts of Germany divided into farms; there are others divided into great estates and worked by laborers. Where will the most solid men be raised? Where will public safety and decency be most insecure? The farm laborer is the complement of the landed proprietor; the city proletarian is the complement of the money king.

The very poor, whose lives are squalid and insecure, are the first victims to temptation. Every added pressure carries some of them out from honesty into crime, as every icy wave loosens a feeble grasp in the spars of the ship-wrecked vessel. M. Parent-Duchatelet examined carefully into the history of 5183 prostitutes in Paris. He found that 2398 had been put on the downward path by some first sin of frailty. 2696 had gone into it because they were generally poor and wretched or without helping relatives; 37 to feed old parents, 29 to maintain younger brothers and sisters, 23 because they found no other way of supporting their own children. Of 3084, whom the same careful investigator examined as to their occupation, he found that only three had a little property, a fixed income of from 200-1000 francs. It is the "fingers thin" that "push from them faintly want and sin." When want becomes too strong, the sin is pushed away no longer. In England, in years of scarcity, the number of youthful prostitutes rises above the average, and falls below it in years of plenty. It would remain to be seen how the percentage would decrease if all the girls had a fair chance of a good living and a happy marriage. To repeat: the outward temptation and the inward desire combine to produce sin. Therefore Christ bids us pray our Father to lead us not into temptation. The church as the Body of Christ is to serve in answering this prayer. It is to lessen temptation and not to increase it. But the existence of wealth increases temptation. It first takes from the poor and renders them needy. Then it comes and tempts them with wealth in accumulated splendor and plunges them in sin. Those who make rent artificially dear make homes hard to form. Those who make coal artificially dear drive the lonely young man or girl into the bright and warm palaces of sin. There are two destructive and dangerous classes. The one is at the top, the other is at the bottom. But it is the strong, who have elbowed their way to the top, who will be held responsible for themselves and for the weak ones whom their climbing feet have pressed down into the mud. And after they have pressed them down, they turn around and ask: "Why are you so dirty? Why do you delight in groveling in the mire?"

Wealth dissocializes society. All that we have said on that score about rank holds of wealth, because wealth today confers rank. The wealthy man is not the brother of the poor man, whatever moral somersaults he may perform to make himself believe so. It would take a great soul indeed for him not to patronize his poor neighbor. And it will take a greater soul yet in the poor man to accept the advances of his rich neighbor as the friendship of an equal. Wealthy men who really try to meet the poor on their own terms are constantly foiled by the suspicions and sensitiveness of the poor. It is the price which they have to pay for their wealth. They gain dollars and lose brothers.

Christianity desires to bind humanity together. Difference in wealth cuts it asunder. Christianity desires to remove the stumbling blocks from the path of the weak. Wealth strews them broad-cast. Shall the enemy who sows the tares be hired to help in the husbandry of the Kingdom of God? Does it seem so strange that Christ demands of high officers in the army of Mammon that they shall resign their position and strip off their insignia before they enlist as soldiers in the army of God?

4. *Wealth is incompatible with the Kingdom.*

Not only does wealth harm its possessor and trip others; but if it does enter the Kingdom, it corrupts Christianity itself. And if the devil can unsalt the salt and sterilize the leaven, he will pat himself for a good day's work.

The admission of wealth into the church has delayed the acceptance of Christ's law. We may as well be frank. We Christians *are* anxious for the morrow. We do not give to him that asks, nor lend to anyone that requires a loan. We do not give our cloak to him that takes our coat. We insist everywhere on strict obedience to the plain commands of Christ, and yet we do not even pretend to obey these precepts. Why not? In most cases probably because we want the things ourselves and do not propose to give them away. But some have actually tried this "promiscuous charity" and have found that it worked harm. What shall we say then? Was Christ less wise than we? Or did he solemnly enjoin duties which he did not expect anybody to live up to till the millennium?

Hardly. The difficulty lies here: Rich men try to make ethics work which were meant for men who live the simple and natural life enjoined by Jesus. If a man has a great pile of wealth, more than other people about him, of course they all lust for it and try to get some share of it, and if it were known that he would give to anyone that asks they would quickly relieve him of his surplus. Indeed, it sometimes seems that the assurance with which people ask of those who possess, and the resentment which they feel when refused, are due to the deeply implanted instinct of human brotherhood. That instinct makes us risk our lives to rescue a drowning beggar. Why should it not make the beggar feel that, if his brother has bread, he has a right to part of it? Here also corruption of the noblest instinct is the worst.

But if a man in want asks the help of one who lives day by day on the produce of his toil, there is nothing much to arouse the man's cupidity. He can only be made free to a seat at the table or to an extra coat. Or if he wants to borrow, he will find no tremendous sums to be drawn. He may borrow a tool or some seed-corn. But whatever he gets, he will always feel that "my brother is stripping himself for my sake; he will eat less; he will have no extra coat." And this sacrifice in the giver does act as a check on the receiver, except in the case of very abandoned characters. Instead of encouraging shiftlessness, it will reprove it.

There are many good, plain people who by natural instinct obey this law of Christ. Their task is made difficult for them by the false conditions created by the wealthy, and by the pauper habits awakened and fostered by the existing inequalities. Many a farmer in times past would never have let a wayfarer pass from his door hungry or without shelter. But since the distress has become frequent in the manufacturing centers, and men out of work first had to take to the road and then by idleness and vicious companionship have learned to love it, the farmer has had to be more careful of the tramp. The just suffer for the unjust. The disease germs bred in a filthy neighborhood float over into the cleanly home. The plain man in the country is hindered from obeying Christ's law by the effect of wealth gathering in the cities.

In the same way Christ's law of trust has been difficult by wealth. He bids us live like the ravens and lilies. But how can a man live so, when it is almost a certainty that he will be laid off two months out of the twelve? When improvements in his trade are projected which will make half the men useless? When twenty men answer an advertisement for a single man? Even the lily would droop if flag-stones were laid about it on every side, catching the rain, and if heavy foilage were trained above it, intercepting the sunshine. Suppose a few ancient ravens should set up a claim of owning the fields and exact every third worm or grain as rent from the new ones for scratching in their fields, would not a look of care come over the new ravens' faces too? Christ bids us seek the Kingdom of God and God's righteousness, and all "these things" would be added to us. It is very true; in the measure in which God's will and God's justice order human society, in that measure will the needs of our lives be satisfied without fretful worry. And those who for private profit keep the Kingdom at a distance make it hard to live a life of trust. The rich cannot well live it. He that has a number of Government bonds between him and starvation may think he trusts God, but in fact he trusts God plus the bonds. And for the poor the life of trust is also made hard. Who will talk of trust to a farmer whose back is bent and whose hands can hardly straighten out, and who yet is running behind every year, thanks to scarce money and a plentiful tariff? Who will talk of trust to a small store-keeper whose trade is being absorbed by the big bazaars, and who cannot keep up a whole store on profits with which they keep up only a single counter? If a man loves wife and children, his very love will throw him into feverish anxiety and make him disobey Christ.

So we lay it upon the disobedience to Christ's primary law against riches that all the minor laws of charitable help and of trust are made impossible to the rich and difficult to the poor. Every step toward the social equalization of wealth would bring Christ's ethics within the bounds of the possible. If the unrighteous sources of wealth were cut off, there would be no such inequality of possession as there is now. There could not be. Men are by nature unequal, but they are not unequal enough to justify anything like the present inequality of wealth. And when the weakness and inertia of generations of poverty shall have been eliminated by plentiful food and intellectual stimulus (and America has proved that it can be done in two generations), then the inequality will be still more reduced, and we shall have that soundest and most delightful society, the society of intellectual and social equals.

Then, with the assured basis of life which nature conquered by man will give, with no haunting fear of starvation, a life of trust in God and of flourishing in the sunshine of his love, will be possible to more than the most heroic souls. Ah, but Christ says: "The poor ye have always with you." Yes, Christ was right, of course. At least eighteen centuries have corroborated his words. Perhaps he foresaw that there would be always people who would seize on a text like that and run it like a hand-spike into the wheels of social progress, and thus keep the poor in society. But there will always be the poor. There will always be slaves to passion who will waste their substance. There will always be the sick who need a friendly hand. There will always be the aged and the very young, who will need protection and love. There will always be the widowed, who have buried their beloved, and the lonely ones, who have never possessed their beloved. Truly there will always be the poor, and opportunity enough for suffering to do its chastening work, and for love to do its healing work. And if all the other poor should fail, there would still perhaps be one so feeble that he could not distinguish a declarative sentence from an imperative, and would insist on changing: "The poor ye have always with you," into, "Strive to have the poor always with you."

In a community governed by righteousness, there would still be opportunity for love. And only there could love do its unhampered work. The fault in our modern charity is that love is made to do the work of justice, an upside-down arrangement which makes even the simple precepts of Jesus appear unwise and impracticable. Such masses of poverty as our great cities possess have not been created by private fault or misfortune but by social injustice, and therefore of course private charity cannot cope with it, but social justice must put a stop to its production. Charity is best administered by personal friends and neighbors. They know best when the other is in need and what he needs, and when they help the suffering one out, it has no pauperizing effect. There is still a vast amount of this mutual help among the working classes. When the number of sufferers becomes so great, or their friends are so destitute, that a great charitable machinery is necessary, it is in itself a proof that there is something wrong in society. And then the best love will be that which, while relieving the greatest distress, labors away to remove the social injustice. Charity can never be more than supplementary to justice. All honor to the workers in the charitable societies; but they know best the weary hopelessness of their task. They know how often they do evil by doing good, and how charity itself becomes destructive. The idea of charitable machinery! That means loving machinery, and how can machinery love, even when loving women are part of it? Truly has Lowell said:

Not what we give, but what we share,
For the gift without the giver is bare.

Modern charity divorces the gift and the giver. The giver does not know the receiver and the receiver does not know the giver. No wonder Christianity of that sort becomes an evil.

This prostitution of religion itself is brought about by the alliance of Christianity and wealth. Religion should do away with riches. Instead, it allows wealth to manufacture poverty and then accepts the alms of wealth to undo in a lame fashion the evil that has been wrought. But instead of undoing it, it adds new evils. And so the evils roll into a snarl that men despair to see unwound. Thus will it be, except in a Christianity that does not fear to be radical and revolutionary. Public justice and then private charity, that is the only true order.

The co-existence of wealth and poverty makes the morality of Jesus difficult of comprehension and still more difficult of obedience. It also corrupts the spirituality of the Christian religion.

Is it not a significant fact that wherever the contrasts of rich and poor in modern civilization are greatest, there materialism and unbelief are greatest also? What great city is there in civilized nations that is not godless? The proportion of church attendance everywhere is smallest in the great cities. Why is this? It would be foolish to assign it to only one cause, but it is surely not wrong to attribute part of it to the existence of wealth and poverty.

The wealthy class, which contaminates the morality of the working classes, also saps their religious faith. The wealthy classes of England and America are still religious after the velvet-bound-prayer-book fashion. Religion is part of respectability. But on the Continent, where the rich have emancipated themselves, they are the bearers of a practical materialism which justifies itself by a cynical skepticism. How has France come to be irreligious? Her irreligion is not of recent growth. It began in the dissolute aristocracy of the last century, which settled God with an epigram. From there lust and unbelief, uniting in a deadlier poison, trickled down into the lower classes. Robespierre objected to atheism because it was aristocratic. The same thing has been true in Germany. A socialist in the Reichstag charged the bourgeoisie with having made unbelief fashionable and with having originated the pessimistic materialism of the common people. And now the wealthy classes in Europe, having made religion contemptible to the people by their ridicule of it, make Christianity hateful by enlisting the church on their behalf. They have found that the wind they have sown has raised them a harvest of whirlwind. They tremble at the red terror and beckon to the priest to exorcise it. And the priest founds charitable institutions with the rich man's money and preaches to the masses that "the rich and the poor must dwell together," and that we must "give honor to whom honor is due."

Another cause for the religious indifference of the great cities is the grinding hardness of the life of the poor. To live away from the mountains, the meadows, the sea, and from all the handiwork of God; to be cooped up in a tenement-walled street with nothing but brick and iron; to live all the day among whirling wheels making a few mechanical motions; to drag a weary body home only to find a querulous wife, a sloppy supper, a dingy bed; if these are not enough to take the ideal thoughts and aspirations to which religion appeals out of a man's heart, what is? What is there of God in the dreary labyrinth of the East End of London, or in the drearier rectangles of the East Side of New York? What language would God speak to a Job living in a tenement? How would he make known his majesty to one who has never seen the Pleiades through the city smoke, who sees the treasures of the snow only in the slush and inspects leviathan and behemoth behind the bars at Central Park? How can we complain if the socialists' ideal is an idealized factory and a glorified tenement house? That is what we have shut the working people up to. How can we complain that they believe in materialism and hold the whole world to be a great machine with merciless cogs, a world of matter in which brute pleasure is the aim and brute force and selfishness are the means? That is the sort of world they live in. The marvel is that any trace of the ideal remains in them. This unbelief and religious indifference of the masses are another count in the indictment against our unjust and loveless civilizations, and since Christ and humanity cannot call the whole corporation to account just yet, the warrants are out against its directors and agents, the protagonists, the embodiment, tools, and profiters of the evil. Let not the wealthy classes protest indignantly against the judgement beginning everywhere. It is God's judgement through humanity.

But the most effectual damage done to Christianity lies in wealth and power gaining control of the church and using it as a tool. Constantine was the far-seeing man to begin it, and in the most varied forms it has continued to this day. The process is very natural. The clergy are educated. They find more affinity among the wealthy than among the poor and ignorant. Their natural tendency is to draw away from the poor. Only a powerful spiritual impulse and conviction can keep the clergy down with the people. The same is true of labor leaders and all other leaders of the people. Then, when the interests of the poor clash with those of the rich, they incline to side with those who possess so much more enlightenment and refinement, everything that passes for a higher life with all except the most spiritual eyes. Also, with the help of the wealthy and powerful so much good can be done. Have influence with a king, and you can get immunity from taxation for the church lands. Have influence with a rich man, and you can build a hospital. Is it not the duty of the servants of God to cultivate the wealthy, persuade them to consecrate their talents to the service of the Lord, and then teach the people gratitude to their benefactors? Would it not be wrong to offend them by hasty words?

Some of the best impulses have made good men subservient to the wealthy and have silenced their tongues against wrong. The wiser among the wealthy know the power of ideas and of a clergy rising as tribunes of the people. They are trained and dexterous in using influence, social favor, and patronage to tie the young reformer with silken bands.

It cannot be denied that the church as a whole, while it contains good democratic material, is largely under aristocratic management. The Roman Catholic Church has its monarchical constitution. In the established churches of Protestant countries, the minister is allowed considerable freedom of movement, but there are limits, as he knows after he has passed them and as his wife knows before he passes them. Our American churches are the continuation largely of dissenting movements in Europe, which sprang up among the people and therefore contain a more popular religion and a more democratic form of government. But even in the freest denominations wealth is making its power felt. The forms of worship are becoming refined. The aesthetic element is becoming more prominent. There are wealthy congregations and poor congregations. The wealthy churches make their power felt in the denomination, for from them come the sinews of war. Religion needs money, a great deal of it, and therefore those who have money are important persons to the Kingdom of God. They are elected into the boards of Home and Foreign and City Mission Societies, Education Societies, Church Edifice Societies, every sort of society. The men of whom Jesus said that they shall with difficulty get into the Kingdom have checkmated him. They have got in and they run things. The minds that have discovered the ways of making money out of the poor sit in the board and devise ways of carrying good tidings to them. The hearts that have proved their proficiency in worldly wisdom now meditate the deep things of the Spirit. Above all, they deliberate on "how to reach the masses." Ah, the confession that lies in that threadbare phrase! So we have to reach them? There is a gulf fixed between us? We are not the masses, not of them, not in them; we are above somewhere, discussing how to reach them. The cork is trying to dive into the water. There was a time when the Christians were the masses, fishermen, tent-weavers, low-browed slaves, garlic-eating Jews, a sinister mass to fill the mind of the philosopher with disgust and the mind of the statesman with vague alarm. That is all changed now. The cross is on our highest domes. We wear it as an ornament in gold and jewels. Christianity now is great, recognized as a power. The princes of the world lay their trophies at its feet.

And there are the people down yonder. We ought to reach them. We ought to persuade them that "at the foot of the cross alone the social question can be solved." But they run after agitators and demagogues.

It was the first Sunday in May. I rode through London on the top of a bus. It was very quiet. Well-dressed people were going into the churches. Well-dressed people were going into the chapels. Fine quarters and dingy quarters; but where was the vulgar herd? Ah, here it comes, a mob rolling through the street, ragged boys, jeering girls, a little string of blue and red in the middle, a big drum, a few plain, sober, bright-eyed faces. God bless them, they are still of the people. We approach Hyde Park. What a crowd! Thousands, tens of thousands, hundreds of thousands. They are talking, making love, lying on the grass, eating oranges. These are the people. There is no end to the march, brawny union black-smiths, haggard non-union sweated tailors. Yonder are the platforms, a dozen of them, every one with a band of speakers. There is John Burns, that yonder is Tom Mann. John Burns is the man who for weeks got up every morning at four, haranged the starving dockers, infused courage into them, persuaded them not to use violence, and then went off to his shop to earn his living. Tom Mann is the fellow who heard that in a certain trade chemicals were used, dangerous to health. He got himself employed and worked till his hands were raw and bleeding that he might help the men by knowing the business. There is a cart with an Episcopalian minister side by side with a Jewess, the daughter of Karl Marx.

I met a friend, a cultured American gentleman. I thought of the churches in Belgravia and these crowds, and I asked: "Where would Christ be if he were in London?" "He would be here, for he had compassion on the multitude." "Would he speak from the tail of a cart as he spoke from the tail of a boat?" "Probably."

A few days later I walked into Westminster Abbey when they were consecrating three bishops. Over the heads of the congregation I caught a glimpse of a solemn procession in the nave, garments, robes, gilt crucifixes. I returned an hour later; they were still consecrating the bishops. I went off for lunch and came back; the bishops were still on the make. Now, how can we more readily imagine Jesus, in an archibishop's robe bowing, kneeling, marching, wheeling, and all that to get a man fit to be a successor of the apostles and to draw a salary—or on the tail of a cart talking to the multitude on the social question? Which would seem to him more important for the Kingdom of God on earth?

The interests of the leaders of the various churches and the interests of Jesus do *not* go in the same direction. The public sentiment of the churches as expressed in the most influential religious papers (with a few notable exceptions) sympathizes with the movements of the common people only when they are directed by the wealthy, and not when they are indigenous in the masses. Religious papers scarcely ever announce the success of a strike but seldom fail to announce the collapse of one. Yet more strikes succeed than fail. It shows where the editorial sympathy lies in the weary struggle of the people.

> Have ye builded your thrones and altars then
> On the bodies and souls of living men?
> And think ye that building shall endure
> Which shelters the rich and crushes the poor?

I have given much space to this discussion, not because I love it but because it is sorely needed. The secular and religious press extol the rich and their works and represent them as prime movers of social progress and pillars of godliness. Christ's teaching flatly contradicts that. And since his teaching on this point has been so generally suppressed, the reasonableness of his opposition to the gathering of wealth must be set forth fully and re-stated once more.

He desires that every man shall work and live on the proceeds. He forbids us to insure ourselves against the future by the hoarding of wealth, because we are sure to fasten our heart to our treasure. He bids us not worry about the future, but to seek the establishment of the Kingdom of God on earth, and a life of simple trust will then be easy. He commands us to share with one another as any man needs it, and this mutual help of the community will afford the stability and the insurance against cases of sickness or distress. Any attempt to gather wealth for one's self he condemns. He gives no limit of what is permissible, because in a fraternal community the entire community would rise in comfort, and it would then be lawful for a man to have what would be unlawful if he had it for himself alone. Wealth is relative. He is rich who has more than others. The efforts for prosperity should tend to raise the whole plane of life and not to raise one above the plane. If any man is rich, he should divest himself of his wealth and turn it to public uses.

It will not do for Christians to wait for society as a whole to reach a better life. They must anticipate the progress of society by private action and, by anticipating it, speed it on. Except your righteousness exceeds the righteousness of political economy, ye can in no wise enter the Kingdom.

Such anticipation will of course make it impossible for a man to pluck the best fruits of the existing conditions. It will to some extent keep him poor and despised. How far he has to fall in with present conditions in order to sustain his own life and the life of his family, he must let the Spirit teach him. There is no law for him except the law of the Spirit. If he saves up the seed-corn for next year's harvest, if he lays by something to educate his children, if he lays by something for his wife's old age—who will condemn him until we have a society Christian enough to relieve the individual of self-insurance. If a man has consecrated his ability to the advancement of the Kingdom but feels that it would be equivalent to the destruction of his life to live as low as the lowest, let him take what comfort he needs for his best work. A famished town has often given double rations to the soldiers on the ramparts. A boat-load of ship-wrecked sailors would do well to allow a double portion of crackers to the mate who alone knows navigation. The worker for the Kingdom will find that the poor are very ready to allow him better comfort than they have, if they see that he is fighting their battles. All is his, provided he is Christ's. And if a man finds that he would injure his brother by giving him what he asks, let him refuse it. A father or elder brother may refuse something to a lad whom he dearly loves. But let such a man look to it that his refusal is due to the love he bears the lad and not to the love he bears himself. The new law of Jesus is no law set in ordinances.

It prescribes no dead rules. It is a compass pointing ever to the perfection of justice and love. He that carries it is free to turn out of his way for trees and rocks. Perhaps at times a man may obey Christ's law best by disobeying it. The Spirit is the freest taskmaster. He that has it can go and come at pleasure, and yet he is absolutely bound, a bound servant of Jesus Christ.

But to anticipate the development of society by private action does not exhaust our responsibility. We know what kind of society Christ desires, and we can further every movement of corporate society in that direction. The abolition of every unjust privilege of wealth-gathering will tend toward the social equality desired by Jesus. It will make a natural life easier for the poor and remove the temptation from the rich. In addition, every social action tending to fraternal co-operation and unity of interest among men will be an incorporation of Christ's thoughts in the institutions of mankind. Negatively the abolition of injustice, positively fraternal association among equals: these are to be simultaneously the social words of the future.

c. Sex and Family

Christ's law of love finds expression in an equal regard for my brother's life and my own life, his honor and my honor, his prosperity and mine. There is one other department of our reciprocal duties, more confined in scope but of the greatest importance: the relation of one half of humanity to the other half, of sex to sex.

It goes without saying that Jesus hated impurity and forbade it. He accepted as a matter of course the ancient law against adultery. But he did not, like the Decalogue, stop with acts of impurity but brought the conscience of his followers to bear on the thoughts which precede and generate the acts. Impure actions are not an absolute standard of guilt. There are those who have never done the wrong but who have always loved it. And there are those who by their evil surroundings have been led to do the wrong before they loved it. Men judge what they see; God looks at the heart, and the followers of Christ must adopt God's standard so far as it is possible for man.

Jesus advocated and represented a higher standard of purity than his times, yet he was freer with women than the customs of his times sanctioned. He freely opened a conversation with a woman whom he chanced to meet alone at a well. The disciples, who represented public opinion, on their return "marvelled that he was speaking with a woman." Moreover, Jesus knew what they did not know, that conversation with this particular woman was not conducive to a good reputation in that neighborhood. Again, in the case of the woman who was "a sinner," he quietly submitted to her approach and touch. There was not the least attempt in the entire scene to keep her at a distance. And in his conversation with his host he made no effort to establish his own prophethood, which had been challenged, but championed the woman by making the noble spring of her action clear. (Lk. 7, 36-50.)

If this was his bearing in extreme cases, he must have maintained the same frank bearing toward women in general. He was a frequent guest in the home at Bethany. Several women seem to have been part of the little traveling company. It would have been safer for him to keep at a greater distance from them. The records of the early church have preserved no slanders against him on this score. But it is hardly possible that the world in his case forgot its readiest resource to blacken a purity that condemns it. It would have been easy for him to assume the reserve which a rabbi's position almost demanded. That he did not do so is itself a declaration. The barriers erected between men and women are confessions of weakness; increase of purity makes greater freedom possible. And greater freedom in turn produces purity of mind.

On the whole there is a surprising scarcity of utterances on this matter in his teachings. When he did speak of it, it was in reply to questions. He did not voluntarily return to it, as he did to the subject of ambition or wealth.

The questions on which his opinion was called out by others covered the debatable ground where conscience is most ready to find excuses for itself and to fortify itself by law and custom. For what causes may a man divorce his wife? May he marry again? May she marry again?

The first principle laid down by Jesus is that marriage ideally does not admit of dissolution. There is that implanted in man and woman at creation which makes a union between them unlike any other human relation, surpassing even the relation between parents and children in closeness. It makes the two one, a complete person. For man to meddle with this union and tear it asunder to gratify a fit of anger, a new lust, or a desire of profit is an interference with the laws of God and an undoing of his doings. (Matt. 19, 1-6.) Only one thing can justify the dissolving of the relation on the part of one: if the other has cut the bond which first united them and which constitutes the peculiarity of marriage. Interference with marriage sows the seed of every trouble. It sends the woman out into life disgraced, torn out of her natural family relation, without means of income and thus peculiarly liable to temptation and herself a cause of temptation. (Matt. 5, 32.) It implicates the man and the family that receives her. The damage done by dissolving the family life is in exact proportion to the fundamental social importance of the family and to its blessings when good. The number of divorces is found to bear a very close correspondence to the number of illegitimate births, showing that there is a unity of cause. Even to-day, when a woman is not nearly so helpless outside the family relation as in Christ's time, divorced women furnish far more than their proportion of criminality. Statistics also corroborate Christ's suspicion of second marriages. In Holland and Saxony the number of divorced women marrying again is twice as great as the equal number of widows marrying again, although in general the widows would be considered more eligible than they. There is therefore very often a second marriage in the background when the divorce begins.

When the Pharisees objected to Christ's position on the indissoluble nature of marriage on the ground that Moses had made regulations about divorce, he replied that Moses had done so "for your hardness of heart, but from the beginning it hath not been so." (Matt. 19, 8.) In other words, Moses came as near the ideal law as the condition of his countrymen would permit. Jesus does not appear to censure such approximate legislation; he merely insists that they shall keep the divine ideal before them and not be content to drop down on a standard or morality set up for past times and evil men. They are not to turn the permission of Moses into a command.

A higher standard yet is a voluntary renunciation of marriage for the sake of the Kingdom of God. (Matt. 19, 11-12.) He who has put his whole life into that is not troubled, as the disciples were, to see marriage stripped of its convenience. But Jesus knew that a life of such devotion is not given to many, and he imposes the duty on no one. (Matt. 19, 11.)

There is one other point on which he expressed himself emphatically. Among the notions of the future life entertained by the Jews was that of the continuance of the sexual relations. The descriptions of the rabbis were often gross and sometimes beastly. The Sadducees used this to ridicule the whole idea of a future life. They imagined the tangle in which family affairs would be after the resurrection, if all the relations of this life were to be resumed. Jesus took the position of neither Pharisee nor Sadducee. He asserted the future life but denied that the marrying and giving in marriage would continue there. (Matt. 22, 23-33.)

This is probably the sum of the distinct teachings of Jesus on the relation of men and women. (The beautiful passage of Christ and the woman in the temple is not authentic.) There are several inferences to be drawn from them, however, upon which I shall touch below.

The teaching of Paul on this subject is very extensive, and its influence on the church has been great. It will be useful to sum it up.

His warnings against impurity are frequent. It was the besetting sin of the Greeks, and all who lived among them were exposed to the contagion. It was constantly invading the church, just as it still is in heathen nations. The council at Jerusalem considered it necessary to except impurity expressly from the general liberty given to the Gentile Christians (Acts 15, 29), and Paul emphatically refused to place it among the actions neither good nor bad in themselves, such as the keeping of days and the eating of certain food. (I Cor. 6, 12-20.) He asserted that it is impossible to hold an act of impurity at arm's length; it involves the whole being and infallibly debases it.

Concerning marriage, he expressed his opinion very fully, though he claimed no categorical authority for his advice but only that consideration due to the thoughts of a man who "has received mercy of the Lord to be trustworthy." (I Cor. 7.) He denies that there is any wrong in marriage and protests against the beginnings of asceticism which were manifesting themselves in the church. (Col. 2, 20-23; I Tim. 4, 1-5.) He holds that for some it means safety, and that they ought to marry. Yet for those who have power over themselves he thinks it best to remain as they are. The time is short till the coming of the Lord. Just as he advises the Jew to remain a Jew and the Gentile to remain a Gentile, the freedman to remain so and the slave to be content as a slave, so he advises the married not to shake off the tie nor the unmarried to enter it. If a man does marry, he will have the distress of seeing his wife and children involved in the coming persecutions. Alone he has only himself to care for. And finally, if a man or woman is married, it is natural and inevitable that part of their interest and work is given to their family, and thus some of the strenuousness of their efforts for the Kingdom will be lost. Paul himself, therefore, remained unmarried. He claimed the right to be married like other apostles but freely renounced it, just as he made no use of his right to receive a salary. He refused to get as much out of life as he could, lest in using the world to the full he should get to serving it.

Several inferences can be drawn from these teachings without doing violence to them.

1. The first evident inference is that *Jesus worked in the direction of the permanence of marriage, and not the reverse.* It is safe to say that he would not sympathize with those who hope for benefits from its easy dissolution. Everything that would tend to make it a union of life and for life would meet with his encouragement; everything which would tend to make it the legalized method of self-gratification, to be dissolved when the passion has lost its fire, would meet with his re-

sistance. No man can dissolve such a relation without secret damage to his own best life and without involving others in sorrow. It would require good cause indeed to perform a psycho-surgical operation of so serious a character.

But as Jesus would resist a pressure against the bond of marriage from within, so he would resist all unnecessary pressure from without. There are such pressures in which no single person but the whole society furnishes the weight. The statistics of morality show that divorces increase in years of scarcity and industrial anxiety. It seems that the worry and anxiety for the future, the snappy temper of a hungry stomach and of feet weary with searching for work, chafe through many a bond that would otherwise endure. Here also God distributes the responsibility justly. But would it not well befit those who profess themselves anxious for the sanctity of marriage to hold aloof from it anything that would endanger it? Another fact of importance is that the proportion of divorces is smallest for the wage-workers and greater for the educated and wealthy classes. This fact is no contradiction of the preceding statement that financial distress increases divorces. For want is a relative term. Want means for every man less than he has been accustomed to have. A businessman would consider himself in great want if he came down to the earnings that seem prosperity to the day laborer. No, this fact indicates that increasing intelligence and education do not solve moral questions but make them more acute. It shows that unless morality keeps progress with education, education contains a menace to society. In France the liberal professions contain about 2.4 percent of the population, but between 1843-67 they brought in 23.29 percent of all the petitions for divorce. This fact supports the assertion that the life of the upper classes is overwrought and unhealthy. A family in which both husband and wife have their stint of daily work to do, in which the pleasures are simple instead of highly spiced and no ennui begs the devil to make the house his home, is fairly safe against the main causes of divorce.

2. The second inference from Christ's teaching is that *he was standing up for the women.* The Pharisees were asking for what cause a man might divorce his wife. Nobody thought of asking when a woman

might divorce her husband. Women were not doing it. In that condition of society marriage was the only vocation, the only road to social respect, the only harbor of safety for a woman. She had everything to gain by its stability. She had everything to fear from a law which put her at the mercy of her husband's moods. That this was the actual bearing of Christ's declaration concerning the permanence of marriage is evident from the rueful exclamation of the disciples: "If the case of the man is so with his wife, it is not expedient to marry." (Matt. 19, 10.)

It is well to bear this in mind, for the decision of Jesus is most often being turned against the women to-day. They are bidden to submit to cruelties and all injuries, so long as the husband does not sin against the one point named. By the change of social conditions, obedience to the letter of Christ's teaching may offend against its purpose.

3. *The entire question of marriage and divorce is better taken hold of before the marriage than after it.* The best way to diminish divorces is to diminish the number of marriages that will end in divorces.

The pairing off of young people always has been and always will be full of uncertainty and possibilities of heart-ache and disappointment. But it is safe to say that it will go on most smoothly where the following conditions are fulfilled: (a) a community without great differences of rank and wealth, so that the choice will be independent of money considerations; (b) a community with a neighborly social life, so that young people can freely meet and take time to develop their predilections; (c) an education and independent position for the girls, which will make them partners joining the firm with an equal stock of working capacity and not suppliants waiting for somebody to support them.

Our highly developed city life furnishes none of these requisites.

(a) The community is stratified, and everybody tries to crawl from one story of the house into the next higher. Young men marry capital for their business. Young women see that their marriage is the one business chance of their lifetime, and they must be on the alert accordingly. These considerations are not yet so decisive in America as they are in "the better classes" in Europe, but we shall inevitably get there if American social conditions go on developing in their present direction. And once love marriages become rare, farewell to the promise of an American stock!

(b) The second condition of a neighborly social circle is almost nonexistent in a modern great city, at least for the mass of its inhabitants. Tenement-house life is the death of family sociability. Young men do not meet their future wives in the sacred atmosphere of the home. They "get mashed on them" on the street, in the Elevated, or in the public ball-room. They fall suddenly in love, and after marriage they fall just as suddenly out of it. They do their love-making under the electric lights of Tomkins Square and whisper their vows amid the shrieks of the merry-go-round at Coney Island. Our great cities are sand-heaps, piles of human atoms. They lack the elementary structures of a social organism within which the family can build itself up. This also is upon the heads of those who are robbing the people of homes by their avarice.

(c) Finally, it is notorious that women are not on an equal footing with men in view of marriage. It is a crying pity to see how girls are forced out of their natural modesty by their false position. Everything is involved for them in being well married. They have to study to be attractive. They have to use means of attraction which operate more speedily, but which for that very reason give a less permanent basis to love. They are compelled to take a man whom they respect little and love less, because their mothers whisper that there may not be another chance. On the other hand, among the young men the bachelor life is becoming more frequent. As single men they can have a standard of living which the support of a family would immediately cut down. They can have the enjoyment of women's society without its burdens. The increase of unmarried men is always a sign of a rotting civilization. Here again the remedy lies deep. Only a healthy society, in which life is simple and a living certain, makes the formation of families safe and desirable for the men and makes woman for her own sake a treasure to be sought after, a helpmate and not a burden, a giver of comfort and not a despoiler of it.

There is perhaps nothing that so concerns the lover of his country and of humanity as the safety of the family life. Corrupt the spring of life and the whole stream is poisoned. Preaching will do something to maintain good morals. But the best way to keep them good is to keep them natural. Unnatural conditions are bound to breed evil. The army is an unnatural life, and consequently the standing armies of Europe furnish the greatest percentage of sexual extravagance and disease, as well as of crime and suicide. Everything that hinders the ready formation of marriages is a cause of social corruption. In Bavaria the percentage of illegitimate births was formerly 22. Later, it sank to 18 percent, and again to 12.79 percent when legal obstacles to marriage and to the freedom of business life were removed. Industrial pressure acts as forcibly as law to diminish marriages. The maximum number of marriages coincides with the minimum price of grain. Those who artificially disturb and depress the industrial prosperity of the people bear the guilt of checking marriage and driving the sexual impulse to seek illicit means of gratification. Women yield to temptation and in turn become tempters. And so the evil perpetuates itself.

Let those who obey Christ and desire purity and a healthy family life begin their work where it will tell best. Let them help to do away with the bitter need of the poor and the rotting superfluity of the rich, which combine to produce prostitution. Let them help to do away with the tenement house by reforming the land system. Let them press forward the education and financial independence of women. Let them in every way help to abolish the chances of dishonest gain, which have poisoned the social body with the malarial fever of covetousness. Money love is the supplanter of family love.

d. The State

The ethical relations so far discussed are the relations of individual to individual, although everywhere a wider outlook has noticed the bearing of individual relations to the whole of human society. As a great writer on ethics has said: "There is no longer any private morality." Humanity is drawing together by a thousand forces. And as vibrations travel fastest through the densest bodies, so the moral movements of the social atom communicate themselves most quickly in the most social society. It is one of the pressing duties of religious men to insist on this fact of solidarity and press its ethical importance home to the conscience of every man.

But in addition to this ever-present social background of private morality, every man is placed over against organized society, the state. The state renders us service and exacts duties from us. What attitude does the Christian take to its demands?

Three cases can arise. The state may demand of us duties which serve our interests and commend themselves to our conscience. In that case our duty is, plainly, to render all assistance required, and more.

In the second case the state may demand of us what conflicts with our interests without conflicting with our conscience, for instance in the levying of burdensome taxes, the vexatious interference with the freedom of personal movement, etc. In such cases the general law of non-resistance to evil holds as anywhere else. So Jesus submitted to the soldiers sent to arrest him. So he paid the temple tax, though his half-smiling colloquy with Peter shows that he did not much relish it. (Matt. 17, 24-27.) And so also he advised the Jews to pay the Roman tax. What if they did give Caesar his own? That did not hinder them from giving God the spiritual service that he demanded. Of course in a modern popular government, with the greater rights, we have also the duty to strive for a change in laws which we consider oppressive and undesirable. But that does not interfere with personal submission to them. A man may courteously pay the custom's duty on a book which he is importing to furnish him the material wherewith he may overthrow that very duty.

The third case presents by far the greatest difficulties. The state may demand of us something which conflicts with our conscience. It may at the same time damage our interests, or possibly benefit them, but it compels us to do wrong. Shall we obey the authority of the state, or the authority of our conscience?

Theologians have in times past given answers to this question which bound the individual conscience under the divine right of the king who could do no wrong. Rebellion was regarded as always wrong. And the stay for this doctrine which has given a long license to wicked men and hindered the enfranchisement of the people was taken from the Scriptures. Does not Paul say: "Let every soul be in subjection to the higher powers; for there is no power but of God, and the powers that be are ordained of God. Therefore he that resisteth the power, withstandeth the ordinance of God"? (Rom. 13, 1-7.) So it was argued that whatever government exists is of God, and to resist it is rebellion against God. But they refused to see the reason which Paul assigns for his advice: "For rulers are not a terror to the good work, but to the evil. . . . He is a minister of God, an avenger for wrath to him that doeth evil. Wherefore ye must needs be in subjection, not only because of the wrath, but also for conscience sake." Obedience therefore is due because civil government stands up for good against evil and thus demands the free approval of our moral judgement. But suppose there is a government which persistently terrorizes the good and favors the evil? Suppose that it approves itself, not by isolated errors, but by its settled policy, a minister of Satan, an avenger for wrath to him that doeth good? Then what? Paul's command falls to the ground with the reason given for it. One may object that Paul wrote this injunction of obedience while evil men wore the imperial purple. It is true; yet the injustice of Roman rule has often been exaggerated. It was burdensome, it was cruel when its own supremacy was endangered. So is the rule of England in India; but like the English rule, the Roman government was the most just, on the whole, that the world had seen. Even the much abused Pilate stood firmer in the defense of innocence than many an American police justice would do, if all the Irish politicians of his district demanded the committal of an obnoxious Italian. To him it was a question between his own political existence and the life of a strange fanatic with a touch of sublimity. He was only not absolutely just.

A passage in the first epistle of Peter (2, 13-17) throws light on the purpose of Paul's command. Peter bids his friends be subject to anything that the king or his deputies command, because they are set to punish evil and reward good. "For so is the will of God, that by well-doing ye should put to silence the ignorance of foolish men; as free, and not using your freedom for a cloke of wickedness, but as bondservants of God." These young Christians had been drinking of the new wine of freedom, and they were getting unsteady on their feet. Paul was always warning against the abuse of freedom in private morality. The same danger threatened in public life. The Christians, conscious of having in them a higher form of life, were inclined rudely to walk across established customs and civil laws, and thus to create the impression that they were refractory and impertinent disturbers of society. The same danger is noticeable on foreign mission fields. The converts are inclined to hold their heads very high and make themselves obnoxious. It is the danger of every transition period. It is the same vexatious and amusing swagger that we all know in lads outgrowing their boyhood. In the early days of Christianity this was a serious matter. Christianity was a new phenomenon and was being observed with a critical and unfriendly eye. Men would judge it by its worst. These immature members who used their new freedom as a pretty covering for what after all was self-indulgence, were endangering the whole movement. Both Paul and Peter told them that one of the chief uses of freedom is not to use it, and that existing institutions had a solid foundation of justice and usefulness underneath them and were not to be lightly set aside.

But this free and manly submission to existing institutions, though known to be imperfect, is a very different thing from a slavish obedience which surrenders the personal conscience to the keeping of government. There was nothing servile about John the Baptist before Herod. There was not the budging of one inch in Jesus before the high priest: "If I have spoken evil, bear witness of the evil; but if well, why smitest thou me?" (John 18, 23.) He met the foxy curiosity of Herod with impenetrable silence, and the polite incredulity of Pilate with a self-possessed dignity that is admirable. Certainly there was nothing cringing in the bearing of Stephen before the Sanhedrin (Acts 7, 51-60), nor in that of Paul: "God shall smite thee, thou whited wall; and sittest thou to judge me according to the law, and commandest me to be smitten contrary to the law?" (Acts 23, 1-5.) We love him as much for this passionate outburst of insulted innocence, as for the courteous self-control that followed. But the plainest declaration of the Christian position was made by Peter before the Sanhedrin. He boldly charged them with injustice in their official capacity and refused obedience to their commands insofar as they ran contrary to the will of God. (Acts 4, 10, 19.) "We must obey God rather than men." (Acts 5, 29.) And, what is the crucial point, he claimed the right to interpret the will of God for himself and to set his interpretation over against the interpretation of the highest authority that he knew. It was the Declaration of Independence of the individual conscience, which received its ultimate expression by Luther at the Diet of Worms.

If the state demands that a citizen shall believe, say, or do what he, after due deliberation and consultation with others, considers wrong, he may and must refuse obedience. Abolitionists were right in disobeying the fugitive slave law. The Quakers were right in refusing to take oaths. The Mennonites were right in refusing to serve as soldiers. When the wrong consists in any single demand, passive resistance to that one demand coupled with open protest against it will usually be effective, though it always entails suffering on some. After much chicanery the Mennonites have wrested exemption of military service even from the Russian government. An interesting case is told of a chaplain in the Civil War. It was against his conscience to kill anybody, but he was no coward. In battle he was forward in every charge, whooping and shouting, but carrying his rifle idle in his hands.

The matter is more complicated when the national wrong cannot be so directly reached but is bound up in the general life of the state. In civilized politics the peaceful redress of injustice is now so open that it would be wrong for anyone to take more stringent measures until he has done all that is possible along the prescribed course of redress. But there are cases where a passive refusal to be implicated in a wrong might become necessary. For instance, if England should begin another opium war, would it not be right for Christian citizens to refuse the payment of taxes, part of which would be used for the maintenance of iniquity?

I am speaking only of passive resistance, because I believe it to be in the end the quickest, the most effective, and the cleanest method. Jesus rejected armed resistance even against the most crying wrong. (John 18, 36.) Those who do not share that conviction against the use of force will have difficulty in showing why armed resistance against a wrong done by civil government is not permissible. If one nation may fight another nation to resist the searching of ships on the high seas, if a colony may fight the mother country to resist an oppressive tax—why may not part of a nation resist another part inflicting a wrong upon them? It may justly be demanded that those aggrieved shall seek redress peacefully. But what if peaceful redress is denied? What if, as in Russia, the public voice is stifled, even the humblest petition draws down cruel punishment on the petitioners, and the aspirations of patriotism and popular devotion, which would be the pride of other countries, are treated as crimes? What if in the struggle of an oppressed class for its rights the oppressors should pack juries, procure special legislation, mislead public opinion by corrupting the press, slander the champions of the poor, and in every way defeat the legitimate efforts for justice? What if experience should gradually lead the oppressed to despair of making headway by the peaceful presentation of their rights, and should teach them that there are some men with whom a little fright goes farther than much argument? What if some state should one day appear not to be the organized people at all, but an organized class rebelling against the unorganized people? Then those who believe in the use of force against rebellion would find the same guns used, only pointed in the opposite direction, and they could raise no just protest against it.

This is the attitude of the Christian toward government: devoted assistance when government seeks the right; submission to troublesome burdens if they fall on him and do not compel a participation in wrong; passive resistance and public protest against compulsory participation in wrong-doing; and establishment of a new genuine state when the previous one becomes a fraud, a class pretending to be a state. The judgement in every case lies with the individual conscience which, however, is bound before God to have sought all light and wisdom obtainable, and to act in concert with others wherever possible before it sets itself against public action.

5

THE NEW MORALITY

The moral life of man is active in three directions: in his relations to his fellow-men; in the conscious maintenance of his own personality; in his fellowship with God. In the preceding section I have attempted to set forth Christ's law concerning the relations between man and man. I pass now to the moral actions which turn back on the man's own life. Of course, in point of fact the two divisions run into each other. A man's bearing toward his neighbor determines his own life, and a man's personal integrity affects his neighbor.

a. Duty to Self

The first duty of man to himself is to maintain his consistency, his unity of life, his truth. Hypocrisy, double-mindedness, is one of the few sins to which Jesus gave no quarter. A man may be bad and a slave to his passions, but as long as there is an acting connection between his outward moral bearing and his inward moral life, moral power can be exerted upon him to help him. But when you talk truth to a man and he answers you seriously, and yet his heart is far from what he says, what can you do for such a man? He is like a patent churn with a broken shaft; you turn the crank, the cogs rattle, but the wheel stands still.

The simplest form of truthfulness is to speak the truth, to let your yea mean yea and not nay.

Men find that inconvenient. Lying is very easy. So they lie. But that again is inconvenient, for there are occasions when truth is really necessary, for instance, in making a contract or in bearing witness in court. Then the universal distrust of one another is felt to recoil on every one concerned. So they have invented a method of securing truth and fidelity in these special cases. They compel the person bearing witness or giving a promise to call on some higher being, or something sacred to him, to visit punishment on him in case of an untruth, and they trust to the man's superstitious fear to keep him from untruth in that case. This is called swearing, and false swearing has ever been considered very wicked, while false talking is of little importance.

Christ levels this artificial distinction. He ridicules the invoking of heaven or earth which are the throne and footstool of God and have nothing to do with the wee unit of a man who stands there swearing. Swearing is based on superstition, and its special influence falls both for him who believes that God hears nothing and for him who believes that God is present at his lightest word as well as at his solemn oath.

But the worst feature about swearing is its untruthfulness. It proceeds from a consciousness of untruthfulness which needs a special asseveration. The really truthful man says "yes" and is done with it. It does not occur to him that anything more is necessary to secure belief. The untruthful man suspects distrust and seeks to prevent it by confirming his words by oaths. While the Decalogue demanded veracity only in witnessing in court, Jesus demands truth everywhere. While the old law forbade false swearing, Jesus forbade all swearing and expected his followers to be so genuine in their truthfulness that their yea would mean yea to all men. If they should yield to the custom of swearing, there was danger that in their minds also the distinction between solemn utterances for which truth is necessary and common occasions at which untruth is permissible would be built up again.

It does not appear that the Christian world has made much progress in the obedience to this command of Jesus. It has outlawed profane swearing and perhaps diminished the kind of swearing into which Peter dropped in the court of the high priest. But the solemn swearing is still in vogue, and it is often maintained that Jesus made no reference to that. But that also is condemned by its fruits. The oath of Herod and the vow of Jephtha are typical cases of how men become entrapped by an oath to do what they know to be wrong. (Matt. 14, 1-12; Judg. 11, 30-40.) The oath of loyalty to a sovereign has often in history constrained the consciences of good men to act against the welfare of their country. In his vow of celibacy the young Catholic priest makes a solemn promise, which at the moment of his consecration he may be perfectly minded to keep, but which in after years may become a two-edged sword keeping two lives asunder that ought before God to unite. The vows of secret societies are either superfluous mummeries or, if they mean anything, ought not to be sworn. No man has the right to give his conscience into the keeping of another man or of a soulless corporation. Nor does he have the right to sell his own future by promising forever to abide by rules of conduct which future years may show him to be inadequate or wrong. One may object that matters would not be changed if men regarded their plain yes as good as an oath. Theoretically not; practically they would be changed. Somehow the senseless literalism of the oath does not attach to the plain promise even of the most honest man. He feels bound to the spirit of the promise but not to its mere form, which may be rendered hostile to the spirit by the change of events.

In short, Christ's suspicion of oaths is well founded. The Christian should need no oath to secure belief in his assertions, and he should use no oath to bind himself for a future which he does not know. The inward consistency of his life, the steadfastness of his principles will be a sufficient guarantee for those who have to trust him. And if Christians can use their influence to abolish oaths in civil life, they will probably do no damage. The way the oath is administered in our law courts and by our public notaries awakens neither reverence nor superstition. The main reason why men lie less under oath is because they are liable to prosecution. If that is retained, there will be little decrease in judicial truthfulness. And there will be a gain. At present the word of the most dissolute and of the most honest man in a township are supposed to be of equal value if they are under oath. Yet they are not. A clever rascal may take care to keep within the letter of the law and yet distort the whole case. Why not let the honest man's testimony have the additional weight to which his honesty entitles it, by letting every man's yea and nay stand on its own strength?

In the next place, Jesus taught that a man's words judge him. "By thy words thou shalt be justified, and by thy words thou shalt be condemned." For "out of the abundance of the heart the mouth speaketh." Generally speaking, a man's words are the barometer of his soul. Therefore Jesus treated it so seriously when the Pharisees insinuated that the spirit which was overcoming the demoniacs was a satanic spirit. It is the last stage of a soul's decay when it cannot distinguish between white and black, between God's Spirit and the devil's. About everything else a man may be in doubt, even about the Son of man, and a word against him can be forgiven. But the Spirit comes with immediate conviction to the heart of every man; and when a man by his words shows that he has lost his sense of the Spirit, those words pass an irretrievable judgement upon him. (Matt. 12, 22-37.)

But words do more than express an inward state. They clinch a conviction. This also Jesus recognized. When their minds were ripe for it, he gave the disciples an opportunity to express themselves in regard to him. And when Peter, speaking the mind of all, asserted that he was the Messiah, the Son of the living God, Jesus hailed this expression as an epoch in his work and began from that time to open up a new reach of thoughts to them. (Matt. 16, 13-21.) Such an expression of thought is like a stone put under the wagon-wheel in driving up a hill; it secures the distance that has been gained and gives the horse breath for the next pull. The Declaration of Independence was made with an effort. It was the wave-crest of patriotic daring. Only a part of the young nation rose so high. But when the Declaration was once put forth, it stayed and drew the next step after it.

Therefore Paul couples the believing of the heart and the confessing of the mouth together, like the driving of the nail and the clinching of it. (Rom. 10, 10.) And therefore Christ has instituted baptism as the emphatic public expression of that faith and that committal to obedience which has taken place in the silence of the heart. The two things belong together. The outward expression without the inward reality is vain; the inward reality without the outward expression is incomplete and in danger of dying stillborn.

But Jesus was not the man to judge words superficially. He puts the greatest value on words, and then again he disparages words. Only insofar as to his discerning spirit they really indicated the state of the heart did he care for them at all. If they were contradicted by the acts of the speaker, the words were bubbles of wind. Acts are a more conclusive criterion than words, because they come more slowly and cost more. Therefore not all that say "Lord! Lord!" shall enter the Kingdom, but those who do the will of the Father. (Matt. 7, 15-27.) Words are blossoms, actions are fruit. Not the son who says "I go, sir," is dear to the father, but the son that does go. If Christ has to choose between words without action and actions without words, he prefers the latter. (Matt. 21, 28-32.)

It is the peculiar danger of religious men and religious committees that their words are so likely to be different from their actions. In a community like that of the Jews, like England under the Puritans, or like any church to-day, there is a standard of religious thought and utterance which is adopted without effort and most successfully reproduced by those who have the glibbest tongue. This religious vernacular of the community is modeled on the utterances of really spiritual men, used perhaps in moments of profound emotion. Thus the utterances of the pulpit or the prayer meeting soar high, but the actions dangle down below somewhere. Again it often happens that a man has in his youth possessed a truly living faith, but that under the cares of life and the deceitful influence of riches it has oozed away. The high-water mark is still visible. The man remembers what a life with God is. He retains the expressions which his inward life formed for itself in the springtide of his spirit. So the grasping, covetous old man speaks with the accents of love and damns the religion he praises. Therefore Paul warns against prophesying beyond the proportion of our faith. (Rom. 12, 6.) This religious lying is an awful danger. It is detestable to Christ. It is the fawning kiss with which Judas shows his intimacy with the Christ whom only a little before he sold for thirty pieces of silver. It is the lie of Ananias, who gave a fraction of his possession and hoped thereby to get the credit of a complete consecration. We know how this leaven of hypocrisy had penetrated the Jewish congregation at the time of Jesus. The first Epistle of John shows that it was at work on the early church also to destroy its whole-heartedness. "He that saith, I know him, and keepeth not his commandments, is a liar, and the truth is not in him." (2, 4.) "He that saith he is in the light and hateth his brother, is in the darkness even until now." (2, 9.) "Whoso hath the world's goods, and beholdeth his brother in need, and shutteth up his compassion from him, how doth the love of God abide in him? My little children, let us not love in word, neither with the tongue, but in deed and truth." (3, 17-18.) How the modern church stands condemned before such words! In Lowell's "Parable" Christ revisits the earth to see how men believe on him. The chief priests and elders receive him and show him that in church and palace and judgement-hall his image is high over all. But Christ walks sadly through all the splendor. He leads forth "an artisan, a stunted, low-browed haggard man, and a poor girl." And as the priests and rulers draw back their robes, Jesus points to the two and says: "These are the images ye have made of me." Walk through Fifth Avenue and Madison Avenue, and admire the double rows of lofty spires rising amid sumptuous mansions. Then walk to the East or to the West, as you please, and see the double rows of lofty tenements, ornamented with iron fire-escapes. Add the minus quantity to the plus quantity, and see whether the sum is plus or minus. The real value of a city's or nation's Christianity is represented by its lowest class, not by its highest. And the existence of a sumptuous Christianity in the midst of a destitute population is prima facie evidence of untruth.

The only hope for the church is to push forward to accept Christ's standard of practical life and to put itself into antagonism against gilded wrong. Then it will get into trouble, and the hypocrites will decamp.

Christ abhors double-mindedness. He refuses even the universal loan of truth to those who are not straightforward and genuine. (Matt. 21, 25-27.) He measures the value of an action by its spontaneity. It was the heartfelt sincerity of the multitude's jubilations at the entrance into Jerusalem which made their Hosannas so delightful to him. "Master, rebuke thy disciples," said the Pharisees, who loved shouting only when it was done by salaried Levites from the approved "Pharisaic Hymn and Tune Book." But Christ answered: "I tell you that, if these shall hold their peace, the stones will cry out." There are occasions that call for noise, and then the most disordered shouts are melodious in Christ's ear. But the sweetest music in his honor is like a rattle of tin pans if it is gotten up to order.

It was the spontaneity of Mary's gift which touched him at Bethany. The disciples were speculating about precisely the best way to invest the cost of the ointment in charity. Jesus sided with feminine feeling against masculine hard-headedness. With their prudence they were letting his heart starve for a little love in those days of bitter need. She divided it and lavished the costly stuff on him in a flood of sweetness.

On the other hand, it was the lack of spontaneity which struck a chill into him in the religious devotions that he watched about him. Men gave alms and watched out of the corner of their eyes for public approval. They fasted and advertised the piety of their stomachs by the sadness of their countenances. They prayed and meanwhile calculated their increasing reputation. Yes, by the terrible irony of sin through which the deceiver at last becomes self-deceived, they got so that they thought they could impose on the Almighty himself, and make him mistake the multitude of their words for fervor. (Matt. 6, 1-8.) As an old lady once said to me: "I never feel really blessed in my public prayers 'til the tears come." So she watched the swelling of her lachrymal glands as she prayed to God.

To sum up: Jesus demands wholeness of life, a correspondence of our words to our actions and of both to our inward life. The value of words and acts depends entirely on their ingenuousness and spontaneity. Religious actions lose their value by side-thoughts and calculations of profit. Chronic separation between the heart and its manifestations induces spiritual paralysis and death.

The second duty of man to himself is to keep his higher life supreme. For though a man "delight in the law of God after the inward man," yet he "sees a different law in his members, warring against the law of his mind, and bringing him into captivity under the law of sin which is in his members." That there is this conflict of desires we all know by experience. It is the problem of every religion and philosophy. Everyone who has not darkened the lamp of his soul by lust or by speculation knows it as an absolute verity, that the voice of the spirit is the voice which he should obey when it contradicts the clamor of his body.

Christianity teaches (1) that this inward conflict exists; (2) that it is the common and natural thing to obey the flesh; (3) that this obedience produces inward corruption and ends in death; (4) that by faith in Christ man comes in contact with the life of God and receives power to overcome the domination of sin and to obey the spirit; (5) that the culmination of this progressive victory is eternal life.

But this victory requires constant effort and watchfulness. He that stands always has to take heed lest he fall. The attraction of the world operates on our lower nature as incessantly as the force of gravitation. Our hearts are always in danger of being "overcharged with surfeiting, and drunkenness, and cares of this life." (Lk. 21, 34.) Therefore we must "watch and pray," that we enter not into temptation, for though the spirit be willing, the flesh is weak. (Matt. 26, 41.) There is a limit to every man's strength of resistance. And there is a vulnerable place in every man's life, though as with Siegfried it be only the size of a linden leaf. Every man knows where it is. Therefore let him take heed lest he expose it to the enemy whose spear hovers ready. His weakness is probably bound up with his strongest affections. But though it be dear to him as the apple of his eye or as his trusty right hand, let him cut through, for it will ruin his soul. (Matt. 18, 8-9.) It may be a book, a habit, a companion, an ambition; it very likely is wealth. The best thing is amputation, performed even a little above the diseased spot to make sure. That was Paul's mind for himself. (I Cor. 9.) He saw others venturing very close to the boundary line of the permissible, and he saw some throw up their hands as they went over the precipice. He refused to go as far as he dared to go. He preferred voluntarily to surrender some of his rightful privileges. He had a right to the sweet comforts of married life as well as other apostles. But he knew that the mated bird seeks a nest; the restless missionary would begin to shorten his flights, he would begin to tremble at mobs and dungeons, and the work which God had laid upon his soul would remain incomplete. He shook his head and remained alone. He had a right to support from the hands of these whom he served. If the herdsman everywhere has a right to the milk of the flock which he tends, surely one carrying the highest treasures of truth and knowledge may claim the means of life from those whom he blesses. But Paul refused support. He preferred to stitch tent canvas for a living and preach for nothing. He was bound not to let the noble race of his life slow down into a leisurely amble for his daily bread. If an athlete could freely refuse the delicacies of life to keep his muscles firm and to gain a wreath of pine twigs, surely Paul could abstain from some things to win the unfading wreath of honor which God bestows on a righteous and heroic life.

The abstinence which Christ demands is not weak and colorless. Christian virtue is not absence of faults. Jesus had no love for the negative characters: for the man with one talent who, though he does not waste it, just wraps it in a napkin and does nothing with it; for the virgins who wake up at the critical moment to find that they have no oil and are useless in the procession; for the fig tree that does not do the one thing for which it was planted; for the respectable people who lived in the midst of the poor, the hungry, the naked, but did nothing for them. Decide yourself, says Christ, be either for or against me; if you are not for me, I count you on the other side. The man that is simply not bad is like an empty house free to the first batch of demons that passes by.

Wherever Jesus found energy, daring, insistence, he praised it. What an eye he had for the heroism in John's character. John was none of your reeds wobbling in the wind, none of your pretty courtiers in soft raiment. He was a man, he was a granite pillar and not a plaster cast. Herod could break him but never bend him. There, said Jesus, that is the character of the Kingdom; the men of violence, who storm in by force, are the ones to take it. (Matt. 11, 7-12.) Three men came to him who wanted to follow him. Yes, said he, you may come; but you must come right away, and you will risk being more homeless than the jackal and the swallow. If you are of the sort that puts his hand to the plow but keeps his head turned back with a longing look at the cool fence corner and the lunch basket, you had better stay away. (Lk. 9, 57-62.) The faith that Jesus praises is not the kind that relaxes in an upholstered elevator and tries to believe that the elevator is sufficiently strong to carry it up. Christ's ideal of faith is the kind that mounts on the roof and tears up the shingles if it cannot get in by the door; the kind that climbs into a sycamore tree to see Christ, forgetful of respectability; the faith that without a word leaves nets and boats and follows the call of the nobler future; the faith that leaves the publican's counting house without stopping to balance accounts and collect outstanding debts; the faith that beats a rattattoo on a friend's door at midnight, wears out a judge who cares for neither God nor men, and turns a brusque word of refusal into a still more pleading appeal.

While it is necessary for men to abstain, Jesus does not put the emphasis on abstinence but on energy. He does not pray for his followers that they be taken out of a tempting world but that, living in the world, they overcome it. There are two ways of preserving purity. One way is to keep out of sight and hearing of all that may sully. The other way is to face evil and grapple with it. A lad, delicately nurtured in a pure family circle, may have the purity of innocence. A preacher, living amid vice and foulness, may have the purity of holiness. And that is the Christian purity.

Christ has put himself in contrast with John the Baptist: "John came neither eating nor drinking, and they say, He hath a devil; the Son of man came eating and drinking, and they say, Behold, a gluttonous man, and a wine-bibber, a friend of publicans and sinners!" They were one in their energy. But John's energy carried him out of the world into the desert; Christ's energy carried him out of the desert into the world. And yet he remained pure. Thrust the nozzle of a garden-hose into a street puddle and turn the water on; will the mud of the puddle enter the hose?

It is well known that the Christian church has not always taken this view of Christ's teaching. It has taken John the Baptist as its model more frequently than Christ. The piety of centuries was ascetic. The hermit, the celibate were considered more holy than the married men of business. Flight from the world was the only sure way of salvation. Even to this day the predominant feature of Christianity in the minds of the people is the abstinence from certain pleasures.

It can fairly be maintained that asceticism had an influence for good. It was a passionate protest against the contagious sensuality of pagan life. And there is an abiding reason in it, as we saw in Paul's case. It is better voluntarily to abstain from some things that are permissible than to push liberty to the very edge.

But the great fault of the ascetic tendency is that it substituted the salvation of one's soul for the Christian aim of establishing the Kingdom of God. By that silent substitution the words of Christ took on a different meaning. Jesus spoke of abstinence from marriage "for the Kingdom of heaven's sake." (Matt. 19, 12.) Paul practiced it. It is simply the renouncing of family happiness in order to concentrate one's whole life on the establishment of God's will on earth. In that sense it is only doing with the sublimest and all-inclusive patriotism what many a young volunteer has done who left his bride unwed to fight his country's battles. But a narrower Christianity turned Christ's unselfishness into a selfish love of one's own soul, to the salvation of which our own tenderest impulses and perhaps the happiness of others have to be sacrificed.

Jesus in a measure loosened the bonds of his family and substituted the community of his disciples for it. They were brother and sister and mother to him. It is that loosening of natural bonds and that growing strength of spiritual kinship which every man has felt who has ever consecrated himself to a great cause and joined a noble movement. It is the lot of every revolutionist to turn from the tears of parents or to draw from the clasp of loving hands. And as long as the revolutionary character of Christ's purpose is recognized, there is nothing strange in his demand that every man who comes to him must hate his own father and wife and children and brethren, yea, and his own life. But when that revolutionary purpose is forgotten the command becomes harsh, brutal, inhuman. To give up one love for the sake of a larger love is right and natural. Every man does it who leaves his parents to cleave to his wife. Every man does it who, like Hector of Troy, leaves Andromache and his child, to fall for his fatherland. But to give up the love of others from love of ourselves and our salvation is not an expansion of life but a contraction. A man leaving his family to enter a monastery and spend his time telling beads and singing vigils has no business to take Christ's words into his mouth.

If Christianity is a revolutionary movement for the emancipation of humanity, the Christian doctrine of self-sacrifice is reasonable and noble. Horatius who held the bridge; Winkelried who broke a way for liberty; the Spartan heroes of Thermopylae anointing their hair for the last battle as for a feast; indeed every noble deed that has kindled the imagination of our boyhood, down to that of the last locomotive engineer who drove his engine crashing through the debris on the track to cut a way for the train, they all contain the element of self-sacrifice for others. Christ gave the ultimate expression to it and made it a universal law. It means carrying into action the principle of loving our brothers.

But the whole principle is immediately vitiated if the sacrifice is made for ourselves. If a man cuts down his food to ten boiled peas a day to feed others, it may be unwise but it is grand. But when a man might have more but confines himself to ten peas that he may torture his flesh and win merit with heaven, we wonder at it, but we do not admire it. It is true that devotion for others will bring reward; "he that loses his life for my sake, shall find it"; but if he loses his life in order to find it and not in order to help others, then the other half of Christ's word is applicable, "he that seeketh his life shall lose it."

Asceticism, then, contains a solid basis of sense. When in any given case the natural desires of life conflict either with the rights and well-being of others or with our own nobler nature, there is nothing for it but resistance. So far most will agree. Furthermore, when in surveying our life as a whole we perceive that our dangers lie along certain lines and that even a moderate indulgence may endanger our self-control or chill our spiritual ardor, it is wise to restrict ourselves voluntarily. So far goes the asceticism of the New Testament. It does not go far enough to take a man out of human society or to annihilate the natural impulses with which God endowed him. Christ has once for all demonstrated the possible holiness of common human life. Christianity would lift man up, not by making him less man but by making him truly man. For, as Pascal says, "man is neither angel nor beast; and the trouble is that he who would make an angel of him, makes him a beast."

Wherever Christianity appears to demand a stricter asceticism, it is not asceticism at all but concentrated devotion for the good of humanity. He who gives himself to the Kingdom of God will be scourged like a monk; but unlike a monk it will not be himself that swings the scourge in the lonely cell, but others will swing it over him in public life.

The substitution of personal salvation for the establishment of the Kingdom of God in the teaching of the church is the cause of false asceticism everywhere. It has twisted the words of Christ out of their natural meaning. It has diverted the energy of religious men from public affairs and concentrated it on themselves. It has produced a false type of godliness. Not till the doctrine of the Kingdom of God shall have entered once more into the consciousness of the church, and Christianity shall become a revolutionary movement, will Christian morality lose its unworldly pallor and become once more the sublimest type of civic virtue. Then no Christian revolutionist need be anxious about inflicting pain upon himself. Others will do it for him.

b. The Practice of Religion

We have spoken of the law of Christ as it regulates our actions toward our fellow-men and toward ourselves. It remains to speak of our actions—if there are any such—in which our relation to God is expressed.

In Jewish society a multitude of actions was performed, not because they were a help to man, but because they were supposed to be pleasing to God. Men fasted, not for the good of their digestion but to please God. Men washed their hands, not to get the dirt off but to undo any defilement which might have been contracted in the sight of God by touching somebody who had touched a dead body. Men painfully abstained from work on the Sabbath, not to have a good rest from their work but to please God. In short there were a thousand and one actions which might or might not bring some advantage to men, but which were not performed for the sake of men but for the sake of God. Aside from good effects on men, the actions themselves were supposed to please God by the very fact of their performance.

The most cursory reader of Christ's life must have noticed that ceremonial laws were the main cause of contention between him and the representatives of the orthodox religion, and that Christ differed from them not in the strictness of his observance but in its looseness. A more careful reading shows only one ceremonial law, the observance of which he enjoined, the law commanding a leper who believed himself healed to be examined by the priest and to make an offering of purification. There was a sanitary basis to this law. The priest was the public officer who had to guard the community against the rash readmission of the quarantined lepers. Jesus knew that the men whom he healed were sound, but he desired that they subject themselves to the regular civil procedure. (Mk. 1, 40-45; Lk. 17, 11-14.)

In one other instance Jesus seems to have displayed zeal for ceremonial law. On his last visit to the temple he drove out those who were selling the objects needed for sacrifice, saying: "It is written: my house shall be called a house of prayer; but ye make it a den of robbers." But a closer examination shows that here also his interest was for humanity and against ceremonialism. Those who were marketing the sacrificial animals and changing the secular money of the pilgrims for the temple shekel, which alone was permitted for offerings, were serving the interests of ceremonial worship; but their commercial chatter, their greed of barter robbed the place of its sanctity, sullied the thoughts of reverence with the heat of covetousness, in short, turned the place into a robbers' den. Immediately afterward the blind and lame crowded to Jesus to be healed, and the children took up the cry of the morning's procession and shouted hosannas about the temple court. That Jesus permitted, but now the ceremonialists were indignant. That was their difference of attitude. To their minds the covetous chatter of trade was no defilement so long as ceremonial objects were being bought and sold; but a crowd of dirty beggars limping or leaping about and a rabble of children shouting hosannas to their enemy were an intolerable profanation. Jesus exactly reversed it. Ceremonialism was not sacred to him, the needs and joys of humanity were. (Matt. 21, 12-16.)

Against some of the ceremonial rules of Jewish society Jesus offended by neglect.

He failed to fast like the Pharisees. The disciples caught his indifference and also ate as they pleased. The Pharisees objected. (Mk. 2, 18-22.) Jesus replied: "Why should they fast? They are happy now, and not sorrowful. They are like the friends of the bridegroom, and no one fasts at a wedding. The time of sorrow will come for them, and when it is natural to fast, then let them fast." Jesus also fasted while he was struggling through his temptations in the wilderness. There are times of trial in which fasting is natural, and then it is also legitimate. But Jesus went farther. He implied that fasting was part of an antiquated formalism which would not harmonize with his new life. To put his disciples with their new ideas to observing the old fast days would be like putting fermenting wine into old wineskins, or like patching a piece of harsh, unshrunk cloth on a garment falling to pieces with age. Better keep it off; there will only be a worse cracking and tearing.

Another neglect noticed by the Pharisees was the disciples' failure to perform the ceremonial washings before they took food. (Matt. 15, 1-2, 10-20.) When they took Jesus to task for this, he flatly denied that there was any sense in their purifications, on the ground that what touches a man or what he eats has no influence whatever on the purity of his heart or on his standing before God. That is determined entirely by his inward life and by the thoughts and words and deeds proceeding from him. This was a clean-cut contradiction of the very basis of ceremonialism. No wonder the Pharisees were offended. (Lk. 12.)

There were other ceremonial laws against which he offended, not by neglect but by actual violation of them. One of them was the understanding that every pious man, and especially a rabbi pretending to holiness, should keep at a distance from all suspected and unclean persons. Jesus shook this prejudice thoroughly. He made a point of seeking the society of publicans and sinners and of getting into conversation with Samaritans. In this also he justified himself by the prophetic motto: "Mercy, not sacrifice," showing that he discerned in the protest of the Pharisees the old clashing of ceremonial piety with mercy and love.

But the most frequent conflict was about the Sabbath law. The Jewish regard for the Sabbath was extremely strict. The Gospels narrate six instances in which Jesus broke the law openly and with determination. (Matt. 12, 1-8, 9-14, Lk. 13, 10-17; 14, 1-6; John 5, 1-18; 9, 1-41.) Most of them were cases of healing. Ceremonialism had so hardened the hearts of the religious leaders to the simplest feelings of humanity that they were chagrined to see a human being relieved of suffering. It is amusing to notice the argument which Jesus usually employed to bring their cruelty home to them. He appealed to their selfishness: "Who of you shall have an ass or an ox fall into a well, and will not straightway draw him up on a Sabbath day?" Nobody, of course. But you see, the ox or ass belonged to them, and the suffering man or woman did not, and that makes all the difference in the world.

There was one case, however, in which the violation consisted not in the relief of the sufferings of another, but in the satisfaction of a simple need of nature by the disciples. They were hungry on the Sabbath, and walking through fields of grain they plucked off some ears, rubbed out the corn, and ate it. According to the Pharisaic code this was work, and the Pharisees spoke out their horror. Jesus found a precedent which would avail with their lawyer souls. He reminded them that David and his men had once when hungry eaten the sacred shew-bread, which the priests alone were allowed to eat. Hunger therefore had the right-of-way over ceremonial restriction. The plain needs of humanity are the solid first facts of life, the corner posts, beams, and girders of the social structure; everything else, even their ceremonial and Sababth law, was a supplement of these, and if it contradicted them, it and not they would have to go. "The Sabbath was made for man, and not man for the Sabbath," and therefore the Son of man, as the representative of humanity and the interpreter of its need, is "lord even of the Sabbath." He can reduce its observance back to those limits within which it will be a blessing and not a curse to men. So even the Sabbath is stripped of its ceremonial sanctity, and its observance is based on its usefulness to man. (Mk. 2, 23-28.)

The hostility of Jesus to ceremonialism grew as he advanced in his work. When he declared his allegiance to the law in the Sermon on the Mount, it does not appear that he was thinking of its ceremonial features at all, for the laws he mentions to illustrate his meaning are moral laws. The distinction between moral and ceremonial laws did not exist with the Jews. To them law was law. Jesus did not define the distinction, but he made it, practically. When the attacks of the Pharisees compelled him to explain his attitude on the ceremonial laws, he declared them partly useless, like fasting and washing; partly put on a wrong and unhuman basis, like the Sabbath law; partly imperfect stages in the development of religion, like the hallowing of special places. (John 4, 19-24.) But the more he came in conflict with the Jewish religionists, the more did he perceive that ceremonialism was not merely an imperfection of religion, but very apt to be the most stubborn obstacle to a true religion. Those who were most concerned about the traditions of the elders were most inclined to set at nought the primary commandments of God. Under the pretext of religion they neglected the simplest duties of life. (Matt. 15, 1-9.) Those who were most minute in tithing mint, anise, and cumin were for that very reason likely to pay little attention to justice, mercy, and faith. (Matt. 23, 23-24.) It is just the temper of the ceremonialist to strain out the gnat and swallow the camel. Those who are full of uncleanness within are most likely to ornament and whitewash the exterior by outward performances indicating religious zeal. (Matt. 23, 25-28.) So Jesus has in his parables repeatedly taken the ceremonialist as the type of all that is unlovely and antagonistic to the spirit of the Kingdom. He paints for us the pompous Pharisee, strutting in the very presence of his God because he fasted twice a week and gave the tithes promptly; the surly elder brother, grumbling at the return of the prodigal; the priest and Levite slipping by the man groaning on the Jericho road. Has Jesus anywhere said a good word for ceremonies? He mentioned no ceremonial command in summing up the law for the young ruler. He certainly has woven for the Pharisee "the Nessus garment of ridicule" which he wears to this day and which has made his name and character common property in every literature. He has warned most emphatically against imagining that ceremonial performances can supplant justice and love, or that any sacrifice will be acceptable before God while he who brings it is not at peace with his fellow-men. (Matt. 5, 23-24.)

Jesus recognized no actions as being in themselves holy and for their own sake constituting a service of God. Of course he recognized prayer as the natural expression of loving fellowship with the Father. But even prayer is robbed of its idea of merit. Let a man talk to God naturally as his needs require, but let him not think that God cares for the prayer itself, for the length of it, or the beauty of it, or the set form of it. (Matt. 6, 5-15.) As for the rest, let the acts with which you would serve God, serve man. Receive the most humdrum creature for Christ's sake and you receive Christ, and receiving Christ you receive God. What need of performing ceremonies to please God when you can always please him by serving your neighbor? Christ has not, as the Catholic Church teaches, one vicar on earth, but a billion. If you desire to lay a sacrifice at the throne of the King, his plenipotentiary stands ready, commissioned to receive it. Who? The man next to you. (Matt. 25, 40-45.)

Of the existing acts of a ceremonial nature Jesus left none in existence as ceremonies. He instituted, however, two acts which are in a sense ceremonial, baptism and the Lord's Supper. Each is the expression of an inward relation to the unseen Christ. The one is the bath of consecration, the other the meal of fellowship. The one gives conscious and public expression to the free act of the individual, by which he renounces his old life and stakes his all, for life and death, on Jesus Christ. The other is the common meal by which the Christian brotherhood remembers the free and loving death of its Master and re-affirms its spiritual fellowship with him, its dependence on him, and its loyalty to him. The one marks the inception, the other the continuation of the freely chosen discipleship.

In instituting these outward expressions for spiritual facts, Jesus recognized that necessary trait of human nature which demands a body for the spirit, an incarnation for the unseen, a "local habitation and a name" for the intangible life of the soul. And the acts, which are created by the inward life, in turn strengthen the inward life. The Marseillaise was the embodied spirit of the French Revolution, but the singing of it in turn propagated and confirmed that spirit. The "stars and stripes" are the symbol of American patriotism, but the sight of the flag in turn kindles and fans the flame of patriotism. So baptism and communion are the result of existing spiritual discipleship; but when thus used, they not only express but establish that discipleship. And when these acts, as they ought, coincide in time with their spiritual equivalents, the two are fused into one, like soul and body, and those who speak of the entire procedure may describe it by either of its constitutent parts or by both jointly. That is the New Testament usage.

But it is a very different thing when the outward act is performed with the expectation of thereby creating the spiritual fact; when baptism is performed on an involuntary and unconscious individual, not to declare faith and loyalty and a new life, but to create them; when communion is performed, not as the expression of a fellowship with

Christ strong enough to demand an expression, but as a rite, which by its mere performance conveys some mysterious blessing. Then the body is expected to create its soul and life. That is the same reversal of nature and good sense which Jesus opposed in the Jewish notions of purification: it is not the bodily act which purifies or defiles the soul, but the reverse. As men have turned the democratic simplicity of Christ's commonwealth into an ecclesiastical aristocracy, so they have turned his spiritual worship into a system of rites and performances. It is apostasy, indeed it is heresy, not against the letter of a dogma, but against the very spirit of Christianity. The veneration of rites is due either to religious childhood which has not yet attained to the emancipation of the spirit, or to religious senility which seeks to disguise its impotence by dye and rouge.

Ceremonialism was the first intensive enemy of Christianity. For the enemies who maligned Paul at Corinth and destroyed his work in Galatia were ceremonialists, who insisted on binding up the limbs of a live faith in the grave clothes of a dead religion. The Jerusalem council, under the leadership of Peter, built a dam to ward off this destruction from the non-Jewish Christians. The dead works, against which Paul protested as powerless to save, were not works of justice or love but ritual performances, circumcision, the keeping of feasts and Sabbaths, the eating of some food and the ceremonial rejection of other food. Such actions might at one time have been commanded, he says, but they were only weak and beggarly rudiments; they were a man's shadow falling before him, like him in outline but not in substance. Since Christ had come, the performance of such things was not an advance but a retrogression. It might be necessary for some in a transition period to retain the old forms. Paul himself did so; but they must be inwardly superior to them, freely subjecting themselves to them as to an onerous duty for the sake of those who were still so weak that they could not discern between the Spirit and forms. The heroic battle of Luther against dead works and for faith was also a battle against ceremonialism. The dead works that Luther had in mind were masses, processions, crosses, holy water, relics and all the paraphernalia of outward performances in the Catholic Church of his day.

Ceremonialism is the symptom of spiritual decay. A dying faith utters itself in dead works. The Spirit is life, it can utter its life by anything. Infallibly those who have no life and yet desire the appearance of life seize on the expressions of a living Spirit and turn them into ceremonies.

Therefore the church must forever be on the watch against them. Here also eternal vigilance is the price of liberty.

Christ permits us to utter our filial relation to God in words, only he demands that these words be true and really utter something. He has also given us two acts by which we can more impressively utter the two central facts of our Christian life, and here too the first demand is that they be true and utter what they are meant to utter. All other service of God is to find its vent in the service of man. He that serves man for God's sake, serves God. And he that does not serve man, does not serve God, though he have a callous on each knee by much praying, though he wear out the cushions of his church pew, though he read his Bible every day and allow no fire in his house on the Sabbath, though he pray in public like an angel and exhort like an archangel—it is in the ear of God like the banging of a restaurant gong and like a boy's toy drum.

There remains one more question concerning the law of Christ, a question not about his teaching on any single duty, but about his teaching on the nature of duty, responsibility, and reward.

The fact of our responsibility is self-evident. We know we are responsible, and that is about as much as can be said concerning it. We are responsible for what we are within the limits of our freedom. And we are responsible for our influence or lack of influence on the world according to the law of solidarity. None of us lives to himself. God has kindled no light of any sort in us to have it concealed under a bushel. The mere existence of the light proves that it was meant to shine and bless. The cause and nature of our responsibility are repeatedly represented by Jesus under the likeness of a trust. We are responsible for what we have, because we did not give it to ourselves.

It is a fund entrusted to our management. A trustee differs from a servant in the freedom of his management. He is not under the daily and minute orders of a master. He knows the purpose of his trust, he knows the spirit of him who entrusted it; within those limits he is free to deal. But he is just as responsible as, or even more responsible than, a servant. He will have to give an account of his management some day. And while all allowances are made if he can show that he has acted in good faith according to the purpose of the trust, no allowance whatever is made if it appears that he has appropriated the trust funds to private uses. The parables of the talents and pounds do not bear on money alone. There was probably no great amount of wealth to be managed by those to whom Jesus told the parable of the pounds on the way from Jericho to Jerusalem. It refers to intellectual ability and attainments, hereditary strength of will, knowledge of truth, beauty of person, physical strength, social position, in short, everything which constitutes a working capital in human society. Of course it applies to money also. If any man claims the right to have more property than his fellows, he can justify his claim only by regarding it as a trust. But in that case he will have to demonstrate that he can use it for them better than they could use it for themselves. He places himself voluntarily under the law of trusts, and that law is all the more inexorable because it gives such latitude. Can anyone assert that the wealthy classes on the whole have not yielded to the temptation of trusteeship, the temptation to embezzle trust funds? What business corporation would tolerate such a board of trustees as the people of the United States possess in their wealthy men? The grievance is all the greater because the stockholders of the defrauded corporation are the poor, the widows, the orphans. What shall the master of a steward do who, instead of serving the household, begins to act as its master and tyrant, to "beat the manservants and the maidservants and to eat and drink, and to be drunken"? (Lk. 12, 41-46.) Every trustee against whom there is well-grounded suspicion, by the lavishness of his own outlay and the meagerness of his expenditures for the trust purposes, that he is appropriating the funds may be summoned to give an account. God has reserved the grand jury and the Supreme Court of the world to himself, whither he may summon evil-doers against whom no plaintiff rises and to which those who are unjustly judged on earth may still appeal. But he has instituted a minor court on earth in which humanity sits as jury. Before that court the wealthy classes of the civilized nations are now being called to give an account of their trusts. Humanity is only doing its duty before God in calling them to account.

The degree of our responsibility, according to Christ's teachings, is exactly graded according to our knowledge, opportunity, and ability. The degree of knowledge in the slothful servant measures the number of stripes which he deserves. (Lk. 12, 47.) The opportunities enjoyed by Capernaum, the Galilean cities, and the men who listened to Jesus made their unbelief and disobedience more culpable than the sins of the proverbially wicked, of Tyre and Sidon, of the accursed Sodom, and of Nineveh whose wickedness rose up before God. (Matt. 11, 20-24; 12, 41.) Ability measures obligation: "To whomsoever much is given, of him shall much be required." (Lk. 12, 48.) The Jews, Paul says, shall be judged according to the high law which they possess, and the Gentiles by whatever knowledge they have. (Rom. 2, 12-15.)

And as reproof and punishment fall heaviest on those who have done least in proportion to their great abilities, so praise and reward are meted out most richly to those who with small opportunities have done most. The widow's two mites, in Christ's sight, are more than the large gifts of the rich, because they are a sacrifice, a surrender of part of herself. (Mk. 12, 41-44.) It is effort and sacrifice which tell before God, it is the leaving of houses and brethren and lands for Christ's sake that shall "receive a hundredfold and inherit eternal life." (Matt. 19, 29.) The parable of the talents and the parable of the pounds are alike in their general idea, but there is this difference: In the former, two servants start with unequal capital and present gains which, though unequal in amount, in each case are 100 percent of the capital, and they receive exactly the same commendation. In the latter parable, the servants begin with equal gains, and their reward is unequal and exactly in proportion to the percentage of their gains. (Matt. 25, 14-30; Lk. 19, 11-27.)

This is a principle of obligation which in the world prevails only to a small extent. Some parents have loving insight enough to praise their children according to their efforts and not according to the results of their effort. But the world at large does not reckon that way. It regards the quantity and quality of the finished product and not the effort that lies behind it. It employs women or children to do the work which men did, and for their greater efforts pays them less. It worships success and not sacrifice. Christ's principle of measuring merit would be revolutionary, if applied. It would level some reputations and exalt others. It may be that some day even the reward paid for work will be measured in some degree by Christ's standard. Acclamation can certainly be more justly rendered in the future. Every man can help do that. He can refuse to admire a public benefaction given from a man's superfluity, and he can search out cases in which a sacrifice has been made, and hold them up to admiration. Every such effort will correct the public standard of judgement. The church itself is derelict. I have seen bulky gifts hailed with admiration by religious assemblies. I have heard pastors in ministers' meetings narrate with grief the death of Mr. Dives, who had left $100,000 for a memorial church bearing his name, while ten millions went to his weeping relatives. I have seldom, if ever, heard any public acclamation at the death of a poor woman, whose back had grown bent and whose joints had become rheumatic over the wash-tub and who had yet been cheerful and helpful, bringing up her family honestly, perhaps rising early on Sunday morning to teach a class, and ever with a dollar to spare for the Johnstown flood, the famine in China, or some neighbor poorer than herself. And yet there are many such. Christian men should deliberately refuse to measure gifts and efforts by their size but make the degree of sacrifice, so far as it can be ascertained, the measure of their admiration.

Christianity clearly holds out a reward to goodness and warns wrong of the punishment in store. There is a "righteous judgment of God; who will render to every man according to his works; to them that by patience in well-doing seek for glory and honor and incorruption, eternal life; but unto them that are self-seeking, and obey not the truth, but obey unrighteousness, shall be wrath and indignation, tribulation and anguish upon every soul of man that worketh evil." (Rom. 2, 5-9.) It is inevitable. It must be so. The results of a bad life will be different from those of a good life. This certainly is constantly added in the Christian teachings as an incentive to righteousness. Christ warns us to forgive that we may be forgiven, and not to judge lest we be judged. (Matt. 6, 14-15; 7, 1-2.) In exhorting to plain trust in God he dwells on the uselessness of anxiety. (Matt. 6, 25-34.) Paul assures his friends that their labor is not in vain in the Lord, and he quickens his own weary steps by the thought of the crown of righteousness which the righteous Judge will give to his faithful servant. The Apocalypse is always holding out the reward "to him that overcometh," and John speaks of the richer life awaiting those who are even now children of God, and admonishes them to purify themselves in view of this hope.

But while Christianity plainly and often speaks of the certainty of reward, it forbids us to do the right for the sake of reward. It holds it up as an encouragement, but not as a cause for right action. It asserts the utility of righteousness, but it repudiates the utilitarian basis of morality. It insists that it is blessed to give, but does not command us to give that we may be blessed.

Jesus condemns the alms-giving which is done with an eye to a reputation of benevolence. (Matt. 6, 2-4.) He bids us purposely to single out those actions for which we can expect no return; to invite to dinner those by whom we do not expect to be repaid, to do kindnesses to those from whom we expect no recompense. (Lk. 6, 31-35; 14, 12-14.) The utilitarian morality is the morality of natural selfishness, which even bad men know well how to handle; only the morality which does good for its own sake, independently of considerations of usefulness, allies us to God, who does even so. The "golden rule" contains a rough and ready method of finding out what is right; it does not contain the motive of doing right. We are to do to others *as* we would have them do to us, and not in order that they may do the same to us.

Our heart demands the belief that

> It's wiser being good than bad;
> It's safer being meek than fierce;
> It's fitter being sane than mad.

The moral universe would crash about us, if it were not so. Even the most heroic soul needs that conviction for itself. The good man, standing in the flood of adversity and seeing no star of hope to herald relief or vindication, can yet be calm and hold to the right because it is right and not because it is good. But soon the heart will protest and demand like Job at least to believe that its "avenger liveth and shall stand forth in later days." It may by faith defer the vindication to future ages or another world, but somewhere God must prove himself just.

But this hope is the divine food of the persecuted prophet at the river Kerith, and not the sauce of Ahab's feast. To taste the power of the coming era belongs by right to those who have left the full enjoyment of the present era. It is misused when it is offered as a bait to induce a grudging hand to let slip some present enjoyment.

Jesus had no love for the dickering spirit. He spoke of treasures laid up in heaven, but whenever anyone tried to calculate his savings or asked for the vouchers, he was reproved. When Jesus had asked the young ruler to leave all things and he had refused, Peter, with the naïve selfishness of an Oriental, reminded the Master that the disciples had left all and had followed him: "What then shall we have?" Jesus promised full reward to them and to all who have left anything for his sake. But he immediately went on to narrate a story of a man who hired laborers to work in his vineyard, and when evening came, paid every man justly, but some more generously than seemed right to others. So some began to haggle and demand his generosity as their right, and were rebuked. (Matt. 19, 27–20, 16.) The point of the story is turned against the mercantile spirit of the disciples. He condemns the arrogance which thinks it has not only done all that could be demanded, but has even put the Almighty under obligations. He bids us do our duty cheerfully, and after we have done it all, still regard it as merely our duty. (Lk. 17, 7-10.)

The idea of reward and punishment has been misused in the church. The calculating spirit has been catered to. The Catholic Church sets a price on its prayers and processions. The reciting of one sort of prayer cuts down purgatory by two hundred days and of another by three hundred. This cannot fail to have the effect of misleading the minds of the people. They do good, but the edge is taken off from their goodness by the calculation of how much reward it is going to bring them. The natural bias of man is toward selfishness anyway, and there is no need of giving it artificial incentives. Protestantism meant to cut off the mercantile method of piety by denying all merit whatever to human actions and making every man absolutely dependent on divine grace and mercy. It has, I think, succeeded in eliminating the idea of earning reward from the single acts of goodness, but it has so persistently held up the hope of heaven and the fear of hell as the reasons why men should do right, that these have after all become the dominant incentives of the mass of church members in Protestant countries. The single acts of religion and morality are not supposed to earn anything, but everything is lumped together and reward expected. It is a more long-range selfishness than that which seeks immediate gratification, but it is selfishness still. The farmer who deposits the proceeds of his market sales in the bank on Saturday instead of investing them in a store suit or mixed drinks, is a prudent man; by and by he will use his savings to buy another meadow lot. On Sunday he abstains from carrying in his hay, misses a whole working day, walks three miles in the broiling sun to the meeting-house where he succeeds in keeping awake part of the time. He is looking for "the welfare of his soul," his "eternal well-being." He is the same prudent man in the one case as in the other; it is in each case his "well-being" that he is thinking of; only one investment is to be realized in this world, and the other in the next.

We should not condemn this. It is natural. I doubt if such considerations can ever be entirely eliminated. They are present even in the love of parents to their children, of husband and wife. That self-control which can renounce immediate gratification for the sake of some larger and higher profit in the future is the necessary condition of all noble pursuits and of an established society. We do not even say that the alternative of reward or punishment, of heaven or hell, should not be held out to men to arouse them to righteousness. In the parable of the unjust steward Jesus appealed to the rich by their faculty of forecasting the future. It was perhaps the only nerve of their stunted conscience which could be made to respond to the galvanic current of truth. But it seems to me that the habitual and exclusive use of this incentive in much of the popular preaching even of our day carries with it a serious danger. It hardens men in their selfishness instead of rousing them out of it. It changes the range but not the quantity of it.

Our natural impulse is to sacrifice others to ourselves. The danger of much of our current Christianity is that we learn to sacrifice ourselves to ourselves. True Christianity educates us toward sacrificing ourselves to others, to humanity, to God. That can be learned only if there is an aim constantly before us calling for self-forgetful service and enlisting all our strength. In fixing our mind on that we shall forget to fix it on ourselves. The church must begin once more to preach the Kingdom of God as the central and all-embracing doctrine. That will draw us out of ourselves. And in forgetting ourselves and not seeking our lives because we seek the Kingdom, we shall find our lives. By ceasing to strive for individual perfection, we shall attain a truer and more harmonious perfection. If necessary, let the call be to those who are too engrossed in their gain to care for the Kingdom: "Save yourselves." But to those who do care, let the word be: "The Kingdom of God." And if, in the long and often seemingly hopeless battle against vested wrong and willful ignorance, the heart of the revolutionary soldier of God grows weary, if he looks back at profits spurned and honors untasted, then he can justly look forward to the rest that is reserved for the people of God, and hear by faith the words of his Master: "Well done, good and faithful servant, enter thou into the joy of thy Lord."

c. *Present Prospects*

We have discussed the aim which Christianity has set for itself. We have reviewed the forces and laws at its disposal. It remains for us to examine the methods of its progress and the present condition of the Christian revolutionary movement.

At the outset we are met by an objection: "You propose to examine the methods of the revolutionary progress. Is there any progress at all? Is Christianity a victorious force? Can the aspirations of humanity for purity, righteousness, freedom, and peace produce anything more than the feverish tossings of a prisoner in chains, the oscillating equilibrium of a pair of scales, the rush of the surf up the beach which yet ever retreats with a moan? Will God conquer?"

The heart of faith can give no answer save the answer of Columbus. The ocean waste seems limitless, the promised land is long in appearing; but we refuse to turn back. Every prophetic soul has believed in the ultimate victory of God and right. Isaiah saw the mountain of Jehovah exalted in the last day above every mountain. The seer of the Apocalypse saw one riding forth on whose garment was written: "King of kings, and Lord of lords," and he heard a voice as the voice of rushing waters, saying: "Hallelujah, for the Lord God Omnipotent reigneth." Paul believed that the time would come for every knee to bow in the name of Jesus and for every tongue to confess him Lord. And Jesus? He had a better right to despair of the world than the easy pessimist of to-day. He did his utmost and the world crushed him. Did Jesus believe in the triumph of righteousness? We hear a cry from the darkness: "Eli, lama asaphthani." We see him sigh: "When the Son of man cometh, shall he find faith on the earth"? And yet he believed. In the face of death he asserted the triumph of right in his own person: "From henceforth shall the Son of man be seated at the right hand of the power of God." (Lk. 22, 69.) Even that sigh of doubt was but the fringe of his energetic promise that God will surely avenge his elect who cry to him day and night against their oppressors. (Lk. 18, 1-8.)

To do the right against all considerations of utility is the categorical imperative of duty. To believe in the triumph of right against all appearances of defeat is the categorical imperative of faith. To deny the former is moral suicide. To surrender the latter is religious suicide.

Insofar as Christianity is identical with righteousness and with the cause of God, its ultimate victory is certain. But I am not asserting that it is victorious at all times and all along the line.

Public thought in America is so far from doubting the value of life and the triumph of right that it is in a perpetual chuckle of satisfaction at "the progress of the world." Hoary wrongs are crumbling; the nations are marching toward popular liberty; steamboats are getting faster, kings rarer, creeds more liberal; what more would you have? Give humanity free play and we shall have the millennium here on schedule time.

This hopefulness is probably due partly to our youthfulness and partly to the idea of evolution which has saturated our thought. We conceive of the world rolling slowly out into the light of day; therefore every step must be day-ward, every change must be an improvement, every new idea must approximate more nearly to the truth than the one it supplants, every tendency must be just. That is the way in which evolution has taken hold of the popular mind.

But this view is not accurate. Evolution—granting it proved—teaches the possibility of change for the better, not the certainty of it. Environment may modify backward as well as forward. Degeneration is as much a scientific fact as development. The forces of death and destruction press hard on the forces of life. The assumption that, on the whole, evolution is moving forward and upward rests partly on sight, but even more on faith.

The matter becomes even more doubtful when the idea of evolution is applied to human history. The nations of the earth have not moved forward with unfaltering march. Concerning some, the proof is wanting that they have ever been lower than they are now. Of others proof is abundant that they have been higher than they are now, and, having come down, they apparently propose to stay down. In Egypt, in Central America, in Asia Minor, in Greece the monuments of a higher civilization look down on a degenerate state. In India and China there is stagnation, if not degeneration. In fact it looks as if every nation had its period of childhood and its teens, and then, when growth is most rapid and life most luscious, it is stung by some hidden disease and sapped of its virility. It declines and henceforth is old. Some nations have collapsed quickly. Others have stood erect for centuries and perhaps, like Italy, have risen to a second period of glory. There are only a few nations whose track through the last two thousand years seems headed toward the Kingdom of God. It is a wavering, lagging line, yet it goes forward. And they seem to have the faculty also of planting new and vigorous societies and of putting a thrill of life into their paralytic sister nations.

In short, while we hold fast our faith in the destiny of humanity and in the capacity of every nation to grow up into an ever higher stature and, for aught we know, into an endless bloom of manhood, yet history solemnly tells us that there are lost nations as well as lost individuals. "Many are called, but few are chosen." The Bible itself tells of a nation, elect of God, which failed in the hour of its visitation, and its vineyard has been taken away from it.

History does not encourage the rollicking optimism which trusts men, especially in the United States, to come down every time feet foremost, like a cat. Nations also have to strive with fear and trembling to be saved. For humanity also the gate is narrow and the way to life is straight.

It is a goodly doctrine, that of human progress. It is very sweet to man. It is delightful to know that, after a few more hampering traditions and worn-out institutions are knocked away, humanity will ride down into the perfect life like a ship from her dock into the sea. The presupposition of this doctrine is that man is by nature good and tends upward, if only he is not dragged down by outward forces. I am frank to confess that I once felt all the attractions of this view of life. But I have been obliged to yield it up and to say now with Browning:

> The candid incline to surmise of late that the Christian faith may be false, I find. I still, to suppose it true, for my part, see reasons and reasons; this, to begin: 'Tis the faith that launched point-blank her dart at the head of a lie—taught Original Sin, the Corruption of Man's Heart.

It is not true that man tends by nature upward. It is the downward way that is easy; the upward way is steep and toilsome. It requires no effort for us to yield to temptation; the effort comes when we try to resist. The number of those who overcome even the natural intellectual inertia is small. Educational institutions do not sustain themselves; with few exceptions they would collapse if the benefactions of individuals or the taxing power of the community were withdrawn from their support. We have to pass laws to get children into school and to keep them out of the saloon. In Europe the theatres giving the classic plays have to be subsidized; those rendering adapted French plays need no subsidies.

None of us individually drifts into purity, justice, and unselfishness, as we all know. And humanity as a whole would likewise, if let alone, by no means roll into the millennium, but by a broad and easy track into a hell on earth, into rottenness, beastliness, and self-destruction. What association of men or what human institution does not sag downward? What political party does not grow corrupt? What church does not tend toward formalism and worldliness? What charitable society is not in danger of becoming uncharitable? What educational system or institution does not stiffen into pedantry to the stifling of intellect? What body of law needs no effort to exhume justice buried under its legal decisions like Nero's guests under his shower of roses?

And not only is the natural tendency downward by mere moral inertia. We have to reckon also with the fact that there is such a thing as conscious, determined, malicious love of evil. The natural thing is to do evil because it looks sweet before it is done, then to do it again because it has acquired power, and thus to continue the downward course. But all this while man knows it to be wrong, he wishes that he did not do it, he is pained to see the young and innocent acquiring the same habit. But it seems to be possible for the human spirit to give itself to evil and to love it, to take delight in ensnaring the innocent, to corrupt their minds systematically, to interfere consciously with the efforts to better society, and not only to turn sideward with a hiss at the approach of purity, but to strike a poisoned fang into its heel. If those who have consciously abandoned the principle of selfishness and handed themselves over to love are children of God, then such are children of the devil. They bear the mark of the beast on brow and hand, on intellect and action.

Now, such men and women have power. There are periods of history which, like a forest tract with charred trunks, show the passing of one of these human firebrands. And what these Catilinian spirits have been in the larger territory of history, their smaller kindred, smiling behind the saloon bar, button-holing local politicians, promenading on the city streets, telling anecdotes on the kegs of a village grocery, or laying snares in drawing-rooms, are to the social circle within which they move. If a determined good man has power, so has a determined bad man. He can even with the same exertion of force accomplish more, because he appeals to the lower instincts of lust, hate, pride, and needs only to draw out the pegs to set the log rolling. These forces have to be reckoned with. They add momentum to the natural downward drift of humanity. Therefore our wrestling is not merely with the natural weakness of flesh and blood, but "against the principalities, against the powers, against the world-rulers of this darkness, against the spiritual hosts of wickedness."

Let us have no illusions. The world will not evolve into a Kingdom of God by natural processes. It is uphill work. It is a battle. Every inch will have to be fought for.

But neither let us have *any* cowardice, especially no croaking sloth hiding under a religious garb. We *must* conquer. We may use the old crusaders' cry with a purer right than they: *Deus lo volt*—God wills it!

And what, then, shall lift humanity up, if the force that raises it is not naturally inherent in it? Water cannot rise higher than its source. An effect cannot contain more than its causes. One epoch of history cannot be greater and nobler than the one out of which it has grown, unless an additional force has entered into its composition. Whence does that force come in human history?

The same question has been raised concerning the asserted upward evolution of the organic world below man. If the higher forms of life have developed from the lowest, what has pushed them up? Those who believe in God have not hesitated to reply: God. He is immanent in the world, forever active and working. It is his force and his guidance which moulds his existing works into higher forms through his Kingdom.

We take exactly that position concerning the life of humanity. God is in it. "The Father worketh hitherto." His will is set toward his Kingdom on earth. His Spirit works upon the spirits of men and of nations. Within limits known to him, and for reasons known by him, he suffers their disobedience and resistance. But he wearies not. His force is still put forth. And the medium through which it is most exerted is those human spirits who have freely surrendered themselves to the will and service of righteousness. There God gets a purchase on humanity. There he can grip it. Such spirits he fills with the ideas and impulses which their time needs in order to take the next step forward, and through these channels the forces of God flow out into humanity. These are the prophetic souls. In them and in their work lies the hope of humanity's progress. The upward forces communicated through them have to overcome the downward inclination of flesh and blood, as life in the physical world overcomes the force of gravity.

The hope of the world therefore lies in religion. Politics cannot lift man; at its best it removes hindrances to his uplifting or refrains from laying stumbling blocks in his way; at its worst it defeats the aims of justice and lends tools to the leagued interests of oppression. Its power in either direction is immense. But it never creates moral forces, it simply yields to them.

Even education does not lift man. It enhances his power either for good or evil. It refines his good or evil enjoyments. But it does not make him good. France is the living demonstration of that to our day. They dress better and converse better at Paris than the rest of us do; they write a more brilliant style, coin cleverer epigrams, and see plays more intelligently. But in spite of that, France supplies the world with lasciviousness and with virulent unbelief.

No, as Mazzini said: "You seek to perform a work of regeneration, and you hope to accomplish it by banishing every religious idea from your work! Politics merely accepts man as he is. The religious idea alone has power to transform. It is the very breath of Humanity; its life, soul, conscience and manifestation. Humanity exists in the consciousness of its origin and the presentiment of its destiny; and only reveals itself by concentrating its power upon one of the intermediate points between these two. Now this is precisely the function of the religious idea. That idea constitutes a faith in an origin common to us all; sets before us, as a principle; a common future; unites all the active faculties on one sole center, whence they are continuously evolved and developed in the direction of that future, and guides the latent forces of the human mind towards it." (Essays, p. 36.)

PART III

BIBLIOGRAPHY

1

THE WORKS OF WALTER RAUSCHENBUSCH

a. Books

Christianity and the Social Crisis. New York: The Macmillan Company, 1907.

Subsequent publications in New York: Association Press, 1907, 1908, 1909, 1910, 1911; New York: The Macmillan Company, 1908, 1910, and 1912; (The Macmillan Standard Library), New York: The Macmillian Company, 1913, 1917, and 1920; ed. with new introduction by Robert D. Cross. New York: Harper & Row, 1964.

Translations: *Le christianisme et la crise sociale.* Trans. by Madame J. Vallette-Babut. Paris: Fischbacher, 1919.

Christianizing the Social Order. New York: The Macmillan Company, 1912.

Subsequent publications in Boston: The Pilgrim Press, 1912; in New York: The Macmillan Company, 1913.

Translations: *Le plat de lentilles: Quelques chapitres de Christianizing the Social Order.* Trans. by S. Godet. Neuchâtel: Editions Forum, 1921.

La situation tragique du riche: Quelques chapitres de Christianizing the Social Order. Trans. by S. Godet. Neuchâtel: Editions Forum, 1921.

Agir, comment? Quelques chapitres de Christianizing the Social Order. Trans. by S. Godet. Neuchâtel: Editions Forum, 1922.

Samfundets kristianisering. Trans. by Eugene Hanssen. Oslo: Steen, 1914. Subsequent publications in Oslo: Steen, 1915, and 1916.

Yhteiskuntaelämän uudistus kristinuskon hengessä I (Kristinuske ja yhteiskuntaelämä IV). Trans. by K. Eemil Roine. Porvoo, Finland: Werner Soderstrom Oy., 1917. Subsequent publications in Porvoo: Werner Soderstrom Oy., 1919, and 1920.

Dare We Be Christians? Boston: The Pilgrim Press, 1914.

Translations: *Osons-nous être chrétiens?* Trans. by M. Farelly. Paris: Fischbacher, 1931.

Evangeliums-Lieder 1 und 2, with Ira D. Sankey. New York: The Biglow and Main Company, 1897.
Subsequent publications: *Evangeliums-Sanger 1 und 2*. Kassel: J. G. Oncken, 1907.

Evangeliums-Sanger 1, 2 und 3, with Ira D. Sankey. Kassel: J. G. Oncken, 1919.
Subsequent publications in Kassel: J. G. Oncken, 1929, and 1931.

Evangeliums-Sanger 3: 150 Neuere Lieder für Abendgottesdienste und besondere Versammlungen, with Ira D. Sankey. Kassel: J. G. Oncken, 1907.

For God and the People: Prayers of the Social Awakening. Boston: The Pilgrim Press, 1910.
Subsequent publications in Boston: The Pilgrim Press, 1925; in London: Student Christian Movement, 1927; in Greenwood, S. C.: Attic, 1966.
Translations: *Pour Dieu et le peuple, prières du réveil social*. Trans. by A. P. Bovet. Paris: Fischbacher, 1914.
Für Gott und das Volk: Gebete der sozialen Erweckung. Trans. by Minna Griebel and Heinrich Frick with an appendix by Conrad Henry Moehlmann. Göttingen: Vandenhoeck & Ruprecht, 1928.
Preces Fraternias. Trans. by A. Rocha. Rio de Janeiro: Centro brasileiro de publicidade, 1936.
Per Dio e per il popolo. Trans. and ed. by G. E. Meille. *Bilychnis*, III (May, 1914), 359-64.

A Gospel for the Social Awakening: Selections from the Writings of Walter Rauschenbusch. Compiled by Benjamin E. Mays with introduction by C. Howard Hopkins. New York: Association Press, 1950.

Das Leben Jesu: Ein systematischer Studiengang für Jugendvereine und Bibelklassen. Cleveland: P. Ritter, 1895. Reprinted from *Der Jugend-Herold*. Cleveland: Publikationsverein der deutschen Baptisten-Gemeinden Nordamerikas, 1894-1895.
Subsequent publications in Sonntagsschul-Lehrer-Bibliothek, Kassel: J. G. Oncken, 1898; and Cleveland: P. Ritter, 1909.
Translations: *Vaar mastares liv: En systematisk undervisnigskurs för ungdomsföreningar och bibelklasser*. Trans. by Willi Mascher. Stockholm: B. M.: Bokforlag, 1925.
Leben und Wirken von August Rauschenbusch, by August Rauschenbusch, completed by his son Walter Rauschenbusch. Kassel: J. G. Oncken, 1901.

Neue Lieder, with Ira D. Sankey. Authorized trans. of *Gospel Hymns Number 5*. New York: The Biglow and Main Company, 1889. Subsequent publication in Kassel: J. G. Oncken, 1891.

Die politische Verfassung unseres Landes (Civil Government of the United States): Ein Handbuch zum Unterrichte für die deutsch-amerikanische Jugend. Cleveland: P. Ritter, 1902.

A Rauschenbusch Reader: The Kingdom of God and the Social Gospel. Compiled by Benson Y. Landis with an interpretation of the life and work of Walter Rauschenbusch by Harry Emerson Fosdick. New York: Harper & Brothers, Publishers, 1957.

The Righteousness of the Kingdom. Ed. with introduction by Max L. Stackhouse. Nashville: Abingdon Press, 1968.

The Social Principles of Jesus (College Voluntary Study Courses, Fourth Year: Part I). New York: Association Press, 1916.

Subsequent publications in New York: Association Press, 1927; New York: Grosset & Dunlap, 1943; in Toronto: McLeod, 1943.

Translations: *Les principes sociaux de Jesus.* Trans. by S. Godet. Geneva: Editions Labor, 1922.

Sociální zásady Ježíšovy. Trans. by Frantisek Sedlácek. Prague: Y.M.C.A., 1921. Subsequent publication with preface by J. L. Hromodka, Prague: Y.M.C.A., 1926.

A Theology for the Social Gospel. New York: The Macmillan Company, 1917.

Subsequent publications: The Macmillan Company, 1922; Nashville: Abingdon Press, 1960.

Translations*: *Die religiösen Grundlagen der sozialen Botschaft.* Trans. by Clara Ragaz with introduction by Leonhard Ragaz. Zürich: Rotapfel-Verlag, 1922.

Unto Me. Boston: The Pilgrim Press, 1912.

Translation: "A Moi," by M. le prof. Mailhet, *Le christianisme social,* XXXVIII (March, 1925), 282-93.

b. Published Articles, Reviews, Pamphlets

"About Politics," *For the Right,* I (March, 1890), 2.

"Aim of Social Christianity," *The Gazette.* Delaware, Ohio, 1911. Clipping in Rauschenbusch Scrapbook at Colgate-Rochester Divinity School Library.

* Translations of *A Theology for the Social Gospel* into far-eastern languages were mentioned in "Tributes from Friends, Alumni, Students," *The Rochester Theological Seminary Bulletin, The Record: Rauschenbusch Number,* LXIX (November, 1918), 53 and 74. A request to translate the work into Chinese had been received and a Japanese translation was either already completed or ready for preparation at that time. These translations are yet to be located.

In addition to the previously noted translations, Chinese, Japanese, Spanish, and Russian translations of "some" of Rauschenbusch's works were mentioned in the biographical entry, "Walter Rauschenbusch," *The National Cyclopedia of American Biography.* New York: James T. White & Co., 1926, XIX, 193. These translations and details of publication could not be located for inclusion in this bibliography.

"American Christianity and National Life," *The Standard,* LXII (1915), 1303-5.

"Der amerikanische Katholizismus," "Der Protestantismus: Nordamerika," "Der Katholizismus: Nordamerika," "Der Katholizismus: Zentral- und Südamerika," "Der Katholizismus: Vereinigte Staaten von Nordamerika," "Der Protestantismus: Die Vereinigten Staaten von Nordamerika," *Handbuch der Kirchengeschichte für Studierende.* Ed. Horst Stephan (Tübingen: J. C. B. Mohr, 1909; Rev. ed. 1931), IV, 36-38, 137-42, 174, 254-55, 259-60, 390-404.

"Auch ein amerikanischer Professor: Nachruf von Alfred Hess," *Christliche Welt* (January 2, 1919), p. 9.

"Augustus Rauschenbusch: An Address by His Son, Walter," *Rochester Democrat and Chronicle* (October 27, 1900).

"Autocracy and War: Germany's Evil Heritage," *Rochester Democrat and Chronicle* (July 1, 1918).

"The Baptist Contribution," *Freedom and the Churches.* Ed. Charles W. Wendte (Boston: American Unitarian Association, 1913), pp. 1-10.

"Baptists and Social Progress," *Centennary of Organized Baptist Work, 1912* (Pittsburgh: 1913).

"Be Fair to Germany," *Lutheran Church Work and Observer,* III (November, 1914), 8-10.

"The Belated Races and the Social Problems," American Missionary Association pamphlet (January, 1914). Clipping in Rauschenbusch Scrapbook at Colgate-Rochester Divinity School Library.

"Beneath the Glitter," *The Inquirer* (1887). Clipping in Rauschenbusch Scrapbook at Colgate-Rochester Divinity School Library.

"Breaking Bread," letter, *The Independent,* XLVIII (March, 1896).

"The Brotherhood of the Kingdom," *Brotherhood Leaflets,* No. 2 (1893).

"Can a Christian Be a Socialist?" *The Philadelphia Press* (February 27, 1893).

Cement of Society (Boston: The Pilgrim Press, between 1912 and 1917).

"Centralization of Baptist Polity," *Thirteenth Annual Session of the Baptist Congress* (New York: Baptist Congress Publishing Company, 1896), pp. 57-60.

"Christ the Source of All Our Good," *The Treasury,* XVIII (February, 1901), 757-58.

"Christian Socialism," *A Dictionary of Religion and Ethics.* Ed. Shailer Mathews and G. B. Smith (New York: The Macmillan Company, 1921), pp. 90-91.

"Christian Socialism and the Brotherhood of the Kingdom: an Interview with Walter Rauschenbusch," *The New York Press* (June 3, 1894).

"Christian Union as an Historical Problem." Clipping in Rauschenbusch Scrapbook at Colgate-Rochester Divinity School Library.

"Christianity a Democratic Religion," *For the Right,* II (December, 1890), 4.

"Christlicher Sozialismus einst und jetzt," *Christliche Welt* (June 3, 1909), pp. 538-42.

"The Church and Its Attitude toward the Labor Movement," *The Iron Molders Journal* (January, 1902), p. 3.

"Church and Money," *The National Baptist* (March 23, 1893).

"The Church and Money Power," *Eleventh Annual Session of the Baptist Congress* (New York: Baptist Congress Publishing Company, 1894), pp. 10-17.

"Church and Socialists: An American View," *Evening Gazette* (Aberdeen, Scotland, May 3, 1911).

"The Church and Social Questions," *Conservation of National Ideals.* Ed. Margaret E. Sangster (New York: Fleming H. Revell Company, 1911), pp. 99-122.

"The Church's Duty," *Rochester Herald* (September 4, 1899).

"The Coming of the Lord," *Report of the Amity Missionary Conference,* Fifth Annual Conference Report (1895), p. 3.

"Comments on Strikes for the Eight Hour Day," *For The Right,* I (June, 1890), 2.

"A Conquering Idea," *The Examiner* (July 21, 1892). Clipping in Rauschenbusch Scrapbook at Colgate-Rochester Divinity School Library.

"The Conservation of the Social Service Message," *Messages of the Men and Religion Movement,* Report of the Social Service Commission at the Congress of the Men and Religion Forward Movement in New York, April 19-24, 1912 (New York: Association Press, 1912), II, 121-25.

"Contribution of Jesus to the Social Movement," *The Springfield Union* (Springfield, Mass., January 29, 1910).

"Contributions Socialism Has Made to the Social Feeling of Which We Are All Conscious," *Rochester Democrat and Chronicle* (December 13, 1909).

"The Culture of the Spiritual Life," *Rochester Baptist Monthly* (November, 1897). Clipping in Rauschenbusch Scrapbook at Colgate-Rochester Divinity School Library.

"The Czar's Peace Proposal," *The Pittsburgh Post* (Clipping of sermon preached at the Fourth Avenue Baptist Church, Pittsburgh, March 6, 1899). Rauschenbusch Scrapbook at Colgate-Rochester Divinity School Library.

"The Deacons of the New Testament," *Homiletic Review,* XXXVIII (December, 1899), 539-43.

"Deutsche Trinksitten in amerikanischer Beleuchtung," *Evangelisch-Sozial,* Vol. 17 (July/August 1908), 129-38. Also in Rauschenbusch Scrapbook at Colgate-Rochester Divinity School Library.

"Devotion to Truth," *Colloquium* (November, 1899). Clipping in Rauschenbusch Scrapbook at Colgate-Rochester Divinity School Library.

"Discipling vs. Proselyting," *Report of the Amity Missionary Conference,* Third Annual Conference Report (1893), p. 32.

"Dr. Fox on the Causes of Poverty," *Christian Inquirer* (April 5, 1894).

"Dr. Willmarth and the Kingdom of God," *National Baptist* (December 14, 1893).

"Does the New Testament Provide a Definite and Permanent Church Polity?" *Twenty-Second Annual Session of the Baptist Congress* (New York: Baptist Congress Publishing Company, 1904), pp. 108-15.

"Dogmatic and Practical Socialism," *Rochester Herald* (March 14, 1901).

"Drop a Nickel in the Slot," *For the Right,* I (January, 1890), 3.

"The Economic Basis of Democracy," *Ford Hall Folks* (February 7, 1915).

"The Education of a Jesuit," *The Treasury,* XI (September, 1893), 486-88.

"Der Einzelkelch in Amerika: Brief an Professor Spitta," *Monatsschrift für Gottesdienst und kirchliche Kunst,* IX (October, 1904), 303-6.

"Emotionalism in Religion," *Eleventh Annual Session of the Baptist Congress* (New York: Baptist Congress Publishing Company, 1894), pp. 33-34.

"England and Germany," *The Watchman* (November 16, 1899). Clipping in Rauschenbusch Scrapbook at Colgate-Rochester Divinity School Library.

"Ethical versus Forensic Conceptions of Salvation," *Eleventh Annual Session of the Baptist Congress* (New York: Baptist Congress Publishing Company, 1894), pp. 76-78.

"An Executive Genius, Joseph," *The Sunday School Times* (October 12, 1901).

"*For the Right* does Not Endorse the Citizens' Movement," *For the Right,* I (July, 1890), 1.

"The Freedom of Spiritual Religion," Sermon delivered at Northern Baptist Convention, Chicago, Illinois, May 8, 1910. Reprinted as *Brotherhood Leaflets* (Philadelphia: American Baptist Society, 1910).

"The Fruition of the Spirit," *Report of the Amity Missionary Conference,* Second Annual Report (1892), p. 9.

Funeral tribute to Harrison E. Webster, *Union University,* by Andrew Van Vranken Raymond (3 vols.; New York: Lewis Publishing Company, 1907), I, 378-83.

"Further Discussion," *National Baptist* (December 28, 1895).

"Gambling," *For the Right,* II (November, 1890), 3.

"Gegen den Krieg," *Christliche Welt* (January 2, 1919), p. 10.

"Genesis of *Christianity and the Social Crisis,*" *The Rochester Theological Seminary Bulletin: The Record,* LXIX (November, 1918), 51-53.

"George C. Coleman," *American Magazine,* LXXII (June, 1911), 183-85.

"Die Geschichte der Idee des Reiches Gottes," Reprint of address at the opening of school year of German Department of Rochester Theological Seminary, September 12, 1902. Rauschenbusch Scrapbook at Colgate-Rochester Divinity School Library.

"Good Men and Good Government," *For the Right,* I (August, 1890), 2.

"Handelsgewinn und nationale Ehre" ("Private Profit and the Nation's Honor"), *Christliche Welt,* trans. by Charles Aked (August 12, 1915), pp. 644-47.

"High Rent and Low Morals," *National Baptist* (March, 1889).

"How Rich Have I a Right to Be?" (May 10, 1894) Clipping in Rauschenbusch Scrapbook at Colgate-Rochester Divinity School Library.

"The Ideals of Social Reformers," *Report of the Brotherhood of the Kingdom,* Third Annual Conference Report (1895), and *American Journal of Sociology,* II (September, 1896), 202-19.

"The Imprecatory Psalms," *The Inquirer* (1892). Clipping in Rauschenbusch Scrapbook at Colgate-Rochester Divinity School Library.

"Impressions of the Northfield Meeting," *The Inquirer* (1887). Clipping in Rauschenbusch Scrapbook at Colgate-Rochester Divinity School Library.

"The Influence of Mazzini," *Colloquium* (November, 1889). Clipping in Rauschenbusch Scrapbook at Colgate-Rochester Divinity School Library.

"Is the Baby Worth a Dollar?" *The Ladies Home Journal,* XXVII (October 1910), 19.

"Is the Woman's Movement Going to Save Society?" *Ford Hall Folks* (April 26, 1914).

"It Shall Be: the Kingdom of God Is Coming," *For the Right,* II (March, 1891), 5.

"Jesus as an Organizer of Men," *Biblical World New Series,* XI (February, 1898), 102-11.

"Justice and Brotherhood," *The Path of Labor,* by M. Katherine Bennett *et al.* (New York: Council of Women for Home Missions, 1918), pp. 165-87.

"Kann ein Christ auch ein Sozialist sein?" (Philadelphia: H. R. Grassmann, 1894). Pamphlet in D. R. Sharpe Collection of Rauschenbusch documents at American Baptist Historical Society Archives, Rochester.

"Keep Them Separate: Church and State," *For the Right,* II (January, 1891), 3.

"The Kingdom and the Church," *Report of the Brotherhood of the Kingdom,* Second Annual Conference Report (1894), p. 37.

"The Kingdom of God," *Brotherhood Leaflets* No. 4 (1894).

"The Kingdom of God," *Cleveland's Young Men,* XXVII (January 9, 1913).

"The Kingdom of God," *The Kingdom,* I (August, 1907), 1-3.

"The Kingdom of God," *Rochester Post-Express* (May 13, 1903).

"Der Kirche Kraft," *The Morning Journal, German Edition* (New York: December 2, 1895).

"Kirche und soziale Bewegung in Nord-Amerika," *Christliche Welt* (April 2, 1908; April 9, 1908; April 16, 1908; April 23, 1908), pp. 346-49, 367-70, 395-99, 410-14.

"Labor Day Address," *The Standard,* LXIV (1916), 184-85.

"A Letter: On the War," *The Standard,* LXV (1918), 1409-10.

"Letter Read at Marlborough Conference of Brotherhood of the Kingdom from Marburg, Germany, July 20, 1907," *The Kingdom,* I (September, 1907), 4.

"Limits of Immigration," *Seventh Annual Session of the Baptist Congress* (New York: Baptist Congress Publishing Company, 1888), pp. 86-87.

"The Little Gate to God" (New York: The Federal Council of Churches, 1918). Poem published as pamphlet, in Colgate-Rochester Divinity School Library.

"Living by the Rule of Loving One's Neighbor," *For the Right,* I (February, 1890), 2.

"Loneliness of Noah," *The Sunday School Times* (July 6, 1901).

"The Lure of the Pastorate," *Rochester Theological Seminary Bulletin* (May, 1914), p. 8.

"The Man Who Wrote Acts," *The Sunday School Times* (December 28, 1901). Clipping in Rauschenbusch Scrapbook at Colgate-Rochester Divinity School Library.

"Members One of Another" (December 22, 1911). Clipping in Rauschenbusch Scrapbook at Colgate-Rochester Divinity School Library.

"Mr. Haldeman's Millenarianism," *The Examiner* (June 18, 1903). Clipping in Rauschenbusch Scrapbook at Colgate-Rochester Divinity School Library.

"Most Radical of Revolutionists," *Rochester Democrat and Chronicle* (March 1, 1909).

The Movement Against Alcoholism in America: An Address Delivered at the World Congress of Free Christianity and Religious Progress, Berlin, August 7, 1910 (Goerlitz, Germany: Hoffmann & Reiber, 1910). Pamphlet in Rauschenbusch Scrapbook at Colgate-Rochester Divinity School Library.

"Municipal Ownership," *Rochester Post-Express* (June 21, 1901).

"Natural and Artificial Monopolies," *Eighth Annual Session of the Baptist Congress* (New York: Baptist Congress Publishing Company, 1890), pp. 55-61.

"The New Apostolate," *Brotherhood Leaflets* (1893).

"The New Apostolate," *Report of the Amity Missionary Conference*, Sixth Annual Conference Report (1896).

"The New Evangelism," *The Independent* (May 12, 1904), pp. 1055-59.

The New Evangelism (New York: Rufus Weeks, 1905). Pamphlet for distribution to the Brotherhood of the Kingdom in personal library of Frederic M. Hudson.

"Non-Partisan Political Ideas," *Rochester Democrat and Chronicle* (October 29, 1908).

"The Old Religious Faith and the New Social Gospel Enthusiasm," *Ford Hall Folks* (May 28, 1916).

"Opening Gun for the Czar," *Rochester Democrat and Chronicle* (February 13, 1899).

"Our Attitude Toward Millenarianism," *The Examiner* (September 24, 1896). Clipping in Rauschenbusch Scrapbook at Colgate-Rochester Divinity School Library.

"Our Attitude toward Millenarianism," *Report of the Brotherhood of the Kingdom*, Second Annual Conference Report (1894), p. 41.

"Our Mixed Civilization," *The Examiner* (August 25, 1892). Clipping in Rauschenbusch Scrapbook at Colgate-Rochester Divinity School Library.

"Pensées de Walter Rauschenbusch," *Le christianisme social*, XXXV (October, 1922), 832.

"Political Liberty and Social Equality," *For the Right*, I (September, 1890), 2.

"Practical Application of Christianity to Social Conditions," *The Transcript* (Boston: November 30, 1908).

"Practical Cures for Social Wrongs Under Individualism," *The Treasury,* XVII (April, 1900), 930-34.

"Practical Measures of Socialism," *The Treasury,* XVIII (January, 1901), 710-13.

"Prayer in Time of War," *The Independent* (October 15, 1914), p. 12.

"Prière contre l'impureté," *Le christianisme social,* XXXIV (February/March, 1921), 251.

"La prière d'amour de Saint Paul dans la langue des affaires modernes," *Le christianisme social,* XXXIII, Numero Unique (November, 1919), 55-56.

"Prière pour les femmes qui travaillent," *Le christianisme social,* XXXXIII (February/March, 1930), 270.

"Prière pour les vrais amants," *Le christianisme social,* XXXIV (February/March, 1921), 252.

"Private Profit and the Nation's Honor," *The Standard,* LXII (1915), 1486-87.

"The Present and Future," *Rochester Post-Express* (November 25, 1898).

"The Problem of the Black Man," *The American Missionary New Series,* V (March, 1914), 732-33.

"Professor Vedder's New Book on Socialism," *The Standard,* LIX (1912), 1276.

"Prophetic Character of the Anabaptist Movement," *Rochester Democrat and Chronicle* (September 15, 1903).

"Proposed Cures for Social Wrongs," *The Treasury,* XVII (February, 1900), 768-71.

"The Pulpit in Relation to Political and Social Reform," *Tenth Annual Session of the Baptist Conference* (New York: Baptist Congress Publishing Company, 1892), pp. 127-29.

"Railroads and the Press," *For the Right,* II (March, 1891), 4.

"Regenerate Church Membership," *Rochester Baptist Monthly* (March, 1903).

"The Rejection of Jesus," *The Inquirer* (1889). Clipping in Rauschenbusch Scrapbook at Colgate-Rochester Divinity School Library.

"Relation of Church and State," *Eighth Annual Session of the Baptist Congress* (New York: Baptist Congress Publishing Company, 1889), pp. 138-40.

"The Relation of the Ministry to Social Questions," *The Dawn* (November 21, 1892).

"The Relation of Theology and Religion," *Twenty-Second Annual Session of the Baptist Congress* (New York: Baptist Congress Publishing Company, 1905), pp. 89-92.

"The Relation of the State to Semi-Public Corporations and Their Employees," *Thirteenth Annual Session of the Baptist Congress* (New York: Baptist Congress Publishing Company, 1896), pp. 132-33.

"The Religion of the Passion Play," *The Independent* (September 29, 1910), pp. 689-93.

"Religion the Life of God in the Soul of Man," *The Baptist Magazine* (May, 1909), pp. 1-8.

"Religion the Life of God in the Soul of Man." Reprint of address to New York State Conference of Religion, November 20, 1900. Pamphlet in D. R. Sharpe Collection of Rauschenbusch documents at American Baptist Historical Society Archives, Rochester.

"The Religious Quality of Social Work," *The Christian Commonwealth, Supplement* (London: July 31, 1912).

"Report of Talk to Sunday School," *Rochester Democrat and Chronicle* (January 25, 1913).

"Report of the Y.M.C.A. Committee to Investigate Social Conditions of Men and Boys in Rochester," *Rochester Union and Advertiser* (May 30, 1904).

"Revelation: An Exposition," *Biblical World New Series,* X (August, 1897), 94-103.

Review of *Das Abendmahl im Urchristentum,* by J. Hoffman, *American Journal of Theology,* X (April, 1906), 342-44.

Review of *Die Anschauung der Reformatoren vom geistlichen Amte,* by W. Thomas, *American Journal of Theology,* VI (July, 1902), 631.

Review of *Die Brüder Alfonso und Juan de Valdes,* by Wilhelm Schlatter, *American Journal of Theology,* VII (January, 1903), 162-63.

Review of *Christi Person und Werk in der Predigt,* by D. H. Gebhardt, *American Journal of Theology,* III (April, 1899), 430-31.

Review of *The Church's Task Under the Roman Empire,* by Charles Bigg, *American Journal of Theology,* X (April, 1906), 337-39.

Review of *Ephemeriden des Isch-Schachefeth,* by L. Rymarski, *American Journal of Theology,* II (October, 1898), 959.

Review of *Erkennen und Schauen Gottes,* by L. Weiss, *American Journal of Theology,* III (October, 1899), 859-60.

Review of *Die Evangelisation mit besonderer Rücksicht auf die Heiligungsbewegung,* by T. Hardeland, *American Journal of Theology,* III (October, 1899), 861.

Review of *Genugsamkeit und Vielseitigkeit des Neutestamentlichen Kanons,* by C. F. Nosgen, *American Journal of Theology,* II (July, 1898), 719.

Review of *Das Heil der Welt,* by J. Pierning, *American Journal of Theology,* II (October, 1898), 955.

Review of *Die Heilsordnung,* by Emil Wacker, *American Journal of Theology,* III (April, 1899), 430.

Review of *Ignaz von Döllinger,* by J. Friedrich, *American Journal of Theology,* VII (October, 1903), 733-43.

Review of *Karl von Hase,* by R. Burkner, *American Journal of Theology,* V (October, 1901), 799-801.

Review of *Luther's Auffassung der Gottheit Christi,* by C. von Kügelgen, *American Journal of Theology,* VI (July, 1902), 630-31.

Review of *Lutherische Dogmatik,* 2 vols., by A. von Oettingen, *American Journal of Theology,* V (July, 1901), 611-15.

Review of *Luther's Theologie,* 2 vols., 2nd ed., by J. Köstlin, *American Journal of Theology,* VI (July, 1902), 592-93.

Review of *Die Materialisierung Religiöser Vorstellungen,* by Ernst Bittlinger, *American Journal of Theology,* X (April, 1906), 340-42.

Review of *Das menschlich Anziehende in der Erscheinung Jesu Christi,* by G. Zart, *American Journal of Theology,* III (January, 1899), 221.

Review of *Die Parusie Christi,* by H. Dieckmann, *American Journal of Theology,* III (July, 1899), 602-3.

Review of *Religions et Sociétés,* by T. Reinach *et al., American Journal of Theology,* X (April, 1906), 339-40.

Review of *Das Sakrament des Heiligen Abendmahls,* by J. Gemmel, *American Journal of Theology,* II (July, 1898), 719.

Review of *St. Pauli Brief an die Galater,* W. F. Besser, *American Journal of Theology,* III (October, 1899), 848.

Review of *St. Pauli Brief an die Römer,* by W. F. Besser, *American Journal of Theology,* III (January, 1899), 211.

Review of *Skizzen aus dem Leben der alten Kirche,* by T. Zahn, *American Journal of Theology,* III (July, 1899), 603-4.

Review of *Über die Aussprüche Jesu an Petrus,* by W. Beyschlag, *American Journal of Theology,* II (July, 1898), 719.

Review of *Wesen und Wirkung der Taufgnade,* by H. Cremer, *American Journal of Theology,* III (October, 1899), 859.

"Revolutionary Ancestry of Baptist and Congregational Churches," *The Springfield Republican* (Springfield, Mass.: December 1, 1908).

"Revolutionary Religion," *Rochester Democrat and Chronicle* (March 1, 1909).

"The Rights of the Child in the Community," *Religious Education,* X (June, 1915), 219-25.

"The Saving Efficacy of Money," *The Inquirer* (1887). Clipping in Rauschenbusch Scrapbook at Colgate-Rochester Divinity School Library.

"The Second Commandment: Love to Man," *The Inquirer* (1889). Clipping in Rauschenbusch Scrapbook at Colgate-Rochester Divinity School Library.

"The Service of the Church to Society," *The Treasury,* XVII (September, 1899), 393-97.

"Services Which the Church Can Render to Society," *Canadian Baptist* (November 10, 1910).

"Should Deal with the Living Present," *San Francisco Star* (July 9, 1904).

"Sinful Mercy," *The Sunday School Times* (August 31, 1901).

"The Single Tax," *For the Right,* I (February, 1890), 3.

"The Social Awakening in the Churches of America," *Proceedings and Papers of the Sixth International Congress of Free Christianity and Religious Progress* (Berlin, 1911), pp. 563-67.

"Social Background, Spirit, and Message of the Bible," *Rochester Theological Seminary Bulletin: The Record,* LXIX (November, 1918), 54-63.

"Social Ideas in the New Testament," *The Treasury,* XVII (June, 1899), 155-59.

"Social Ideas in the Old Testament," *The Treasury,* XVI (March, 1899), 871-76.

"The Social Ideas of Paul," *Report of the Brotherhood of the Kingdom,* Sixth Annual Conference (1898).

"Socialism," *Rochester Herald* (November 11, 1908).

"Socialism Is Coming," *The Call* (January 28, 1909).

"Socialism Is of Two Kinds: The Practical and the Dogmatic Contrasted," *Rochester Democrat and Chronicle* (February 25, 1901).

"The Social Mission of Baptists," *Christian Socialist* (November 1, 1907).

"The Social Movement and the Higher Life in Our Country," *Rochester Democrat and Chronicle* (November 16, 1899).

"Some Moral Aspects of the Woman's Movement," *Biblical World New Series,* XLII (October, 1913), 195-99.

"The Social Program of the Church," *The South Mobilizing for Social Service.* Ed. by James E. McCulloch (Nashville: Southern Sociological Congress, 1913), pp. 504-11.

"Some Words About Socialism in America," *For the Right,* I (April, 1890), 3.

"Speaking in Tongues: What Was It?" *The Watchman* (September 30, 1897). Clipping in Rauschenbusch Scrapbook at Colgate-Rochester Divinity School Library.

"The Stake of the Church in the Social Movement," *American Journal of Sociology,* III (July, 1897), 18-30.

"State-Help versus Self-Help, or Paternalism in Government," *Sixteenth Annual Session of the Baptist Congress* (New York: Baptist Congress Publishing Company, 1898, pp. 107-16.

"Suggestions for the Organization of Local Chapters of the Brotherhood of the Kingdom," *Brotherhood Leaflets* (1902).

"Sunday School Lesson on Samson," *The Inquirar* (1888). Clipping in Rauschenbusch Scrapbook at Colgate-Rochester Divinity School Library.

"That Boston Fad," *The Inquirer* (1889). Clipping in Rauschenbusch Scrapbook at Colgate Rochester Divinity School Library.

"Thoughts on Prayer," *Rochester Baptist Monthly* (January, 1901).

"To the Deacons of Our Churches," *Brotherhood Leaflets,* No. 6.

"Tradition as a Formative Influence in Baptist Doctrine and Church Life," *Twelfth Annual Session of the Baptist Congress* (New York: Baptist Congress Publishing Company, 1895), pp. 36-38.

"The Transition from the Present to a Co-operative Order of Society," *Third Year of the Sagamore Sociological Conference* (Sagamore Beach, Massachusetts: Sagamore Sociological Conference, 1909), pp. 15-17.

"Le XIIIe chapitre aux Corinthiens appliqué aux affaires en style moderne," *Le christianisme social,* XXXVI (November, 1923), 869-71.

"The Trend Toward Collectivism," *The City Club Bulletin* (Chicago): V April, 1912), 123-30.

"A Trip to the Pacific," *Rochester Theological Seminary Bulletin: The Record,* LXVI (May, 1915), 50.

"The True American Church," *The Congregationalist* (October 23, 1913), p. 562.

"The True Foundation," *Monroe County Mail* (Monroe, New York: August 11, 1904.

"The Unspoken Thoughts of Jesus," *Modern Sermons by World Scholars.* Ed. by Robert Scott and William C. Stiles (10 vols., New York: Funk and Wagnalls Company, 1909), VIII, 22-32.

"The Value and Use of History," *Rochester Theological Seminary Bulletin: The Record,* LXV (November, 1914), 31-41.

"La vision du nouveau christianisme," trans. by Elie Gounelle, *Le christianisme social*, XXXIII (January, 1920), 3.

"Walter Rauschenbusch's letzter Gruss," *Christliche Welt* (September 4, 1919), p. 576.

"Wanted! A New Type of Layman," *Brotherhood Leaflets* and *National Baptist* (March 8, 1894).

"Wanted: A New Type of Layman," *Rochester Democrat and Chronicle* (February 21, 1906).

"War and Hate: A Reply," *The Standard*, LXIV (1916), 296-97.

"War and the Loss of Love," *The Standard*, LXIII (1915), 1589.

"Welsh Revival and Primitive Christianity," *The Examiner* (June 15, 1905). Clipping in Rauschenbusch Scrapbook at Colgate-Rochester Divinity School Library.

"What Help Does Modern Christianity Give Us on Modern Social Problems?" *The Examiner* (November 3, 1904). Clipping in Rauschenbusch Scrapbook at Colgate-Rochester Divinity School Library.

"What Is a Christian Nation?" *The Materials of Religious Education: Being the Principal Papers Presented at, and the Proceedings of the Fourth General Convention of the Religious Education Association, Rochester, N.Y. February 5-7, 1907* (Chicago: Executive Office of the Association, 1907), pp. 25-30.

"What Is a Christian Nation?" *The Standard*, LIV (1907), 757-58.

"What Stephen Did for the Christian Church," *The Sunday School Times* (February 8, 1902). Clipping in Rauschenbusch Scrapbook at Colgate-Rochester Divinity School Library.

"Where Does It All Come From?" *For the Right*, I (November, 1889), 3.

"Who Shall Educate: Church or State?" *Seventh Annual Session of the Baptist Congress* (New York: Baptist Congress Publishing Company, 1889), pp. 28-31.

"Why Has Christianity Never Undertaken the Task of Social Reconstruction?" *Report of the Brotherhood of the Kingdom*, Twelfth Annual Conference (1906), pp. 28-29.

"Why I Am a Baptist," *The Baptist Leader*, revised reprint of series from *Rochester Baptist Monthly*, edited and introduced by H. H. Barnette (January, 1958), pp. 1-10.

"Why I Am a Baptist," *Rochester Baptist Monthly*, XX (November through March, 1905-6), 203, 85-88, 106-8, 134-6, 156-59.

"Wie die Bedingungen für eine soziale Wirksamkeit des Christentums mit der Zeit sich verändert haben," *Christliche Welt* (May 27, 1909), pp. 511-16.

"Woman's Work in the Church," Report of the *Amity Missionary Conference,* Fourth Annual Conference Report (1894), p. 5.

"A Word for the Little Churches," *The Examiner* (March 19, 1892). Clipping in Rauschenbusch Scrapbook at Colgate-Rochester Divinity School Library.

"Ye Did It Unto Me," *Proceedings of the National Conference of Charities and Correction,* ed. by Alexander Johnson (Fort Wayne, Indiana: Fort Wayne Printing Company, 1912), pp. 12-17.

"Yielding Our Rights," *The Sunday School Times* (July 20, 1901).

"The Zürich Anabaptists and Thomas Müntzer," *American Journal of Theology,* IX (January, 1905), 91-106. Portions republished in *Conrad Grebel* by Harold Bender (Goshen, Ind.: 1950), pp. 282-87; and *Spiritual and Anabaptist Writers,* ed. by George H. Williams in vol. XXV of *The Library of Christian Classics,* ed. by John Baillie *et al.* (Philadelphia: The Westminster Press), pp. 73-85.

c. Unpublished Material

"Advantages of Socialism." Manuscript notes for address at Saint Paul's Men's Guild, February, 1902. In D. R. Sharpe Collection of Rauschenbusch documents at American Baptist Historical Society Archives, Rochester.

"Baptism." Lecture notes of George Fetter, 1913. In American Baptist Historical Society Archives, Rochester.

"The Brooklyn Strike." Manuscript notes for sermon, 1895. In D. R. Sharpe Collection of Rauschenbusch documents at American Baptist Historical Society Archives, Rochester.

"The Christian Movement and the Social Movement." Manuscript notes for *Christianity and the Social Crisis,* 1905. In D. R. Sharpe Collection of Rauschenbusch documents at American Baptist Historical Society Archives, Rochester.

"Church History." Lecture notes of Professor A. J. Bretschneider, 1905. In American Baptist Historical Society Archives, Rochester.

"Church History I." Lecture notes of George Fetter, 1911. In American Baptist Historical Society Archives, Rochester.

"Church History II." Lecture notes of George Fetter, 1912. In American Baptist Historical Society Archives, Rochester.

"Church History III." Lecture notes of George Fetter, 1913. In American Baptist Historical Society Archives, Rochester.

"Church History of America." Lecture notes of George Fetter, 1912. In American Baptist Historical Society Archives, Rochester.

"Church History of England." Lecture notes of George Fetter, 1911. In American Baptist Historical Society Archives, Rochester.

"Church History Outline: Christianity and the Roman Empire, A.D. 303-400." Printed lecture outline in Rauschenbusch Scrapbook at Colgate-Rochester Divinity School Library.

"Church History Outline: Gnosticism." Printed lecture outline in Rauschenbusch Scrapbook at Colgate-Rochester Divinity School Library.

"Church History Outline: Introduction to the Study of Church History." Printed lecture outline in Rauschenbusch Scrapbook at Colgate-Rochester Divinity School Library.

"Church History Outline: Primitive Christianity." Printed lecture outline in Rauschenbusch Scrapbook at Colgate-Rochester Divinity School Library.

"Church History Outline: The Rise of Theology and Dogma in the Ancient Church," Printed lecture outline in Rauschenbusch Scrapbook at Colgate-Rochester Divinity School Library.

"Church History Outline: The Triumph of Christianity in the Roman Empire, A.D. 303-400." Printed lecture outline in Rauschenbusch Scrapbook at Colgate Rochester Divinity School Library.

"Close Intended for Quaker Hill but Not Read." Manuscript notes undated. In D. R. Sharpe Collection of Rauschenbusch documents at American Baptist Historical Society Archives, Rochester.

Correspondence and papers in D. R. Sharpe Collection of Rauschenbusch documents at American Baptist Historical Society Archives, Rochester.

Correspondence and papers in personal library of Conrad Henry Moehlman, New Orleans Baptist Theological Seminary, New Orleans, Louisiana.

Correspondence and papers in personal library of D. R. Sharpe.

Correspondence with Vida Scudder in personal library of Max L. Stackhouse.

"Discussions of Döllinger." Manuscript of paper for American Baptist Historical Society, January 14, 1904. In D. R. Sharpe Collection of Rauschenbusch documents at American Baptist Historical Society Archives, Rochester.

"The Ethics of Thinking." Commencement address at Rochester Theological Seminary, 1886. In D. R. Sharpe Collection of Rauschenbusch documents at American Baptist Historical Society Archives, Rochester.

"The Ethics of Jesus." Manuscript notes of speech given at the first conference of the Brotherhood of the Kingdom, Marlborough, N.Y., 1893. In personal library of Frederic M. Hudson.

"Enoch Pond Lectures on Applied Christianity at Bangor Theological Seminary, January, 1915." Copy by C. H. Hopkins from Bangor, Maine, newspaper. In American Baptist Historical Society Archives, Rochester.

Forty-five volumes of notes for sermons and addresses in English and German from 1886-1905. In D. R. Sharpe Collection of Rauschenbusch documents at American Baptist Historical Society Archives, Rochester.

"Henry George." Manuscript cited in *Walter Rauschenbusch* by D. R. Sharpe (New York: The Macmillan Company, 1932), p. 80. Probably written in 1887, now misplaced.

"Historical Address: the Roman Catholic Church." Manuscript in D. R. Sharpe Collection of Rauschenbusch documents at American Baptist Historical Society Archives, Rochester.

"The History of the Idea of the Kingdom of God." Manuscript of paper for Brotherhood of the Kingdom meeting at Amity Church, New York City, 1894. In D. R. Sharpe Collection of Rauschenbusch documents at American Baptist Historical Society Archives, Rochester.

"Jesus as an Organizer of Men." Manuscript of article for *Biblical World* that was lost, then recovered after Rauschenbusch had dispatched for publication a less complete version which he wrote from memory (1898). In D. R. Sharpe Collection of Rauschenbusch documents at American Baptist Historical Society Archives, Rochester.

"How to Get a Good Wife," Manuscript notes for address to German Department students of Rochester Theological Seminary. In D. R. Sharpe Collection of Rauschenbusch documents at American Baptist Historical Society Archives, Rochester.

"Das Kollektiv-Leben der Menschheit." Manuscript notes for address to German Department faculty at Rochester Theological Seminary, October, 1895. In D. R. Sharpe Collection of Rauschenbusch documents at American Baptist Historical Society Archives, Rochester.

"Life of Döllinger." Manuscript notes for address. In D. R. Sharpe Collection of Rauschenbusch documents at American Baptist Historical Society Archives, Rochester.

"Reminiscences of My Life." Manuscript booklet for Pauline Rother, later the wife of Rauschenbusch (1892). In D. R. Sharpe Collection of Rauschenbusch documents at American Baptist Historical Society Archives, Rochester.

"Social Questions Outlined, Social Questions in the Bible, Social Questions in the Teaching of the Church, Social Questions in the Actions of the Church." Manuscript notes for address. In D. R. Sharpe Collection of Rauschenbusch documents at American Baptist Historical Society Archives, Rochester.

"Special Topics." Lecture notes of George Fetter, 1912. In American Baptist Historical Society Archives, Rochester.

"Stephen." Manuscript notes. In D. R. Sharpe Collection of Rauschenbusch documents at American Baptist Historical Society Archives, Rochester.

"Temperance." Manuscript notes for addresses at Brick Church, and Second Baptist Church, both in Rochester, January and February, 1901. In D. R. Sharpe Collection of Rauschenbusch documents at American Baptist Historical Society Archives, Rochester.

"Topical Grouping of the Parables from the Point of View of the Kingdom and the Kingdom of God in the Parables of Jesus." Manuscript notes for address at Brotherhood of the Kingdom meeting in the church of Mr. Wheat on Long Island, about 1895. In D. R. Sharpe Collection of Rauschenbusch documents at American Baptist Historical Society Archives, Rochester.

Uncatalogued sources from the German Department of Rochester Theological Seminary at North American Baptist Seminary Library, Sioux Falls, South Dakota.

"The Woman Problem." Manuscript notes for projected book in six parts, 1899. In D. R. Sharpe Collection of Rauschenbusch documents at American Baptist Historical Society Archives, Rochester.

2

SELECTED SECONDARY LITERATURE

Abell, Aaron Ignatius. *The Urban Impact on American Protestantism*, 1865-1900. Hamden, Conn.: Archon, 1962.

Ahlstrom, Sydney E. *Theology in America.* Indianapolis: Bobbs-Merrill Company, 1967.

Aiken, John R. "Walter Rauschenbusch and Education for Reform," *Church History*, XXXVI (December, 1967), 456-69.

Allen, Jimmy Raymond. "Comparative Study of the Concept of the Kingdom of God in the Writings of Walter Rauschenbusch and Reinhold Niebuhr." Unpublished Th.D. dissertation, Southwestern Baptist Theological Seminary, 1958.

Baker, Ray Stannard. *The Spiritual Unrest.* New York: Frederick A. Stokes Company, 1910. Esp. Chap. VII, 260-85.

Barnette, Henlee Huxlit. "The Ethical Thought of Walter Rauschenbusch." Unpublished Ph.D. dissertation, Southern Baptist Theological Seminary, 1948.

Battenhouse, Paul F. "Theology in the Social Gospel, 1918-1946." Unpublished Ph.D. dissertation, Yale University, 1950.

Bodein, Vernon P. "The Development of the Social Thought of Walter Rauschenbusch," *Religion in Life*, VI (Summer, 1937), 420-31.

———. *The Social Gospel of Walter Rauschenbusch and Its Relation to Religious Education* (Yale Studies in Religious Education, Vol. XVI). New Haven: Yale University Press, 1944.

Bowden, Henry W. "Walter Rauschenbusch and American Church History," *Foundations,* IX (July-Sept., 1966), 234-50.

Carter, Paul A. *The Decline and Revival of the Social Gospel: Social and Political Liberalism in American Protestant Churches, 1920-1940.* Ithaca: Cornell University Press, 1954.

Carter, Purvis M. "The Astigmatism of the Social Gospel." Unpublished Master's dissertation, Howard University, 1962.

Cauthen, Kenneth. *The Impact of American Religious Liberalism.* New York: Harper & Row, 1962.

Cross, Robert D., ed. *The Church and the City.* ("The American Heritage Series.") Indianapolis: Bobbs-Merrill Company, 1966.

Dickenson, Richard. "Rauschenbusch and Niebuhr: Brothers Under the Skin," *Religion in Life,* XXVII (Winter, 1957-58), 163-71.

Dillenberger, John, and Welch, Claude. *Protestant Christianity: Interpreted Through Its Development.* New York: Charles Scribner's Sons, 1954. Pp. 247-52.

Dombrowski, James. *The Early Days of Christian Socialism in America.* New York: Columbia University Press, 1936.

Dupertuis, Jean. *"Christianisme Social" d'après Rauschenbusch.* Saint-Blaise: Foyer Solidariste, 1911.

Durfee, Harold A. "The Theologies of the American Social Gospel: A Study of the Theological and Philosophical Presuppositions of the American Social Gospel." Unpublished Ph.D. dissertation, Columbia University, 1951.

Everett, John Rutherford. *Religion in Economics.* New York: King's Crown Press, 1946.

Fricke, Ernest E. "Socialism in Christianity in Walter Rauschenbusch." Unpublished Th.D. dissertation, University of Basel, 1965.

Haldeman, I. M. *Professor Rauschenbusch's "Christianity and the Social Crisis."* New York: Charles C. Cook, n.d.

Hammar, George. *Christian Realism in Contemporary American Theology: A Study of Reinhold Niebuhr, W. M. Horton, and H. P. Van Dusen.* Uppsala, Sweden: A. B. Lundequistska Bokhandeln, 1940.

Handy, Robert T. *The Social Gospel in America, 1870-1920.* A Library of Protestant Thought. New York: Oxford University Press, 1966.

———. "Walter Rauschenbusch," *Ten Makers of Modern Protestant Thought.* Ed. by G. L. Hunt. New York: Association Press, 1958.

Hopkins, C. H. *The Rise of the Social Gospel in American Protestantism, 1865-1915.* New Haven: Yale University Press, 1940.

Horton, Natalie R. "The Life, Work and Influence of Walter Rauschenbusch." Unpublished Master's dissertation, Baptist Theological Seminary, 1951.

Hudson, Frederic M. "The Reign of the New Humanity." Unpublished Ph.D. dissertation, Columbia University, 1968.

Hudson, Winthrop. "Walter Rauschenbusch and the New Evangelism," *Religion in Life,* XXX (Summer, 1961), 412-30.

Johnson, F. Ernest. *The Social Gospel Re-Examined.* New York: Harper & Brothers, Publishers, 1940.

Langford, S. Fraser. "The Gospel of Augustus H. Strong and Walter Rauschenbusch," *The Chronicle,* XIV (January, 1951), 3-18.

Liever, Oscar W. "The Idea of the Kingdom of God as Reflected in the American Social Gospel, 1865-1917." Unpublished Ph.D. dissertation, Duke University, 1941.

Lochman, J. M. "Cesta Sociálního evangelia W. Rauschenbusch," *Theologia Evangelica,* I (1948), 217-25.

Locke, Harvey James. "Rauschenbusch." Unpublished Ph.D. dissertation, University of Chicago, 1930.

Marney, Carlyle. "The Significance of Walter Rauschenbusch for Today," *Foundations,* II (January, 1959), 13-26.

McGiffert, Arthur C. "Walter Rauschenbusch: Twenty Years After," *Christendom,* III (Winter, 1938), 96-109.

McKelvey, Blake. "Walter Rauschenbusch's Rochester," *Rochester History,* XIV (October, 1952).

Mead, Sidney E. *The Lively Experiment: The Shaping of Christianity in America.* New York: Harper & Row, Publishers, 1963.

Meille, G. E. "La scomparsa di un profeta americano," *Bilychnis,* XII (November-December, 1918), 273-75.

"The Memorial Service," "Reviews of Major Books," "Tributes from Friends, Alumni, Students," *Rochester Theological Seminary Bulletin: The Record,* LXIX (November, 1918).

Meyer, Donald B. *The Protestant Search for Political Realism, 1919-1941.* Berkeley: University of California Press, 1961.

Meyer, F. W. C. "Walter Rauschenbusch, Preacher, Professor and Prophet," *The Standard* (1911), pp. 662-63.

Miller, Robert Moats. *American Protestantism and Social Issues, 1919-1939.* Chapel Hill, North Carolina: University of North Carolina Press, 1958.

Moehlman, Conrad H. "Life and Writings of Walter Rauschenbusch," *Colgate-Rochester Divinity School Bulletin,* I (October, 1928), 32-7.

————. *A Rauschenbusch Sourcebook with Commentary.* Los Angeles: 1953 (Microfilm).

————. "Walter Rauschenbusch and His Interpreters," *Crozer Quarterly,* XXIII (January, 1946), 34-50.

Moellering, R. L. "Rauschenbusch in Retrospect," *Concordia Theological Monthly,* XXVII (August, 1956), 613-33.

Muelder, Walter G. "Walter Rauschenbusch and the Contemporary Scene," *The City Church,* VIII (March-April, 1957), 10-12.

Müller, Reinhart. *Walter Rauschenbusch: Ein Beitrag zur Begegnung des deutschen und des amerikanischen Protestantismus.* Leiden: E. J. Brill, 1957.

Naumann, K. "Die Theologie des 'Social Gospel' in Amerika." Unpublished Ph.D. dissertation, Tübingen, 1943.

Niebuhr, H. R. *The Kingdom of God in America.* New York: Harper & Brothers, 1937.

Niebuhr, Reinhold. "Walter Rauschenbusch in Historical Perspective," *Religion in Life,* XXVII (Autumn, 1958), 527-36.

Nixon, Justin Wroe. "The Social Philosophy of Walter Rauschenbusch," *The Colgate-Rochester Divinity School Bulletin,* I (November, 1928), 103-9.

Noble, David W. *The Paradox of Progressive Thought.* Minneapolis: University of Minnesota Press, 1958.

Oxnam, G. Bromley. *Personalities in Social Reform.* New York: Abingdon-Cokesbury, 1950. Esp. Chap. II.

"Professor Rauschenbusch as 'a German,'" *The Journal and Messenger* (February 7, 1918), p. 7.

Ramsey, Paul. "A Theology for Social Action," *Social Action,* XII (October, 1946), 4-34.

Robins, Henry Burke. "The Contribution of Walter Rauschenbusch to World Peace," *The Colgate-Rochester Divinity School Bulletin,* XII (May, 1940), 149-54.

————. "The Religion of Walter Rauschenbusch," *The Colgate-Rochester Divinity School Bulletin,* I (October, 1928), 37-43.

Schlesinger, Arthur M., Jr. "Reinhold Niebuhr's Role in American Political Thought and Life," *The Politics of Hope* (Boston: Houghton Mifflin Company, 1962), pp. 97-125.

Schneider, Carl E. "Americanization of Karl August Rauschenbusch, 1816-1899," *Church History*, XXIV (March, 1955), 3-14.

Sharpe, Dores R. *Walter Rauschenbusch*. New York: The Macmillan Company, 1942.

Singer, Anna M. *Walter Rauschenbusch and his Contribution to Social Christianity*. Boston: Richard G. Badger, Publisher, 1926.

Smith, H. Shelton, *et al. American Christianity: An Historical Interpretation with Representative Documents*. Volume II: 1820-1960. New York: Charles Scribner's Sons, 1963.

Smith, H. Shelton. *Changing Conceptions of Original Sin*. New York: Charles Scribner's Sons, 1955.

Smucker, Donovan E. "Multiple Motifs in the Thought of Rauschenbusch," *Encounter*, XIX (Winter, 1958), 14-20.

————. "The Origins of Walter Rauschenbusch's Social Ethics." Unpublished Ph.D. dissertation, University of Chicago, 1957.

————. "Rauschenbusch's View of the Church as a Dynamic Voluntary Association," *Voluntary Associations: A Study of Groups in Free Societies*. Ed. by D. B. Robertson (Richmond, Virginia: John Knox Press, 1966), pp. 159-70.

Starr, Edward Caryl. "Walter Rauschenbusch, 1861-1918." Unpublished manuscript in American Baptist Historical Society Archives, Rochester.

Stormer, John A. *None Dare Call It Treason*. Florissant, Mo.: Liberty Bell Press, 1964.

Visser t'Hooft, W. A. *The Background of the Social Gospel in America*. Haarlem: Tjeenk Willink and Zoon, 1928.

Vulgamore, Melvin L. "The Social Gospel Old and New: Walter Rauschenbusch and Harvey Cox," *Religion in Life*, XXXVI (Winter, 1967), 516-33.

INDEXES

INDEX OF SCRIPTURE REFERENCES

Judges 11:30-40 253

Isaiah 80
2:2-4 82
2:4 71
3:13-15 71
19:18-25 82
24:21-22 71
40–66 83
42 90
44:3-4 133
54:13 133

Jeremiah
4:2 82
16:19 82
31:31-34 133

Ezekiel 80

Daniel 80

Joel 2:28-29 133

Micah 4:1-4 82

Habakkuk 2:14 82

Zephaniah 2:11 82
3:10 82

Zechariah 14:9 82

Malachi 3:2 71
3:5 71

Matthew 4:16 160
5:3-9 197
5:10-12 70
5:23 182
5:23-24 183
5:32 238
5:38-42 184
5:40 166
5:43-48 182
6:1-8 257
6:1-18 196
6:2-4 275
6:5-15 268
6:10 109
6:14-15 ......183, 275
6:19-20 208
6:25-34 ......207, 275
6:33 109
7:1-2 275
7:15-27 255
7:21-27 106
8:11 106
8:18-22 159
9:36–10:1 157
10:5-6 83
10:24-25 150

Matthew—*cont'd*
11:2-5 90
11:3-5 109
11:7-12 260
11:11 109
11:20-24 273
11:27 123
11:28-30 197
12:1-8, 9-14 266
12:22-29 90
12:22-37 254
12:28 ....109, 147
12:34 109
12:38 89
12:41 273
12:46-50 ......149, 153
13:7-22 208
13:24-30, 47-50 106
13:57 70
14:1-12 253
15:1-2 266
15:1-9 268
15:1-20 161
15:10-20 266
16:13-21 254
17:24-27 ..165, 166, 245
18:1-4 197
18:8-9 258
18:15-17 183
18:15-20 155

Matthew—*cont'd*
18:20 155
18:21-35 183
19:1-6, 8 238
19:11-12 239
19:12 261
19:16 276
19:16-22 209
19:23-26 208
19:27–20:16 276
20:20-28 196
20:25 197
20:28 197
21:12-16 265
21:23-27 181
21:25-27 257
21:28-32 255
21:31 109
22:11-14 106
22:15-22 165
22:23-33 239
23:5 196
23:6-7 195
23:8-12 196
23:15 158
23:16-22 180
23:23-24, 25-28 268
23:29-36 70
23:34 83
25:1-13 106
25:14-30 274
25:31-46 ..106, 167, 182
25:40-45 269
26:26-29 150
26:41 258
26:50-53 185
26:51-52 91
26:52 193
27:42 89
28:19 158
28:20 148

Mark 1:40-45 264
2:18-22 265
2:23-28 ......161, 267
9:11-13 70
10:23-24 218
12:41-44 273
19:29 273

Luke
1:51-53, 71, 74-75 .. 73
2:34-35 73
3:10-14 208
3:15 71
4:1 147
4:14 147

Luke—*cont'd*
4:16-21 72
4:18 147
5:3-9 219
6:20-26 219
6:30-34 207
6:31-35 275
7:26 70
7:36-50 237
9:19 70
9:57-62 260
12 266
12:11-12 147
12:13-21..165, 166, 208
12:22-31 207
12:41-46 272
12:47 273
13:10-17 266
13:34-35 70
14:1-6 266
14:7-11 195
14:12-14 275
14:25-35 159
16:1-13, 14 209
16:19-21 208
16:19-31 209
17:4 183
17:7-10 277
17:11-14 264
18:1-8 279
18:9-14 196
18:18-30 159
19:1-10 209
19:11-27 274
20:4-18 70
21:12-15 147
21:34 258
22:24-27 196
22:25 197
22:69 279

John 3:3 99
3:3-6 135
3:20 149
4:19-24 267
5:1-18 266
5:44 200
6:14-15 72
6:30-31 89
6:35 150
6:57 97
6:66-68 91
9:1-41 266
11:47-50 72
12:42-43 200
13:1-17 197
13:33-34 153

John—*cont'd*
14:4 149
14:12 147
14:14 ....147, 149
14:16-19 148
15 150
15:5 148
15:8 160
15:14 149
18:22-23 185
18:23 247
18:36 .....91, 185, 249
18:36-37 91
20:22-23 155

Acts 1:4-8 133
1:8 147
1:15-26 152
2 134
2:44-47 208
4:10 248
4:19 ....147, 248
4:31 147
4:32-35 208
5:29 248
5:41 147
6 147
6:1-6 ....152, 173
6:5 147
7 147
7:51-60 248
8:14 134
8:29 147
9:31 145
10:38 146
10:44 134
11:1-18 152
12:12 173
13:2-4 147
15:1-29 152
15:28 147
15:29 239
16:6-7 148
17:7 78
19 161
19:1 134
20:37 173
23:1-5 248

Romans 2:5-9 275
6 158
7:15–8:11 135
8:9 ......134, 135, 148
8:14 134
8:23 148
8:26 148
9:1 148

Romans—*cont'd*
10:10 255
12:6 256
12:12-21 185
12:17 185
12:20 184
13:1-7 246
13:11-14 106
14 153
14:14-15 135

I Corinthians
1:26-29 160
2:6-16 133
2:15 148
3:1, 3 146
3:16 137
6:7 185
6:12-20 240
6:15-20 135
6:19 137
7 240
7:29-31 105
7:40 147
9 259
10:2 158
12:4-11 146
12:13 144
13:1-3 182

II Corinthians 3:6-18 . . 138

Galatians 2:20 148
3:1 134
4:4 107
4:21–5:1 137
5:1 138
5:16-24 135
6:2 182

Ephesians 1:13 148
2:22 137
3:10 160
3:14-21 148
5:18-21 135

Philippians 2:1 146
2:3-8 198

Colossians 2:20-23 240

I Thessalonians 1:5 134
4:13-18 106
4:15-17 106
5:15 185

II Thessalonians 2:1-12 . 108

I Timothy 4:1-5 240
6:5-10 211
6:6-10 218

James 48, 49
1:25 181
2:1-9 198
2:26 179
3:11 182
5:1-4 77
5:7-9 106

I Peter 1:5 106
2:13-17 246
2:19-24 185
3:8-18 185
4:7 106

I John 2:4 . . . . . 179, 256
2:9 256
3:16 182
3:17-18 256
4:20-21 182

Revelation (Apocalypse)
48, 49, 77, 103, 125, 148, 279

INDEX OF PERSONS AND SUBJECTS

Abolitionists, 248
Abraham, 85, 210
Abstinence, 259, 260
Adam, 124
Almsgiving, 275
Ambition, 195, 205
American Baptist Historical Society, 17, 19, 20
Amos, 82
Anabaptists, 40, 129
Ananias, 155, 256
Anxiety, 275
Apocalypse, *see* Index of Scripture References: Revelation
Asceticism, 240, 261, 263

Background of the Social Gospel in America, The (Visser 't Hooft), 28n
Banking, 213-14
Baptism, 39, 255, 269
Baptist Congress, 17
Barth, Karl, 21, 27
Beaven, A. W., on Rauschenbusch, 15
Bennett, John, 59n
Bible as resource, approaches of Bultmann and Rauschenbusch contrasted, 45-59
Bodelschwingh, 175
Bonhoeffer, Dietrich, 14
Brotherhood of the Kingdom, 17
Browning, Elizabeth Barrett, 201
Browning, Robert, 199, 281
Brunner, Emil, 27
Bultmann, Rudolf, use of biblical sources, 45-59
Bushnell, Horace, 14

INDEX

Calvinism
history and, 30
as social philosophy, 20, 21
Carter, Purvis M., 33n
Catholic Church, *see* Roman Catholic Church
Charles I, of England, 193
Cicero, 127
Civil rights, churches and, 25
Columbus, Christopher, 279
Communications media, 214
Conscience, authority of, 245-50
Conservation of National Ideals (Sangster), 18n
Covenant, 95
Cromwell, Oliver, 102, 132n, 193
Cullmann, Oscar, 45
Christ, *see* Jesus Christ
Christ-event, Kingdom of God and, 37-39
Christian Realism (Bennett), 59n
Christianity
American, 14
Christian culture, 23
Christian realism, 23
"higher life" of man and, 258-63
Judaism and, 47-48, 55
new society and, 143-46
power of, 161-62
prospects of, today, 279-85
relation to demands of state, 244-50
revolutionary character of, 70-78, 110-16, 118-32, 132-49, 149-78
rules vs. spirit, 167
social philosophies, 20-26, 168-72
wealth and, 229-36
Christianity and the Social Crisis (Rauschenbusch), 15, 29n, 35n, 36n, 38n, 48n, 51n
Christianizing the Social Order (Rauschenbusch), 15, 35n, 36n
Church, the
action and, 172-78
as body of Christ, 174-76, 224
Broad Church thinkers, 159
as community, 149-62
divisions within, 63-64
duty of, 160, 171-72
functions of, 153-62
individual and, 55-56
Kingdom of God and, 39-41
missionary activity of, 157-62
moral leadership, 154-56, 168-78
prophetic office of, 168
as protector of faith, 153
in the world, 162-78
see also Denominationalism; Free church; denominations by name
Daniel, 107
Dare We Be Christians? (Rauschenbusch), 34n
Das Leben Jesu Christi (Neander), 160
Daudet, Alphonse, 204
David, 72, 122, 267
Deacons, 190
Decalogue, 236, 252
Decision making, historicity and, 58-59
De Laveleye, 145
Denominationalism, 22, 39n
conciliar denominationalism, 22-26
Dent, Frank Lloyd, 37n
Dilthey, 45
Display tactics
churches and, 94-95
Jesus and, 93-94
Dives, 166, 209, 210, 222
Divine Imperative (Brunner), 27
Divorce, 242-44; *see also* Marriage
Dodd, C. H., 45
Duty, categorical imperative of, 279

Ebionites, 209
Ecumenism, sectarian church and, 39n
Education, 282, 284
Edwards, Jonathan, 14
Elijah, 85, 123, 185
Elisha, 85
Ely, Richard T., 23n
Emerson, Ralph Waldo, 14
Energy, 259, 260
Environment, 280
Epistle to the Romans (Barth), 27
Equality, of mankind, 205-6
Essays (Mazzini), 285
Essenes, 160
Evangelicalism, history and, 30
Evolution, 280-81
Existentialism, 45
Exteriority, 55

Faith
categorical imperative of, 279-80
Jesus' ideal of, 260
Family, 261-62; *see also* Marriage; Sex
Fasting, 265
Federal Council of Churches, 15
Felix, 78
For God and the People (Rauschenbusch), 15
"For the Right," 15
Forgiveness, 183
Formation and Life of the Social Organism, The (Schäffle), 154, 161, 171
Fosdick, Harry Emerson, 33n
Fox, George, 180

Frederick William I, of Prussia, 108
Free church, 39-40, 45
  on law and gospel, 55
French Revolution, 143, 173, 269

Garrison, William Lloyd, 67
George, Henry, 34
German Protestants Face the Social Question (Shanahan), 18n
Geschichte des Materialismus (Lange), 161
Gideon, 159
Gnosticism, 49-50, 55
God, holiness and love reconciled in, 130; *see also* Spirit of God
Golden Rule, 275-76
Gospel and law, 55-56
Gospels, concept of Jesus in, 125
Gossett, Thomas F., 33n
Grace, 55
Grant, Frederick, 45
Gustafson, James, 59n

Handy, Robert T., 23n
Harnack, Adolf von, 45
Herod, 247, 253, 260
Hillel, Rabbi, 121
Historical Jesus and the Kerygmatic Christ, The (Braaten and Harrisville), 45n
History
  Kingdom of God and, 41
  lessons of, 281
  significance of, 28-30
Hosea, 82
Howard, John, 175
Hudson, Frederic M., 17n
Hume, David, 31

Impurity
  Jesus on, 236-37
  Paul on, 239
Incarnation, 57
Individual
  church and, 55-56
  Kingdom of God and, 37-39, 110-16
  regeneration of, 110-16
  value of, 95-98
  world and, 98-105
Interiority, 55
Interpretation of Christian Ethics, An (Niebuhr), 15n
Isaiah, 82, 279

James, William, 14
Jephtha, 253
Jeremiah, 84, 123

Jesuits, Order of, 104, 155
Jesus Christ, 279
  attitude toward women, 236-37, 241-42
  ceremonialism and, 264-70
  concept of, in early church, 124-25
  and Kingdom of God, 132-49
  and the law, 180-95
  law of love, 235-36
  law of trust, 226-27
  in lives of others, 149-52
  on marriage, 238-41, 261
  and Messianic hope, 81-98, 254
  personality of, 122-32
  on relation of man to man, 195-206
  on responsibility, 271-74
  revolutionary character of, 74-77, 120-21
  on sacrifices, 120
  second coming and the Kingdom, 105-10
  secular society and, 165-67
  on sexual relations in future life, 239
  spiritual means employed by, 91-95
  teachings of, 63-69, 98, 119-22
  on truth, 252-54
  use of force, 90-91
  use of power, 89-90
  and value of the individual, 96-98
  on wealth, 206-36
  see also Christ-event
Jesus and the Word (Bultmann), 48n, 49n, 51n, 52n
Jesus Christ and Mythology (Bultmann), 57n
Joel, 82
John the Baptist, 39, 47, 48, 49, 55, 71, 74, 77, 81, 85, 109, 130 247, 260-61
  and the Messiah, 133
John Birch Society, 24n
Jonah, 122
Josiah, 84
Judaism, 117
  missionary activity of, 83
  Paul's work and, 78
  ritual in, 137-38, 161, 264-70
Judas Iscariot, 256
Justice, 191-92, 216, 218, 282

Kerygma and History (Braaten and Harrisville), 45n
Kerygma and Myth (Bultmann), 57n
Kingdom of God, 177
  Bultmann on, 50-54
  Christ and, 118-32
  concept of, 30-45, 79-116
  establishment of, 77, 101, 283

Kingdom of God—*cont'd*
  extension of, 98-105
  interior and exterior life of, 86-88
  Jesus' conception of, 83-84
  marriage and, 239
  material wealth and, 225-36
  meaning of Kingdom on earth, 110-16
  personal salvation and, 263
  principal dimensions of, 32-39
  rank order in, 196-97
  Roman Catholic Church and, 163
  and second coming of Christ, 105-10
  spiritual bases of, 85-86, 88-95
Koinonia, 55

Land, and economic system, 34-35, 212-13
Lange, A., 161
Lassalle, 122
Law
  and gospel, 55-56
  Jesus and, 180-95
  see also Liberty; Love; Trust
Lazarus, 166, 209, 210, 222
Levites, 257
Liberty, law and, 181
L'Immortel (Daudet), 204
Lincoln, Abraham, 14
Little, H. Ganse, 45n, 56
Little Journey in the World (Warner), 219
Logos, 133
Lord's Supper, 269-70
Louis XVI, of France, 193-94
Love, 153, 216, 217, 218,
  law of, 181-95, 206, 235-36
Lowell, James Russell, 161, 228, 256
Luther, Martin, 248, 270
Lying, 252, 256

MacGregor clan, 131, 132n
Mankind
  animal nature of, and Spirit of God, 134-35
  doctrine of progress, 281
  duty to self, 251-63
  historicity of, 58-59
  moral life of, 251
  supremacy of "higher life," 258-63
Marriage
  Jesus on, 238-41, 261
  Paul on, 240, 261
Marx, Karl, 233
Mazzini, 172, 284
Meekness, 197
Melville, Herman, 114
Men, religious life and, 113-15
Mennonites, 248
Messiah, Jesus recognized as, 254
Messianic hope, 71-74, 80-81, 132
  defined, 81
  Jesus' attitude toward, 81-98
  spirituality of, 84-88
  universality of, 82-84
  warrior-king concept, 88
Messianic theocracy, *see Theocracy, messianic*
Micah, 82
Montanists, 107
Morality
  "New Morality," 251-85
  see also Church: moral leadership
Moses, 158, 238
Müller, R., 39n

Nature, Kingdom of God in, 33-35
Neander, 160
Neighbor concept, 67
Nero, 167
Newman, John Henry, Cardinal, 180
Nicea, Council of, 127
Nicene Creed, 127
Niebuhr, Reinhold, 27
  on Rauschenbusch, 15, 43-44
None Dare Call It Treason (Stormer), 24n

Oaths, 252-54
Obedience, to state, 246
Obligation, principle of, 274
Oden, Thomas C., 45n
Onesimus, 167
Oxnam, G. Bromley, 15n

"Parable" (Lowell), 256
"Paracelsus" (Browning), 199
Paraclete, 133
Parent-Duchatelet, 223
Pascal, Blaise, 263
Patents, 215
Paul, 47, 49, 55, 89, 103, 106, 108, 117, 137, 138, 146, 148, 152, 158, 167, 198, 210, 218, 246, 247, 248, 255, 256, 259, 261, 270, 275, 279
  Christ in, 150
  church and, 153, 160, 174
  church vs. Kingdom, 99-100
  concept of Jesus, 124
  on impurity, 239
  on marriage, 240, 261
  and nationalism of Judaism, 83
  overcoming evil with good, 184, 185
  on salvation, 199
  Spirit of God and, 133-38
  work of, 77-78, 161

Person, personality, 37n; *see also* Individual
Personalities in Social Reform (Oxnam), 15n
Personhood, 55
Peter, 106, 146, 152, 154, 166, 173, 198, 245, 247, 248, 253, 254, 270, 276
Pharisaism, Pharisees, 90, 120, 131, 158, 166, 180, 196, 209, 238, 239, 241, 254, 257, 265, 266, 267
Philemon, 167
Philo of Alexandria, 121
Pilate, 78, 91, 132, 185, 246, 247
Plato, 121, 172
Politics, 284-85
Post, Elizabeth, 15n
Poverty, 219-21, 227-36
Pragmatism, 31
Prayer, 268-69
Prayers of the Social Awakening (Rauschenbusch), 15
Pride, 196, 199
Priestcraft, Spirit of God and, 138-41
Primitive Christianity (Bultmann), 48n, 49n
Principle, meaning of term, 37n
Progress and Poverty (George), 34
Property, 210-13
Prophets (Old Testament), 118, 149, 210-11
  character of, 70-71
  and the individual, 95-96
  message of, 82-83
  Messianic salvation, 84-85
  and Spirit of God, 132-33
Protestantism, 94, 277
Punishment, reward and, 277-78
Purification, Jewish, 270
Purity, 282; *see also* Impurity

Quakers, 129, 248

Race relations, 33; *see also* Slavery
Race: The History of an Idea in America (Gossett), 33n
Radical Obedience: The Ethics of Rudolf Bultmann (Oden), 45n
Rauschenbusch, August, 39n
Rauschenbusch, Walter
  books by, 15, 17-20
  life summarized, 14-20
Rauschenbusch, Mrs. Walter, 15n, 17
Rauschenbusch Reader, A (Landis), 33n
Raymond, J. E., 15n
Real estate, 212-13
Red Cross, 175
Reformers, the, 93
Reformation, 107, 145
Religion
  as hope of world, 284
  power of, 129
  practice of, 264-78
  religious superstition and Spirit of God, 135-38
  see also Christianity; Judaism
Religion (Ramsey), 59n
"Reminiscences of My Life" (Rauschenbusch), 14n
Remnant, concept of, 84
Resistance, passive, 249-50
Responsibility, 271-74
Retribution, 186, 193
Revelation, 56-57
Rewards, 274-78
Righteousness
  Christianity and, 280
  individual vs. collective, 102-5
  and Kingdom of God, 86-87
  Ritschl on, 18
Righteousness of the Kingdom, The (Rauschenbusch)
  concepts in, 20-59
  writing of, 17-20
Ritschl, Albrecht, 25, 27, 45
  influence on Rauschenbusch, 18
Rob Roy (Scott), 132n
Robespierre, 229
Roland, Madame, 139
Roman Catholic Church, 93, 94, 162-63, 164, 231, 271, 277
  social philosophy, 20, 21
Roosevelt, Theodore, 42
Rousseau, Jean Jacques, 143
Russian Revolution, 14-15

Sabbath, laws concerning, 266-67
Sacrifice
  Jesus on, 120
  self-sacrifice, 262-63
Sadducees, 72, 90, 239
Salvation, 44
  individual vs. world, 99, 263
  Messianic, 84-88, 96-98
  Paul on, 199
Salvation Army, 155
Samson, 141
Sangster, Margaret E., 18n
Sapphira, 155
Schäffle, 154, 161, 171, 172
Schleiermacher, Friedrich, 25, 45
Schmidt, Nathaniel, 17, 20
Schweitzer, Albert, 53, 54
Scott, Sir Walter, 132n
Scudder, Vida, 15n
Selfishness, 142

Seneca, 127
Sermon on the Mount, 180, 267
Service, life of, 197-98
Sex, 34
  in future life, 239
Shanahan, W. O., 18n
Sharpe, D. R., 14n, 19, 30n
Simeon, 73, 85
Sin
  causes of, 190
  and grace, 55
Slavery, 167, 194; *see also* Race relations
Smucker, Donovan E., 16n
Social ethics
  biblical studies and, 59
  law vs. spirit, 167-68
  New Testament and, 45-59
Social Gospel
  vs. existential gospel, 46
  relevance of, 25-26
  social sciences and, 23
Social Gospel in America, The (Handy), 23n
Social order, Christian, 35-42
Social Principles of Jesus, The (Rauschenbusch), 15, 35n, 37n, 38n, 39n, 40n
Social Teaching of the Christian Churches, The (Troeltsch), 20
Socialism, 30, 35, 122
Society
  Christian influence and, 187-95, 207-8
  church and, 162-78
  Jesus and, 165-67
  regeneration of, 110-16, 152
  Spirit of God and, 141-46
  stratification of, 199-206, 224-25
  wealth and, 224-25
Socrates, 121
Solomon, 122, 210
Spirit of God, 132-49, 254, 271
  and man's animal nature, 134-35
  power of, 146-49
  and priestcraft, 138-41
  and religious superstition, 135-38
  revolutionary character of, 134-49
  and society, 141-46
Spinoza, Baruch, 125
Stackhouse, M. L., 30n
Starr, Edward, 19
State
  church and, 162-78
  relation of Christian to, 244-50
Stephen, 147, 248
Stocks, speculation in, 214-15
Stoics, 127
Stormer, John A., 24n
Strauss, D. F., 125
Swearing, 252-54
Systematic Theology (Tillich), 27

Theocracy, Messianic, 32-35, 40, 41, 43, 79-98, 118
  church and, 149-78
  Spirit of God and, 132-49
Theology for the Social Gospel, A (Rauschenbusch), 15, 54n
Tillich, Paul, 27
Titles, use of, 196
Troeltsch, Ernst, 20, 22, 25
Trust, law of, 226-27
Truth
  embodiment of, 127-28
  power of, 91-95
  self and, 251-54

"United Church" movements, 22
Universalism, 44
Unselfishness, 282

Vatican Council II, 21, 22
Visser 't Hooft, W. A., 28n
Voluntary Associations (Robertson), 16n

Wage system, 217
Walter Rauschenbusch (Müller), 39n
Walter Rauschenbusch (Sharpe), 14n, 30n
Ward, Harry F., 24n
Warner, Charles Dudley, 219
Wealth, material, 206-36
  Christian virtues and, 218-22
  as destroyer of character, 221-25
  Kingdom of God and, 225-36
  sources of, 212-16
Wilder, Amos, 45
  on Rauschenbusch, 52n
Williams, Leighton, 15n, 17
Wilson, Woodrow, 14
Women
  ambition and, 205
  Jesus' attitude toward, 236-37, 241-42
  place of, 242-44
  religious life and, 41, 113-15

Xenophon, 121